ISRAEL—
EMPOWERED
BY THE SPIRIT

ISRAEL – EMPOWERED BY THE SPIRIT

by
WALLACE E. SMITH
and
BATYA RUTH WOOTTEN

Israel— Empowered by the Spirit

Wallace E. Smith and Batya Ruth Wootten

© 2009, Wallace E. Smith, Las Vegas, NV; Key of David Publishing, St. Cloud, FL.

Cover Painting, "Blessed Move of the Ruach" by David Hardin, Las Vegas, NV. © 2008. Used by Permission.
Cover Design by John Diffenderfer, Artistream, Lebanon, TN, 615.547.1555. www.artistream.info

Published and Distributed by:
Key of David Publishing, PO Box 700217, Saint Cloud, FL, 34770
www.keyofdavidpublishing.com
Distributed by:
Messianic Israel Marketplace, PO Box 3263, Lebanon, TN 37088 (800.829.8777)
www.messianicisrael.com

Printed in the United States of America.
All quotations are used by permission.
Unless otherwise noted, Scripture quotations are from the *New King James Version of the Bible* (NKJV), copyright © 1979, 1980, 1982, Thomas Nelson, Inc.
Verses marked NNAB are from the *New American Standard Bible*, © Quick Verse for Windows, 1992-2009, Craig Rairdon and Parsons Technology.
Verses marked KJV are from the *King James Version* Bible.
Verses marked NIV are from the *New International Version*, © 1995 by The International Bible Society, Zondervan Publishing, Grand Rapids.
Verses marked ISV are from the International Standard Version, © 2008, as listed at: http://isv.org/index.htm
Verses from *26 Translations of the Holy Bible*, © 1985 by Zondervan Corporation, Mathis Publishers, Atlanta, are marked according to the particular translation.
Note: To emphasize some Scriptures, *italics*, or an alternate word choice has been used, especially for the names of the Father and Son. Also, brackets [] indicate text added by the authors.

ISBN 1-886987-28-9

In Appreciation

First and foremost I want to give thanks for the inspiration given by our Lord and King, Yeshua, the anointed Messiah, without whom we cannot take our next breath.

I want to send special love notes to my wife Kathy: You are my number one support and helpmate. Thank you for allowing me to take time away from you to accomplish this work. Thank you for your help in editing this book. You are my spell-checker in time of need. I thank you for your love, both for Yeshua and for me. God knew I needed you. He blessed me when He sent you my way.

To my immediate family, I want to extend my gratitude for putting up with me when I least deserved it. You have seen me through my self imposed bumps and ruts as I have followed God's leading into the Messianic life. Thank you!

Thanks to Mary Taylor and Susan Hardin for wielding your "big red pen," and to David Hardin for your excellent cover painting. Your depiction of the dove taking flight from an almond branch perfectly captures the essence of this book, it speaks of the soon coming outpouring and renewal of the *Ruach haKodesh*, the Holy Spirit.

A special "Thank you," goes to Batya Wootten. Your enthusiasm over this project and your input has been inspirational. Your compassionate mothering style has truly transformed this book into one that can now be easily comprehended by one and all.

Wally

Editorial Appreciation

I have many to thank for helping with this work.

First, I thank my husband, Angus, who never fails to think outside the box and thus make great contributions. Also, my friend, Sandy Bloomfield, an accomplished editor and ghost writer, put her red pen to the text. And, friend and editor, Chaun Stirling, also reviewed the work and helped me to clarify certain points.

Calligrapher, Anita Robertson (www.thescribeandscroll.com), has a degree in English, and she is said by her husband Al to have "an insatiable desire to pull weeds out of public flower beds and to correct manuscripts." Thanks to Al and Anita, our "garden" is now a more pleasant place.

Tawnie Manning, with *Abba's Olive Tree*, also made encouraging and helpful suggestions, as did friend and neighbor, Larry Shock.

Special thanks go to Larry Schmidt (Messianic Israel Talk Group, www.yahoo.com) for his careful scrutiny; a dedicated student of the Word, he added some fine points to the text. Another knowledgeable contributor to the MIT Group is Scott Skaggs, who thankfully lent his theological talents to the pool. Pamela Moore, who has a Ph.D in Biochemistry, graciously helped us with our research. Many in the Group contributed in various ways: John Conrad, David Pennington, Miguel Demelli, Wanita Panza, Christine Miller, and several others. My thanks to each one, and to Scott and Jane Diffenderfer for the comments they made.

Finally, my deepest thanks go to Wally Smith for allowing me to take part in this important work. Wally has an unending desire to reach those in the Church, and he allowed me to join him with my cry for Messianic Believers to likewise open their hearts. May our combined efforts in this book be used to help Believers from all walks of faith grow in their empowerment by the *Ruach haKodesh*, the Holy Spirit. May we all come to better know the Comforter who is lovingly sent to us by the God of Israel.

Batya

YHVH— יהוה

We will occasionally use these four letters to indicate the Name of the One True God, which is often translated as "the LORD." Historically, Judaism avoided its use and Christianity followed suit. The Father's Name is spelled with four Hebrew letters, יהוה, yod, hey, vav, hey, and is variously translated: Yahweh, Yahveh, Yehovah, etc. We sometimes use the four English letters that best duplicate the sound of the Hebrew letters, as pronounced in modern Hebrew: YHVH. We also sometimes use *Elohim*, which is Hebrew for *God*, and Yah, which is short for YHVH (Isa 12:2).

YESHUA— ישוע

Yeshua is the Messiah's Hebrew/Aramaic name. A shortened form of Yehoshua (Joshua), it means "Salvation" (Neh. 8:17; Mat 1:21). Jesus is derived from the Greek *Iesous*. They changed His name because their language did not have a "sh" sound, and they often added an "s" to the end of male names. This Greek transliteration (sound) was converted into English when the English letter "J" had a sound like that of today's "Y." It was pronounced "Yesus," much like the Greek name. However, with the hardening of the sound of the English "J," it began to be pronounced as "Jesus." We choose to transliterate His name from Hebrew into English, and as "Yeshua."

EPHRAIM— אפרים

Ephraim is the given name of Joseph's second son. It means "doubly fruitful." Jacob/Israel prophesied that Ephraim's heirs would become a "fullness of Gentiles." The name "Ephraim" was used to describe the Ten Tribes of the Northern Kingdom, also called the Kingdom of Israel. The term "Ephraimite" was sometimes used to describe these people (as opposed to the Southern Kingdom of Judah). The people of Ephraim lost their identity after they were exiled by the Assyrians (around 722 B.C.). We will use this name to describe those known as the "Ten Lost Tribes," and to broadly speak of non-Jewish Believers in the Messiah of Israel, who also are deemed in Scripture to be of Israel's commonwealth (Gen 41:52; 2 Ki 17:34; 1 Ki 12:21; Eze 37:15-28; Eph 2:11-22).

TORAH— תורה

Torah means teaching, instruction, direction. This Hebrew word is often translated as the "Law." Our God says He loved Abraham because he kept His Laws (Gen 26:5). Abraham kept the spirit of the Torah before the letter of it was given to Moses. Everyone who wants to be a success should likewise look to our Father's precepts for guidance. Moses said of them, "Keep and do them, for that is your wisdom and your understanding in the sight of the peoples who will hear all these statutes and say, 'Surely this great nation is a wise and understanding people'" (Deu 4:5-6). King David said, "How blessed are those whose way is blameless, who walk in the law of the LORD. How blessed are those who observe His testimonies, who seek Him with all their heart. They also do no unrighteousness; they walk in His ways .... Oh that my ways may be established to keep Thy statutes! Then I shall not be ashamed" (Psa 119:1-6).

King David also said of the Father's Word, "The sum of Your word is truth, and every one of Your righteous ordinances is everlasting" (Psa 119:160). Messiah Yeshua, in a prayer for those who would follow Him, said of the written Word of His day, "Sanctify them in the truth; Your word is truth" (John 17:17).

As New Covenant Believers, we are saved by grace through faith, and not by works, but by the shed blood of our Messiah and by the word of our testimony. It is with this understanding of all that our Messiah has done for us, and of the wise and simple faith of our forefather Abraham, that we speak of honoring the eternal wisdom of Torah and walking in its lifestyle.

We also note that Adam and Eve were sent outside the Garden for their sin, and that Israel was scattered among the nations for hers. Not until Messiah returns us to His Promised Land, and sprinkles us with "clean water," will we be fully empowered to walk in His eternal Torah. Until then let us nonetheless seek to have it written on our hearts, by His Holy Spirit, and to walk in its ways, as it is promised (Jer 31:31-33; Eze 36:23-28; 37:15-28).

Take out our heart of stone, O God, and give us a heart of flesh that always seeks after You and Your ways! Amen!

CONTENTS

FOREWORD

Once, when a dear friend was introducing me, he said, *"The reason Batya keeps hammering us about the Holy Spirit is because it is so important to our movement...."*

The truth is that I had been (and still am) persistent in speaking about the Holy Spirit at every opportunity I get. I had not thought of myself as being that way, but when I heard John Conrad's humorous introduction, I knew his words were true.

The reason I talk about the *Ruach haKodesh*, the Holy Spirit, is because most of my adult life has been dedicated to the restoration of the whole house of Israel. I am devoted to the reunion of a repentant and restored Israel, one that includes both houses, Ephraim and Judah. I look forward to the day when their two sticks are made one in the holy hand of the Almighty. Every book I have written has to do with this subject. And it is the very reason why I wanted to help with the book you now hold in your hand.

My heart's desire is to see the whole house of Israel restored, but I realize that we cannot get to that goal apart from empowerment by the Spirit.

The problem is that our movement, in trying to leave behind the errors of the Church, has made the mistake of throwing one of those proverbial babies out with the bath water.

It is my understanding that this bath water saying began because, before we had running water in our homes, the whole family had to bathe in the weekly family bath water, starting with the father. By the time they got to the poor baby, the water was so dirty they could miss the child when they threw the water out.

We do not know whether this story is true, but we do know that there is lots of dirt in the family bath water of Christianity, and Judaism too, for that matter. However, as we seek to rid ourselves of the mistakes of the past, we must not throw out the "baby" that is the eternal truth that our God still works through His Spirit Most Holy.

We who love Israel, above all people, must guard this truth in our midst. We must seek to grow in our understanding of true rebirth and immersion in the Ruach haKodesh— because it is in this hour, even as it was for Zerubabbel of old: *"This is the word of the LORD..., 'Not by might nor by power, but by My Spirit'"* (Zec 4:6).

My hope is that you will prayerfully read this book while asking the Holy One to protect you from anything that might not be from Him, and at the same time, ask Him to fully immerse you in everything that is from Him.

This book is written with a holy fear of possibly offending or misrepresenting The Spirit Most Holy. The material herein is thus presented in all humility. Our goal is not to claim that we have all the answers, but to encourage Believers to ask the Father for more of His Holy Spirit, and to empower us to operate in His gifts in a way that truly pleases Him.

May it be so in our day…

Yours for the Salvation of the Whole House of Israel,
Batya Wootten
Author, Co-Director, Key of David Publishing

PREFACE

*A*re you crazy?
    You're really asking for it this time!
You really want to open that can of worms?

These are a few of the responses voiced when I confided in a few friends that YHVH was leading me to address some concerns regarding the baptism with the Holy Spirit in today's Messianic movement.

I was concerned because it is generally accepted that a majority of Christians (from Pentecostal/Charismatic persuasions), having discovered their Hebrew Roots, came out of the Sunday Church and were re-planted in the Messianic Movement. And, we must concede that the Pentecostal/Charismatic movement can be fraught with high-octane emotion that lends itself to both real and counterfeit manifestations of the gifts of the Holy Spirit.

Comparatively, the Messianic Movement can bubble over with emotion as well; however, its focus has not been collectively on the *Ruach haKodesh*, the Holy Spirit, but has centralized on the intellectual pursuit of Torah and on honoring and obeying it.

This focus has led many within our movement to ask, *"Where are manifestations of the Ruach among us?"*

We must realize that the Messianic movement is comprised of Messianic Judaism and Messianic Israel, and it should not be concluded that there is a total absence of the Ruach among those who call themselves Messianic. This entire movement is a leading of the Ruach; it is as scripturally prophetic as the Second Coming. This also is not to say that there have not been manifestations of the Ruach on individual lives within the movement. However, many have seemingly put the Ruach on a back burner.

What is at the root of this Messianic phenomenon that resists the Spirit? This question becomes pronounced when we consider that Messianic congregations are predominantly populated by members who are familiar with the moving of the Spirit.

We will investigate this prophetic phenomenon that has resulted in the birth of today's Messianic movement, and we begin with words from the prophet Ezekiel:

> "Moreover the word of the LORD came to me, saying: 'Son of man, when the house of Israel dwelt in their own land, they defiled it by their own ways and deeds; to Me their way was like the uncleanness of a woman in her customary impurity. Therefore I poured out My fury on them for the blood they had shed on the land, and for their idols with which they had defiled it. So I scattered them among the nations, and they were dispersed throughout the countries; I judged them according to their ways and their deeds. When they came to the nations, wherever they went, they profaned My holy name— when they said of them, "These are the people of the LORD, and yet they have gone out of His land." But I had concern for My holy name, which the house of Israel had profaned among the nations wherever they went. Therefore say to the house of Israel, Thus says the Lord GOD: "I do not do this for your sake, O house of Israel, but for My holy name's sake, which you have profaned

among the nations wherever you went. And I will sanctify My great name, which has been profaned among the nations, which you have profaned in their midst; and the nations shall know that I am the LORD, says the Lord GOD, when I am hallowed in you before their eyes.

"For I will take you from among the nations, gather you out of all countries, and bring you into your own land. Then I will sprinkle clean water on you, and you shall be clean; I will cleanse you from all your filthiness and from all your idols. I will give you a new heart and put a new spirit within you; I will take the heart of stone out of your flesh and give you a heart of flesh. I will put My Spirit within you and cause you to walk in My statutes, and you will keep My judgments and do them. Then you shall dwell in the land that I gave to your fathers; you shall be My people, and I will be your God'" (Ezekiel 36:16-28).

Historically, ancient Israel was at its peak during the reigns of King David and King Solomon. Solomon was endowed with divine wisdom from God, constructed the Temple, and expanded Israel's influence. However, as a part of this expanding influence, Solomon married many foreign wives and was greatly affected by their false religions. He built temples and high places to their pagan gods and participated in their worship. Because of this, God declared that the united Kingdom of Israel would be divided, and He promised to give Jeroboam, who was a servant of Solomon, the Ten Northern Tribes:

"Then Ahijah took hold of the new cloak which was on him and tore it into twelve pieces. He said to Jeroboam, 'Take for yourself ten pieces; for thus says the LORD, the God of Israel, Behold, I will tear the kingdom out of the hand of Solomon and give you ten tribes (but he will have one tribe, for the sake of My servant David and for the sake of Jerusalem, the city which I have chosen from all the tribes of

Israel), because they have forsaken Me, and have worshiped Ashtoreth the goddess of the Sidonians, Chemosh the god of Moab, and Milcom the god of the sons of Ammon; and they have not walked in My ways, doing what is right in My sight and observing My statutes and My ordinances, as his father David did'" (1 Ki 11:30-33, NASB).

The Northern Kingdom of Israel, also known as the House of Ephraim, broke away from their brothers in the Southern Kingdom, who were also known as the House of Judah.

After Solomon died, his son, Rehoboam, came to power (in the territory of Judah), but Jeroboam rightfully assumed power in the newly formed Northern Kingdom. Ultimately, because Jeroboam began to fear for his position, he resisted reunion with Judah and instead established heathen worship centers for those of the Northern Kingdom of Ephraim/Israel (1 Ki 11:31; 12:26-30).

Israel and Judah remained separate political entities for the next two hundred years. There was some intermingling between them, as there were Northern Israelites who remained faithful to YHVH and thus moved south (for a season) and integrated themselves in Judea. Then, between the years 734 to 721 BC, the Assyrian Empire attacked, subjugated, and dispersed many of Northern Israel. It was the Assyrian custom to subdue conquered peoples, abolish their religion and displace them by intermarrying them with others in foreign conquered lands. Since that time, the House of Israel/ Ephraim was corporately swallowed up among the nations. They were completely assimilated and lost their identity.

The Southern Kingdom, the House of Judah, the Jewish people, has been the only "known" representatives of Israel since that time. While experiencing their own dispersions at the hands of Babylon and Rome, and even terrible events like the Inquisition and Holocaust, Judah has remained faithful to his Jewish heritage and thus, the Jews are the only identifiable race of Israelites today.

In the end of days, and prior to the Messiah's return, it is prophesied that the scattered House of Ephraim will return to their heritage as part of the people of Israel, and that, many will return to the Land of Israel. For the LORD promised them, "I will take you from among the nations, gather you out of all countries, and bring you into your own land (Ezek 36:24). At that time, all Israel will have one King, Yeshua the Messiah, and they will all be observing the eternal truths of the Torah, also known as the "Law of God," and sometimes as the "Law of Moses."

> "My servant David will be king over them, and they will all have one shepherd; and they will walk in My ordinances and keep My statutes and observe them. They will live on the land that I gave to Jacob My servant, in which your fathers lived; and they will live on it, they, and their sons and their sons' sons, forever; and David My servant will be their prince forever. I will make a covenant of peace with them; it will be an everlasting covenant with them. And I will place them and multiply them, and will set My sanctuary in their midst forever. My dwelling place also will be with them; and I will be their God, and they will be My people. And the nations will know that I am the Lord who sanctifies Israel, when My sanctuary is in their midst forever" (Ezek 37:24-28, NASB).

(For an excellent study of Israel's identity and the reunification of Judah and Ephraim, we recommend the book, *Redeemed Israel: Reunited and Restored* by Batya Ruth Wootten. [a])

While it is exciting to see this awe-inspiring truth, we also need to see that, before this ultimate reunion of Judah and Ephraim, before the return of Yeshua our Messiah, YHVH says that He will institute a phenomenal move of His Spirit:

> "I will put My Spirit within you and cause you to walk in My statutes, and you will keep My judgments and do them.

---

[a] © 2006, Key of David Publishing, St. Cloud, FL 34770. ISBN: 1886987211

Then you shall dwell in the land that I gave to your fathers; you shall be My people, and I will be your God" (Eze 36:27-28).

This promised outpouring of the Ruach is certain, Ezekiel defined it, and through him we see how it applies to us.

"The hand of the LORD came upon me and brought me out in the Spirit of the LORD, and set me down in the midst of the valley; and it was full of bones. Then He caused me to pass by them all around, and behold, there were very many in the open valley; and indeed they were very dry. And He said to me, 'Son of man, can these bones live?' So I answered, 'O Lord GOD, You know.' Again He said to me, 'Prophesy to these bones, and say to them, O dry bones, hear the word of the LORD! Thus says the Lord GOD to these bones: Surely I will cause breath to enter into you, and you shall live. I will put sinews on you and bring flesh upon you, cover you with skin and put breath in you; and you shall live. Then you shall know that I am the LORD.' So I prophesied as I was commanded; and as I prophesied, there was a noise, and suddenly a rattling; and the bones came together, bone to bone. Indeed, as I looked, the sinews and the flesh came upon them, and the skin covered them over; but there was no breath in them. Also He said to me, 'Prophesy to the breath, prophesy, son of man, and say to the breath, Thus says the Lord GOD: Come from the four winds, O breath, and breathe on these slain, that they may live.' So I prophesied as He commanded me, and breath came into them, and they lived, and stood upon their feet, an exceedingly great army. Then He said to me, 'Son of man, these bones are the whole house of Israel. They indeed say, Our bones are dry, our hope is lost, and we ourselves are cut off! Therefore prophesy and say to them, Thus says the Lord GOD: Behold, O My people, I will open your graves and cause you to come up from your graves, and bring you into the land of Israel. Then you shall know that I am the LORD, when I have opened your graves, and brought you up from your graves. I will put My Spirit in you, and you shall live, and I will place you in your own land. Then you shall know that I, the LORD, have spoken it and performed it,' says the LORD" (Ezek 37:1-14, NASB).

YHVH is causing our dead bones to live again. He is assembling the whole House of Israel, both Judah and Ephraim. In the years of this movement, bones have been brought together and sinews have formed— that which connects the bones, which is our Hebrew roots, our heritage. Flesh or muscle has been added— which gives strength and allows us to stand upright. Strengthening comes from realizing the eternal truths of YHVH's Torah: "You shall therefore keep every commandment... so that you may be strong and go in and possess the land..." (Deu 11:8). Skin has covered the flesh— which makes one identifiable. In the Messianic movement this would be, Messianic Judaism, Messianic Israel, Messianic Independents, etc. (It is not our intent to be exclusive, but to broadly define our meaning here.)

However, our God does not want brother Judah, those who have yet to recognize Yeshua as Messiah, to be left out of this bone assembly. Verse 11 reads, "Son of man, these bones are the whole house of Israel." We want to include both Judah and Ephraim.

We are on the precipice of the fulfillment of verse 14: "I will put My Spirit in you, and you shall live." We are at the juncture where our God is about to put his Ruach, His breath of life, into our lives and our movement. Then, He will bring us back to our own land.

God's Word is sure. It is going to happen. We are going to return home to the Promised Land. That time is soon and very soon. We can be sure of this promise because we already see a partial fulfillment in the return of the House of Judah to the modern State of Israel. YHVH says He will "save the tents of Judah first, so that the glory of the house of David and the glory of the inhabitants of Jerusalem shall not become greater than that of Judah" (Zec 12:7).

The tents of Judah have been and are presently being established in the Land. The Jews have been returning to the modern State of Israel in record numbers for decades now. They are truly being established "first." Logic dictates that if there is a first then there must be something that comes after. That is the day Messianic Israel, the House of Ephraim, is looking forward to: their return and the restoration of all things. One day soon, Ephraim and Judah will dwell together in the land of Israel. Our God will have His way. His Kingdom will be established in His Land. At its center will be His chosen capital, Jerusalem. But before this occurs, there shall be a tremendous outpouring of His Holy Spirit, the Father's Divine Ruach.

That is what this book is about. It is meant to be a tool that will help us get ready for that awesome day. To prepare, we must take an accounting; we must take a good hard look at ourselves. An audit is never enjoyable, and sometimes it will cost us. But, an audit is always beneficial, because it sets our house in order.

The prayer behind this book is that it will help with that audit.

With the Ruach haKodesh being corporately placed on the back burner, it is now time for us to put our house in order— time to make way for our return to the Land and the return of our Messiah— by the power of the Ruach.

We suggest you read this book with a Bible in one hand and pen and notebook in the other. There is no hurry. Prayerfully read with an attitude open to the Spirit of Truth. You will surely experience the joy of a Biblical explosion of new understanding, your entire being will be baptized and empowered.

Because of our Wonderful Messiah,
Wallace E. Smith
Founding Pastor, House of Israel Fellowship
A Free Congregation of Messianic Christians
Las Vegas, Nevada
www.houseofisraelfellowship.org

I

By My Spirit...

Speaking of the latter days, Zechariah the prophet said to Zerubbabel, *"This is the word of the LORD..., 'Not by might nor by power, but by My Spirit'" (Zec 4:6, NASB).*

We who want to see the Kingdom restored to Israel will have to abide by this holy standard. Restoration will come to Israel— but only by the *Ruach haKodesh* of her God. It will happen by the power of the *Spirit Most Holy*, otherwise it will not happen at all.

Who, what group of Believers, most needs to hear and understand this decree? Why is it a problem to some? What do we see in the earth today that works to hinder Israel's full restoration? And, how do we overcome that which hinders us?

Who needs to hear and understand? Messianic Believers. Why is it a problem? There is enmity between some Messianics and the Church. What hinders Israel's full restoration by the Spirit? Misrepresentation and misunderstanding of the truth, wrong attitudes... (this list could go on ad infinitum).

How do we overcome that which hinders us?

We reexamine our positions based on Scripture and, we then embrace the truths we find about the Holy Spirit.

This book is about the problems that interfere with that embrace. It is a plea and a prayer in print. It is first a plea for both sides to truly hear legitimate complaints and then to seek a more Scriptural understanding of the matter.

This work is presented with a prayer, that change might come to those with ears to hear, that empowerment from on High would descend upon us with a mighty outpouring, and that individually and collectively we might begin to walk in a way that helps bring restoration to the whole house of Israel— by the power of the Spirit Most Holy.

This book will not try to "sell the idea of speaking in tongues as though it were an 'end-all.'" We will instead show them to be a sign that should point to something that is even greater than the gift itself. We also will show that speech is holy to our God, and that we should have careful Scriptural regard for it, in all its forms.

This book will not claim to provide all of the answers about the vast subject that is the Holy Spirit— or His fruits and giftings. However, we will seek to address related issues as accurately as we know how. Yet, in the end, our only sure claims will be that, we who want to "move in the Spirit," we who want to see Israel restored, need to sincerely reexamine the issues involved. And that, to make it through the difficult times that are now upon us, we need to be filled with and empowered by the Ruach. Moreover, if we have misrepresented the Holy Spirit to others, or entertained wrong attitudes, or neglected to fully embrace all that the Father wants to give us, now is the time for us to repent. It is time for us to enter into all that our God has for us in this hour.

With this plea and prayer in mind, we now humbly and prayerfully begin our study about the Holy Spirit and His precious giftings.

2

EMPOWERMENT IN THE HOLY SPIRIT: OUR OBJECTIVE AND GOAL

L eaving the elementary teaching about the Christ, let us press on to maturity, not laying again a foundation of repentance from dead works and of faith toward God, of instruction about washings [baptisms] and laying on of hands, and the resurrection of the dead and eternal judgment. And this we will do, if God permits.(Heb 6:1-3, NASB).

We live in difficult times. More so than ever before, we need to *mature* and *press on* in our faith, especially when it comes to understanding being born of, and baptized (washed), immersed in, and empowered with the Holy Spirit, the *Ruach haKodesh.*

Scripture says *baptisms* are *plural,* an *elementary* principle, and the *milk* of our faith. In Scripture, *meat* is *doing,* and it is now time for us to move on, to the *meat* of our calling. More so than ever before we need to be *empowered* to do the works of our Father. To do His work, we begin our walk when we first repent of our sins and are reborn of His Spirit. This inward happening should then be followed by the outward ritual of water baptism, which should be followed by the infilling, or *empowerment* with the Holy Spirit (Mat 3:15; Luke 24:49; John 3:3; 4:34; 1 Cor 3:2-2; Heb 5:12-13).

In water baptism our witness is usually a minister, or recognized official of the church, and the medium is water.

The Greek word for baptism is *baptizo* and means to make *whelmed*. It is the root for our English word *overwhelmed*. Further definition of the word mean to make *fully wet* or to *immerse*. [2]

In regards to *baptism/empowerment* with the Spirit, the baptizer is Yeshua haMashiach, Jesus the Messiah, the medium is the *Ruach haKodesh*, the Holy Spirit (Mark 1:8; Luke 3:16; 24:49).

John the Baptist ministered a "baptism of repentance." This baptism is symbolized by water baptism, which is a ceremonial ordinance that allows Believers to publicly declare their faith in Yeshua, by being momentarily submerged in water (Mat 10:33). This act depicts the death of our old self-life, and our rebirth into a new life in Yeshua. It is an outward sign that is meant to depict an inward state. This baptism of repentance is a shadow, a type, a blueprint, a physical illustration of that which is to come.

It speaks of our promise of being resurrected into eternal life in Messiah— if we leave our old man, our carnal nature, behind.

Immersion in the Holy Spirit is the living reality to which water baptism points, and it has been so from the onset. Holy Spirit baptism/empowerment is the goal and the primary baptism.

Water baptism is a symbolic ceremony. We learn a great deal from it with respect to the baptism with the Holy Spirit. It can be likened to a general contractor's learning of the details about a building by studying the architect's blueprint.

In this ceremonial blueprint, we see an outline of the baptism with the Ruach haKodesh. When a repentant Believer goes through the waters of baptism and seeks to build a new life, through this act he figuratively declares to the world his two important objectives:

---

2 *Strong's* word # G907. From *Strong's Hebrew and Greek Dictionaries, Electronic Edition, STEP Files* © 1998, Parsons Technology, Inc., Cedar Rapids (hereafter: *Strong's*).

- Burial of his old sinful nature
- The desire to rise again— by the power of God— to live a new life of righteousness

Spiritual resurrection is the picture that is painted in water baptism. In it, the washed Believer arises to build a new life of righteousness, by the power of the Spirit, and in accordance with God's Word. Various verses illustrate this point.

> "[You were] buried with Him in baptism, in which you also were raised with Him through faith in the working of God, who raised Him from the dead. And you, being dead in your trespasses and the uncircumcision of your flesh, He has made alive together with Him, having forgiven you all trespasses." .... "Do you not know that as many of us as were baptized into Christ Jesus were baptized into His death? Therefore we were buried with Him through baptism into death, that just as Christ was raised from the dead by the glory of the Father, even so we also should walk in newness of life. For if we have been united together in the likeness of His death, certainly we also shall be in the likeness of His resurrection, knowing this, that our old man was crucified with Him, that the body of sin might be done away with, that we should no longer be slaves of sin" (Col 2:11-13; Rom 6:3-7).

These objectives find fulfillment in a Ruach-baptized Believer. They are not a figurative exercise as is water baptism and need to become recognizable in the Believer's life.

The sign of Holy Spirit *rebirth* is depicted in water baptism and points toward another baptism: That of being immersed in, and empowered to live by the Spirit. Like our Messiah, we too, are to be "led by the Spirit" (Mat 4:1). These two different baptisms speak of:

- Outward sign of inward burial of the old sinful nature
- Rising to a new life of righteousness and obedience, and being empowered to live that life by the Holy Spirit

Water baptism is an outward action that speaks of a rebirth that has roots in our inward desire for change. Holy Spirit *immersion/ empowerment* is an inward experience. Its good fruit in our lives becomes outwardly visible to those who are around us.

Having experienced these things, these signs should be present in our life: True rebirth, water baptism, and outward evidence of beginning inward change based on immersion in and empowerment with the Holy Spirit.

Unfortunately, some only look for evidence of speaking in tongues as proof that one has been baptized in the Spirit. However, the Evil One, *haSatan*, the Accuser of the Brethren, is a liar and thief who comes to kill and destroy. He also is a counterfeiter. His *modus operandi* is to twist and distort the Word, and thus to deceive the seed of Adam (John 8:44; Rev 12:10). Since Satan works to deceive us with inferior duplicates, we should beware having only one evidence to confirm immersion in the Holy Spirit.

If we think, the only sign of the baptism with the Holy Spirit is speaking in tongues, that can lead us to miss its higher meaning, which is *a new walk of holiness*. It is true that the first evidence that people had been baptized with the Spirit was speaking in tongues (Acts 2:4). However, the more important point is where that empowerment in the Spirit is supposed to ultimately lead us.

Speaking in tongues helps us communicate with our God, but as with Adam, our God is ever asking certain questions of His creation. When Adam sinned, the Father asked him two questions: *"Where are you?"* And, *"Who told you that you were naked?"*

YHVH is all knowing and did not need to get information from mortal Adam. Instead, His rhetorical questions were asked in hopes of getting Adam to examine his self. In the same way, we too need to examine ourselves (2 Cor 13:5). We want to ask of our self, *"Where am I? Who told me the things I am basing my life on?"*

And, *"Am I truly listening to the Father's voice?"* [3]

---

3 *The Voice… Hearing the Almighty* by Batya Wootten, 2009, Key of David Publishing.

Tongues are a "sign," but signs generally point to something else (1 Cor 14:22). They indicate information about something that lies ahead. Signs also help us to know that we are on the right path.

TONGUES ARE A "SIGN," BUT SIGNS GENERALLY POINT TO SOMETHING ELSE

Speaking in tongues should be regarded as a sign that our lives are in the process of being transformed by the Holy Spirit. Tongues should not be viewed as the *end result*, but as a *beginning sign* of something greater, it being that we are on our way to complete transformation in and by the power of the Ruach haKodesh.

We do not want to camp out at the foot of the sign and think we have arrived. Instead, we want to continue moving forward, toward that which the sign is pointing.

If we see a "Yield" or "Divided Highway" sign on the road, we do not stop at the sign and think we have "arrived."

No. We continue to go down the road and then— we experience what the sign was pointing to. If we do not move beyond the sign, we will not really know what it was about.

If we follow the wrong signs, at the very least, it will hinder our arrival at our chosen destination. And this is a special danger in our day. The father of lies wants to keep us off track, and does not want us to arrive at our final destination, so we especially want to beware misleading signs.

As for the various signs of the Holy Spirit, we will see that they point to our call to holiness, and that the Father gives them to help us along life's way. With this idea in mind, we see that holiness is an important accompanying sign of Holy Spirit Immersion.

We serve a jealous God who is calling us to be like a pure virgin. We need to serve Him in simplicity and purity. But we also need to beware, because, even as the serpent deceived Eve, so the evil one is ever at work, he is ever seeking to deceive Messiah's Bride (2 Cor 11:2-3; Col 2:4-18).

Let us be wise enough to realize that our process of purification does not stop with speaking in tongues. Our transformation ends when we arrive at a certain promised level of holiness. When we are at last adorned as Messiah's Bride, when we are found to be without spot or wrinkle, then our process is complete (Eph 5:27).

So it is that, *even if we speak in tongues*, we could be lacking something…

3

BURYING OUR SINFUL NATURE— LEARNING TO BE OBEDIENT

We are at war.

All the days of our earthly sojourn find us trapped in a war of, flesh against spirit. We are all born with a worldly, carnal mind that is inherently sinful. We poisoned our minds in the Garden. There, we were told, "Of every tree of the garden you may freely eat; but of the tree of the knowledge of good and evil you shall not eat, for in the day that you eat of it you shall surely die" (Gen 2:16-17).

With our great mind, we decided against what we were told, we ate, and we have been cursed with having to choose between good and evil ever since. As part of the "chosen people," we now have to choose, every day, whom we will serve. Moreover, we choose the Spirit of Truth, because He will guide us into all truth. [4]

---

4 Chosen/Choose: See, Exo 19:4-6; Deu 4:37; Josh 24:15; John 16:13; 1 Pet 2:9-10; and *Strong's* # H 977. Also see, *The Voice... Hearing the Almighty* by Batya Wootten, chapter 5, "Forever Chosen To Choose," 2009, Key of David Publishing, Saint Cloud, FL.

Romans 8:7 says of our fleshy minds, "The carnal mind is enmity against God; for it is not subject to the law of God, nor indeed can be" (NKJV). "This is so because the corrupt nature has a hostile attitude toward God. It refuses to place itself under the authority of God's standards because it can't" (God's Word®). "The mind that focuses on human nature is hostile toward God. It refuses to submit to the authority of God's law because it is powerless to do so" (ISV). "The wisdom of the flesh is an enemy to God; for it is not subject to the law of God, neither can it be" (Douay-Rheims Bible). [5]

The true character of our rebellious mind becomes apparent when it is called upon to follow the Torah of God. (We define "Torah" as His *eternal* teachings and instructions: See "Torah" definition, page viii). As New Covenant Believers, we do not seek to obey these instructions as though we might be deemed righteous by keeping them, because all have turned aside and fallen short of His high standard. Apart from the forgiveness we find in Messiah, there is none righteous (Rom 3:10-24). We instead speak of following His Torah teachings, His "Instructions," because, in them, we find strength and wisdom (Deu 4:5-6; 11:8).

However, when faced with the prospect of obedience, our unregenerated mind naturally rebels. So we are told, "Do not be conformed to this world, but be transformed by the renewing of your mind, that you may prove what is that good and acceptable and perfect will of God." Our minds must be renewed, *empowered*, *transformed*. This happens, "not by works of righteousness which we have done, but… through the washing of regeneration and re-newing of the Holy Spirit," (Rom 12:2; Titus 3:5). Our carnal mind will not subject itself to YHVH's Torah and cannot be made holy. We need to learn to think anew— according to the truth of the Word and not according to the mind of man. The Spirit begins this washing when we are reborn. We then bury our sinful nature, our "old man" (Col 3:9), in a water baptism of repentance.

---

5 Various Translations. See http://bible.cc/romans/8-7.htm

Before we enter into that water, we determine in our heart that our old man will be left below. We also determine that, by the power of the Ruach, we will rise and begin a new life in the Messiah, wherein we will begin to have our mind constantly washed and renewed, by the Holy Spirit and by the Word.

In water baptism, death and burial of the carnal nature is figuratively expressed when the repentant one is placed under water, symbolically buried in a watery grave. This experience also speaks of a new beginning in our life.

When we are filled with and empowered by the Holy Spirit, death and burial continually takes place in the spirit realm. Paul said, "I die daily," meaning, his flesh man was dying on a regular basis; every day it had less hold on him, because it was being subjected to the leading of his spirit man (1 Cor 15:31).

Water baptism is more than a symbolic exercise. The death of our flesh man begins to become visible fact, evidenced in that the Spirit begins to purge us of our death-destined ways. As we begin our walk of faith, our sinful nature is progressively slain, and one day, we will not sin any more (Eze 37:23; 1 Cor 15:31; Phil 1:6).

Like *salvation*, our death is a process. Messiah says, if we endure until the end, we *"will be saved"* (Mat 10:22). The Greek word translated "saved" is *sozo*. It means to save, deliver, protect, heal, preserve, and to be made whole; however, this word is in the present tense and should rightly be translated as "being saved." This tense speaks of something that happened in the past and is continuing to happen. [6] Our God does the saving, we cannot do it ourselves, but it is nonetheless a process in our lives.

OUR DESIRES BEGIN TO CHANGE

As we seek to allow our spirit man to rule, rather than our flesh man, and begin to be washed and led by the Spirit, and as our sinful nature is put to death, our *desires* change.

---

6 *Strong's # G 4982.*

In fact, the first inner sign of Holy Spirit baptism is *a desire not to sin*. We no longer desire to *practice* or *continue* in lawlessness.

John says, "No one who has been born from God *practices* sin, because God's seed abides in him. Indeed, *he cannot go on sinning, because he has been born from God*" (1 John 3:9, ISV).

To understand this verse, we must take note of the key word, "practices." [7]

As for practicing sin, *in essence*, John further says:

We are God's children, but what we will be like has not been revealed yet. When Messiah is revealed, we will be like Him. This is our hope, so we want to keep ourselves pure for Him.

If we keep living in sin, we are practicing disobedience. There is no sin in Messiah and to continue in sin suggests we do not really know Him. Once we are truly born anew of the Holy Spirit, we cannot bear to continue in sin. If we do *practice* sin, our habits testify that we instead belong to the evil one.

If we practice Yah's righteousness, we will love our brothers, but, practicing righteous will cause the world to hate us. Yet, we must continue in His love, not just in words but in deeds. We seek to honor His commandments and do what pleases Him. Because He has given us His Spirit, and is in us, we can do His will. Because we love Him, we do not habitually continue in sin, but instead, out of love for Him, we make a habit of practicing love of the brethren.

In the Spirit, we have imputed righteousness, but it is our job to implement that righteousness in this life. If we do miss the mark and fail and transgress, the Ruach convicts us. That is His job. He is sent to convict the world of sin, righteousness, and the judgment to come (see Gen 4:7; John 14:15-16; 16:8; 1 John 3).

Finally, we know we are making a mistake, or missing the mark of our high call, if and when we are ashamed of our actions. When we want to hide our actions from others, it is probably because what we are doing is wrong. The Spirit is convicting us; our innate conscience is thus accusing us, and we need to repent (Rom 2:15).

---

7 *Strong's #'s* G4160 and 4238.

We want to be quick to repent, because we serve a God who has told the whole world about King David's sin and He will not hide our sins. "Be sure your sin will find you out" (Num 32:23).

TEMPTATION

Our goal is sinlessness. Yet, we all fall short of this high call— and yet again, we must not entertain sin nor let it abound in our life (Rom 5:20).

If we are tempted, it does not mean that the Holy Spirit has failed. For, what we experience today in Holy Spirit baptism is not the *fullness* or complete baptism. We will experience full empowerment with the Spirit in the future. At that time, YHVH's people "will no longer defile themselves with their idols, or with their detestable things, or with *any* of their transgressions." At that time, He will deliver us from our scattering and fully cleanse us from our sins (Ezek 37:23).

Later, we will examine *when* this complete cleansing takes place, when this full baptism with the Ruach haKodesh occurs.

For now we note that, while sinlessness is the Father's goal for us, and that we must not *practice* sin, that does not mean we will not be *tempted* in this life. However, temptation in itself is not sin. Temptation can lead to transgression, especially if we allow it to leaven and rise in our soul, and then act upon it. But, once we are empowered by the Ruach, transgressing the Torah goes against our new nature. We may make errors in judgment or leave tasks undone; or like a child, we may have a lot to learn, but we no longer knowingly *desire* to sin. Moreover, in the Spirit, we are better equipped to resist Satan's old tricks and beware his traps.

As for temptation, the Word says of it:

The Devil tried to tempt Messiah Yeshua. And Yeshua said we should pray that we might not be led into temptation but instead be delivered from its evil snare. [8]

---

[8] Mat 4:13; 6:13; 26:41; Mark 1:13; 11:4; 14:38; 22:40-46; Luke 4:1-13; Heb 11:37.

Not resisting temptation can lead to falling away.

Satan can successfully tempt us if we lack self-control; so we first pray that we might be granted this important spiritual gift. [9]

Temptation by Satan is common to man; but God is faithful and promises that He will not allow us to be tempted beyond what we are able to endure. [10]

Satan, and not our God, is the source of temptation.

Moreover, temptation takes root in us when it feeds on our personal lusts: "Let no one say when he is tempted, 'I am being tempted by God'; for God cannot be tempted by evil, and He Himself does not tempt anyone. But each one is tempted when he is carried away and enticed by his own lust"(James 1:13-14, NASB).

Again, we need to pray, on a daily basis, that we might be strengthened in our inner man and delivered from temptation.

We also need to realize that a great company of Believers *will* achieve this high standard. For, John said:

> "I looked, and behold, a Lamb standing on Mount Zion, and with Him one hundred and forty-four thousand, having His Father's name written on their foreheads. And I heard a voice from heaven, like the voice of many waters, and like the voice of loud thunder. And I heard the sound of harpists playing their harps. They sang as it were a new song before the throne, before the four living creatures, and the elders; and no one could learn that song except the hundred and forty-four thousand who were redeemed from the earth. These are the ones who were not defiled with women, for they are virgins. These are the ones who follow the Lamb wherever He goes. These were redeemed from among men, being firstfruits to God and to the Lamb. And in their mouth was found no deceit, for they are without fault before the throne of God" (Rev 14:1-5).

---

9 Luke 8:13; 1 Cor 7:5-9; 9:25; Gal 5:22-25; 6:1; 1 Tim 6:9; 2 Pet 1:4-11.
10 1 Cor 10:13; Heb 2:18; 4:15; James 4:7-8; 2 Pet 2:9.

John spoke of Believers who are faultless. This high standard can, and will be reached. Men like Asa and Job did so in the past:

> "The high places were not removed: nevertheless Asa's heart was perfect with the LORD all his days." And, "The LORD said to Satan, 'Have you considered My servant Job, that there is none like him on the earth, a blameless and upright man, one who fears God and shuns evil?'" (1 Ki 15:14, KJV; Job 1:8).

The sign that follows a valid baptism in the Holy Spirit is a righteous life. The Believer does not merely stop *practicing* sin (this indicates what he *does not do*), but he rises from water baptism to begin *living a life of righteousness* (which indicates what he *does do*). The Spirit-baptized Believer, in short, will not want to sin (Sign 1) and will go on to do righteous deeds (Sign 2). He will seek to obey and desire to be led by Torah's eternal principles. He not only tries to stop breaking the Law of God, but now desires to honor it.

In symbolic language, righteousness (obedience) is referred to as "good fruit." When John the Baptist saw that true righteousness was missing from the lives of those who came to him for baptism, he said to the multitudes who came out to be baptized by him:

> "You brood of vipers! Who warned you to flee from the wrath to come? Therefore bear fruits worthy of repentance, and do not begin to say to yourselves, 'We have Abraham as our father.' For I say to you that God is able to raise up children to Abraham from these stones. And even now the ax is laid to the root of the trees. Therefore every tree which does not bear good fruit is cut down and thrown into the fire" (Luke 3:7-9).

This man of God, who Yeshua called the greatest prophet of all, knew very well that, if righteousness (right actions, good fruit) did not follow water baptism, then their symbolic exercise was essentially pointless.

The same is true of speaking in tongues.

John was looking for good fruit— true repentance followed by obedience in the lives of those who came to him. When he didn't find it, John's denunciations were voiced in no uncertain terms. He said, "Every tree which does not bear good fruit is cut down and thrown into the fire."

Messiah Yeshua said something similar:

> "Beware of false prophets, who come to you in sheep's clothing, but inwardly are ravenous wolves. You will know them by their fruits. Do men gather grapes from thorn bushes or figs from thistles? Even so, every good tree bears good fruit, but a bad tree bears bad fruit. A good tree cannot bear bad fruit, nor can a bad tree bear good fruit. Every tree that does not bear good fruit is cut down and thrown into the fire. Therefore, by their fruits you will know them" (Mat 7:15-20).

In summary, a Ruach baptized Believer will endeavor to live a righteous life. They will be eager to honor YHVH's Torah (John 10:30; 14:15). They will seek to abide by His Covenant, which means, they will honor His Ten Commandments (Deu 4:13). [11]

Not only will Spirit-baptized Believers not want to sin (Sign 1), they will go on to produce good fruit by seeking to obey His Torah Instructions (Sign 2).

Now we will examine baptism's third sign…

---

[11] See *Redeemed Israel: Reunited and Restored*, Batya Ruth Wootten, chapter 27, "True Torah Nurtures the Hearer," 2006, Key of David Publishing, Saint Cloud, FL.

4

A Third, and Very Important Sign

A third, and very important yet often overlooked, sign that accompanies Spirit-filled Believers is their supernatural power to be a witness for Messiah Yeshua.

"Being assembled together with them, He commanded them not to depart from Jerusalem, but to wait for the Promise of the Father, which, He said, you have heard from Me; for John truly baptized with water, but you shall be baptized with the Holy Spirit not many days from now. Therefore, when they had come together, they asked Him, saying, 'Lord, will You at this time restore the kingdom to Israel?' And He said to them, 'It is not for you to know times or seasons which the Father has put in His own authority. But you shall receive power when the Holy Spirit has come upon you; and you shall be witnesses to Me in Jerusalem, and in all Judea and Samaria, and to the end of the earth'" (Acts 1:4-8).

When we broadly consider this matter of supernatural power, we find that it manifests itself in a variety of ways, such as:

- The gift of tongues and prophecy
- Words of knowledge and wisdom
- Supernatural healings and miracles

However, strictly speaking, the supernatural power that Yeshua was referring to in Acts 1:8 was not the power to do these kinds of miracles. The disciples already had that power. Some three years before, Yeshua had called them together and given them supernatural power and authority over all devils and to cure diseases (Luke 9).

Therefore, the power they were to receive at the baptism with the Holy Spirit was not the kind of power they already possessed. It was instead a completely different kind of power.

Bear in mind that many of the prophets of old manifested supernatural power. Elisha, for example, raised the dead through power from God (2 Ki 4:32-36).

The power mentioned in Acts 1:8 was an entirely new kind of power. It has to do with speech. Beyond tongues, it is the power to witness about our resurrected Savior on a supernatural scale. The gift of tongues is a sign that points to our ability to speak with life-changing power about our Messiah.

Yeshua said of this gift:

> A THIRD...
> SIGN...
> POWER
> TO BE A
> WITNESS...

"But you shall receive power when the Holy Spirit has come upon you; *and you shall be witnesses to Me* in Jerusalem, and in all Judea and Samaria, and to the end of the earth" (Acts 1:8).

When the disciples received this new kind of power— which is the power to witness effectively— they turned the world upside down.

Supernatural Speech About
A Supernatural Kingdom

Within a few years the gospel they preached had penetrated areas where even a thousand miracles might have gone unheeded (Luke 16:27-31).

The unique, different power they received on that *Shavuot* Day (Pentecost) was the great power of the Ruach to open the eyes of the spiritually blind, to unstop the ears of the spiritually deaf and to raise the spiritually dead. That is the power Spirit-baptized Believers are promised in Acts 1:8. We are given the power to witness to people, with spectacular, life-changing results. We are given the power to do the spiritually impossible! That kind of power had never been known before. It was new. It is still with us today and is for every Believer. It is ours for the asking.

The supernatural power conferred on us by the Ruach, in short, is not to be confined only to speaking in tongues, or to receiving great insights, or to having power to do amazing physical miracles. These things are given to help us be effective witnesses. They help us to minister to individuals, to pointedly speak and declare the vitally important gospel of Messiah Yeshua's reunited and fully restored Kingdom of Israel (Mat 24:14; Acts 15: Eph 2:15).

That power can change lives for all eternity!

Spiritual manifestations are extremely important, but let us keep them in proper perspective: The primary reason for baptism with the Holy Spirit is to empower us to walk in righteousness and obedience. Next is that we might be *witnesses* for Messiah and His Kingdom. (We are *witnesses* in both our actions and speech.) Third are the various gifts of the Spirit— which are given to help us with the first two goals: Walking in righteousness and being effective witnesses. The Spirit, who knows the minds and hearts of all men, knows exactly what each individual needs. If we will listen to Him, He will tell us exactly what to do and say with each individual.

In this way, we will produce supernatural results, as the disciples did in the early days of the first century church.

The secret to our success is to have "ears to hear" the Spirit. He is all-knowing and He will lead us in His way if we will but listen to Him. Messiah Yeshua said, "Do not worry beforehand about what you are to say, but say whatever is given you in that hour; for it is not you who speak, but it is the Holy Spirit.... [He] will teach you in that very hour what you ought to say" (Mat 10:19; Mark 13:11; Luke 12:12).

With such potential power at our disposal, we do not want to resist the Holy Spirit in any way; we instead want to clearly hear His voice and be led by Him (Acts 7:51; Rom 8:14; 11:8).

Again, we do not want to camp around the signs, but instead want to move in the direction of the glory to which they point. Such signs give evidence that we are on the right route. They signify a divine path to others. They confirm to us that our feet have been set on a Highway of Holiness. Genuine manifestations of the Holy Spirit affirm that we are on our the Road to Zion!

SUPERNATURAL POWER: REAL OR COUNTERFEIT?

Beware. Supernatural power, at its secondary level, meaning, *the power to do physical miracles*, is not confined to "the Church."

Pause and meditate. Think on this important statement.

The power to do physical miracles is found in many religions, pagan and otherwise. Satan is a counterfeiter. In India, Africa, China and the Middle East, and in most nations of the world, there are heathen spiritual leaders who possess miraculous powers, and believe it or not, *many of them speak in tongues*. Like the magicians of ancient Pharaoh, they are very capable of duplicating most of the miracles done by the prophets of God (Exo 7:11,22). [12]

Beware. Snakes can beget snakes.

---

12 Most scholars agree that one sign of demonic possession is speaking in unintelligible tongues. Other signs include divulging future/hidden events, display of powers beyond age or condition, superhuman strength, fits, convulsions, and personality changes. This does not mean that all "speaking in tongues" is demonic, but beware, such things are common in non-Christian, occult, satanic, and Hindu faiths: www.geocities.com/Athens/Rhodes/3543/pentcsl.htm; also http://en.Wikipedia.org/wiki/Speaking_in_tongues

False miracle workers can produce miracles of sorts.

Those who speak lies sometimes also speak in tongues.

The commonly known expressions of supernatural power (miracles, healings, tongues, etc.), wonderful though they may be, absolutely should not be taken as singular signs of the baptism with the Holy Spirit. There is ample evidence that heathen religious leaders often achieve similar spectacular miracles. And, their powers do not emanate from YHVH, the Holy One of Israel.

Moreover, we should not accept something as being from God simply because it is accompanied by a miracle. Let us realize this: Satan can control his own. He can cause demons to release people from various bondages— and he does so in order to deceive people into believing in the abilities of one of his workers.

The false miracle worker may himself be deceived into thinking the miracle came from the Almighty God, when, in fact it is the work of one who wants to be like God: Satan.

Again, a unique sign of the baptism with the Holy Spirit is supernatural witnessing power— about Yeshua haMashiach and His coming Kingdom— and, it is done with apostolic effect.

Power. The power to effectively change lives, to bring people closer to the Messiah of Israel, is a clear sign of the baptism with the Holy Spirit. A Spirit-baptized-Believer should be one who tears down strongholds and builds up people in Messiah.

The spirit-baptized Believer must recognize their call to holiness. YHVH says, "Be holy, because I am holy." We are called to master sin (Gen 4:7; Lev 11:44; 1 Pet 1:16). In our rebirth, we begin to desire to turn from sin, and baptism with the Spirit empowers us to implement that desire and to master sin.

A valid Ruach haKodesh rebirth and baptism should begin with an inward desire for forgiveness, then be evidenced by righteousness (Scriptural obedience) and power to preach the Gospel of the Kingdom with life-changing results. Various gifts are given to us to help us reach these goals, but the gifts are not the end, they are instead, a means to an end.

If traits of holiness are missing in one who claims to be baptized with the Spirit, we are not seeing a proper example of Holy Spirit baptism. [13] It instead indicates that something is lacking. They need to be shown a more accurate way, to repent, or both (Acts 18:26).

EMOTIONS, ARROGANCE, AND TRUE GIFTS

We must never put our emotions or experiences above Scripture. If Scripture counters what we believe, it is time for us to change what we believe.

If someone claims to speak in tongues, but is arrogant about it and thinks they are more spiritual because "they have a gift," they are not properly representing the Holy Spirit. The boastful will not stand before YHVH. He will remove from our midst the proud and will leave among us a humble people (Psa 5:5; Zep 3:11-13).

To be boastful about the gifts of the Spirit is no better than boasting about supposedly keeping the Law. Errant boasting proves we are in error. Scripture asks us, "What do you have that you did not receive? And if you did receive it, why do you boast as if you had not received it? (Mat 20:25-28; Rom 2:23; 3:27; 1 Cor 4:7).

True humility is controlled strength. To be humble is to be modest about one's strengths. If we are to possess this gift, we must possess it in true humility.

In conclusion, we begin our walk with an inward desire to turn from sin, are born anew of the Spirit, then baptized in water. As reborn sons, we are to keep Messiah's commandments, and the Spirit empowers us to do that. Spirit empowerment is seen in Scriptural obedience— honoring the One True God with obedience is one of its most true measures. True manifestations of the Holy Spirit help point the way to Zion. [14]

---

13 Thanks to the following for several of the insights presented in chapters 2 and 3: Stewarton Bible School, www.atschool.eduweb.co.uk.
Malcolm Smith Tapes Series, "Lights and Perfections," www.malcolmsmith.org
14 Mat 3:11; John 14:15-17; Rom 4:3; 2 Cor 5:21; Col 1:27.

5

COUNTERFEITS AND DISOBEDIENCE

I t is a fact that Satan has, over the centuries, produced a counterfeit version of nearly everything God has done. There is not one area of activity, in which He is engaged, that Satan will not, sooner or later, produce one or more inferior, counterfeit versions. Moreover, his counterfeit works, his cheap imitations, have worked their way into the Church.

Thus we find, in various Jewish and Christian circles:

- False Prophets who pose as ministers of righteousness
- Counterfeit Sabbaths, Festivals or Holidays that are being palmed off as genuine Sabbaths, Festivals or Holy Days of our God
- Antichrists and bogus Messiahs pretending to be agents of the One True God
- Miracle workers with phenomenal powers who claim they are instruments of YHVH

These are hard words, but the truth is, in these and many other areas, Satan has counterfeited the true work of YHVH. So we ask, should we naively suppose that, in the matter of the baptism with the Holy Spirit, Satan has been and now is idle?

Not a chance! In this arena the Devil and his demons are extremely active. He has already deceived many into thinking they have been truly baptized with the Holy Spirit. It is a deception of enormous magnitude, and the time has come to expose it. Again, these are hard words, but Scripture proves them to be true.

THE LYING SPIRIT

Many Believers have not even heard of the Lying Spirit. Yet, he is probably the most skilled and effective agent among those who do the work of the Evil One. The Lying Spirit is very skilled in the art of deception. He will succeed where all other agents fail, mainly because he never comes in recognizable garb. He instead poses as the Spirit of Truth. He also transforms himself into an Angel of Light, when, in fact, he is but a messenger of darkness. He inhabits the wolf in sheep's clothing; he is the lamb that speaks like a dragon, the miracle-working False Prophet, from whose mouth proceed falsehoods and deception that are usually sprinkled with a touch of truth.

In the Church this spirit speaks through the mouths of the false prophets, as well as ministers and pastors who blatantly reject the commandments of God— yet think they are following His Son.

Among these are those who instruct their hearers that the baptism with the Holy Spirit is "not for today's Christian," but instead claim that it "ceased with the passing of the last Apostle." Or they claim that "it is of the Devil!" They contend that baptism with the Holy Spirit is obsolete and they disregard God's Torah.

On the other hand, some acknowledge that the baptism with the Holy Spirit is for today, but they proudly parade their supernatural gifts, claiming they serve as evidence that their teachings are "correct." But, the working of wonders does not necessarily prove the verbiage used is truth. Furthermore, the Lying Spirit knows how to be a wonder worker.

We see the methods used by the Lying Spirit in 1 Kings 22:

"Now three years passed without war between Syria and Israel. Then it came to pass, in the third year, that Jehoshaphat the king of Judah went down to visit the king of Israel. And the king of Israel said to his servants, 'Do you know that Ramoth in Gilead is ours, but we hesitate to take it out of the hand of the king of Syria?' So he said to Jehoshaphat, 'Will you go with me to fight at Ramoth Gilead?' Jehoshaphat said to the king of Israel, 'I am as you are, my people as your people, my horses as your horses.' Also Jehoshaphat said to the king of Israel, 'Please inquire for the word of the LORD today.' Then the king of Israel gathered the prophets together, about four hundred men, and said to them, 'Shall I go against Ramoth Gilead to fight, or shall I refrain?' So they said, 'Go up, for the Lord will deliver it into the hand of the king.' And Jehoshaphat said, 'Is there not still a prophet of the LORD here, that we may inquire of Him?' So the king of Israel said to Jehoshaphat, 'There is still one man, Micaiah the son of Imlah, by whom we may inquire of the LORD; but I hate him, because he does not prophesy good concerning me, but evil.' And Jehoshaphat said, 'Let not the king say such things!' Then the king of Israel called an officer and said, 'Bring Micaiah the son of Imlah quickly!' The king of Israel and Jehoshaphat the king of Judah, having put on their robes, sat each on his throne, at a threshing floor at the entrance of the gate of Samaria; and all the prophets prophesied before them. Now Zedekiah the son of Chenaanah had made horns of iron for himself; and he said, 'Thus says the LORD: With these you shall gore the Syrians until they are destroyed.' And all the prophets prophesied so, saying, 'Go up to Ramoth Gilead and prosper, for the LORD will deliver it into the king's hand.' Then the messenger who had gone to call Micaiah spoke to him, saying, 'Now listen, the words of the prophets with one accord encourage the king. Please, let your word be like one of them, and speak encouragement.' And Micaiah said, 'As the LORD lives, whatever the LORD says to me, that I will speak.' Then he came to the king; and the king said to him, 'Micaiah, shall we go to war against Ramoth Gilead, or shall we refrain?' And he answered him, 'Go and prosper, for the LORD will deliver it into the hand of the king!'

"So the king said to him, 'How many times shall I make you swear that you tell me nothing but the truth in the name of the LORD?' Then he said, 'I saw all Israel scattered on the mountains, as sheep that have no shepherd. And the LORD said, "These have no master. Let each return to his house in peace."' And the king of Israel said to Jehoshaphat, 'Did I not tell you he would not prophesy good concerning me, but evil?' Then Micaiah said, 'Therefore hear the word of the LORD: I saw the LORD sitting on His throne, and all the host of heaven standing by, on His right hand and on His left. And the LORD said, "Who will persuade Ahab to go up, that he may fall at Ramoth Gilead?" So one spoke in this manner, and another spoke in that manner. Then a spirit came forward and stood before the LORD, and said, "I will persuade him." The LORD said to him, 'In what way?' So he said, 'I will go out and be a lying spirit in the mouth of all his prophets.' And the LORD said, 'You shall persuade him, and also prevail. Go out and do so.'

"Therefore look! The LORD has put a lying spirit in the mouth of all these prophets of yours, and the LORD has declared disaster against you.'

"Now Zedekiah the son of Chenaanah went near and struck Micaiah on the cheek, and said, 'Which way did the spirit from the LORD go from me to speak to you?' And Micaiah said, 'Indeed, you shall see on that day when you go into an inner chamber to hide!' So the king...said, 'Take Micaiah, and return him to Amon the governor...and to Joash the king's son; and say, "Thus says the king: Put this fellow in prison, and feed him with bread of affliction and water of affliction, until I come in peace."' But Micaiah said, 'If you ever return in peace, the LORD has not spoken by me.' And he said, 'Take heed, all you people!'" (1 Ki 22:1-28).

This illuminating chapter depicts one of the greatest deception this world has ever witnessed. In addition to being an account of the times in which they were written, these prophetic verses speak of a symbolic prediction that is coming true in our day.

In these words we see that God had determined to hand the disobedient Ahab over to destruction because, even after Elijah's spectacular victory on Mount Carmel (chapter 18), Ahab was still allowing his wicked wife Jezebel to corrupt the nation of Israel.

We also see how each spirit, in turn, proposed a plan to trick Ahab to his death. But, only the Lying Spirit's plan would work. And, his plan was to speak through the mouths of the prophets of Israel. These were not the prophets of Baal— they had been taken out two chapters earlier. These men were instead the respected spiritual leaders and prophets of Israel!

The deluded prophet Zedekiah was wearing a pair of iron horns (verse 11), which symbolize supernatural power. But even with all of his great power and numerical advantage (said to be 400 to 1 in verse 6), Zedekiah was nonetheless delivering a false message. Worse yet, he was totally unaware that the Lying Spirit was using his tongue. Even the righteous King Jehoshaphat believed in the false prophets, and he almost lost his life as a result.

This ancient experience was recorded in the Hebrew Scriptures because it contains an important message for us. We are those who live in the closing days of this present age. And the Word tells us that "all these things happened to them as examples, and they were written for our admonition, upon whom the ends of the ages have come" (1 Cor 10:11).

The above narrative serves as an example, a type, an illustration. It depicts a great spiritual deception that is destined to come upon this world in the end of days. And, that awful scheduled time has already begun...

A BLUEPRINT FOR THE LATTER DAYS

As we further examine this important matter, we see that the story provides a spiritual blueprint, a dramatized prophecy, it depicts "world-encompassing deception," and it is sweeping through the Church in our day.

The pattern portrays a deception that was the work of the Lying Spirit of old. And strange as it may seem, YHVH is again allowing multitudes of rebellious souls to believe that same Lying Spirit. YHVH is allowing this because, just like Ahab and Jezebel, the people of our day do not really want to obey YHVH's instructions. And they are then deceived into working with false prophets.

We read in 2 Thessalonians 2 of Satan using "all power, signs, and lying wonders" to work "deception among those who perish," because they did not "love the truth." Because they do not receive the truth (about "The Truth," Yeshua) YHVH sends them a "strong delusion, that they should believe the lie" (vss. 2:1-12; John 14:6).

The Lying Spirit is once more at work. He is again posing as the Spirit of Truth. As in the days of old, his spokesmen of today have supernatural, occult power, like that of the iron-horned Zedekiah (1 Ki 22:11; 2 Chr 18:10). Once more, the Lying Spirit has a majority on his side and is deceiving many into thinking his people speak the truth. But in the end, even those whom this false spirit deludes will find out that he was a liar— that the truth was not in him.

Now, consider an amazing, similar, end-time scene that is described by our Lord, Messiah Yeshua. He said:

> "Not everyone who says to me, 'Lord, Lord,' shall enter the kingdom of heaven, but he who does the will of my Father in heaven. Many will say to me in that day, 'Lord,

COUNTERFEITS AND DISOBEDIENCE

Lord, have we not prophesied in your name, cast out demons in your name, and done many wonders in your name?' Then I will declare to them, I never knew you; depart from me, you who practice lawlessness!" (Mat 7:21-23).

This is one of the most amazing spiritual pictures portrayed in the Bible. It staggers the imagination. Think about it. It describes many supposed Believers who:

- Openly profess Jesus as their Savior (they say, "Lord, Lord")
- They have prophesied in His Name
- They have cast out devils in His Name
- In His Name they have done many wonderful works and have even performed miracles!

Sadly, for all their preaching and wonder-working powers, Yeshua will refuse these people entry into His Kingdom. Yet this is the same Yeshua who said, "He who comes to me I will in no wise cast out."

What is the reason for this seemingly astonishing rejection?

It is important that we understand this point lest we, too, fail to qualify for the same reasons.

Scripture tells us they will be rejected because they are evildoers, workers of iniquity, lawless ones. Messiah will say to them, "I tell you I do not know you, where you are from. Depart from Me, all you workers of iniquity" (Luke 13:27). In the New International Version (NIV) this verse reads, "I don't know you or where you come from. Away from me, all you evildoers!" Yeshua also says to them, "I will declare to them, 'I never knew you; depart from me, you who practice lawlessness!'" (Mat 7:23).

So, what is this lawlessness, who is working it, and how so?

Strong's Greek Dictionary reveals that *workers* is translated from *ergates*, which can be used figuratively to speak of a *teacher*. Moreover, *iniquity* is from *adikia*, which speaks of *injustice*, of wrong character and unrighteousness. *Lawlessness* is taken from *anomia*, which means violation of law, wickedness, iniquity, transgression.

It is taken from *anomos*, meaning one who does not subject themselves to the Law; and by implication is thus a Gentile, a heathen— specifically, one that is not counted among the chosen, separated, covenant, people of Israel. [15]

THE MYSTERY OF INIQUITY...

What is it that invalidates the powerful arguments these Believers put to Messiah? What is this lawlessness that disqualifies these wonder-workers from the Kingdom of Heaven?

The answer is, *iniquity*— and it is said to be a "mystery" that is "now at work" (2 Th 2:7, KJV). Iniquity, or lawlessness, is deliberate, persistent sin, it is willful refusal to acknowledge one's sin and turn from it and instead obey the voice and instructions of the Almighty (Heb 3:10-12). Lawlessness is absolute rejection of YHVH's commandments. It is disobedience of the worst kind. It is an act of spiritual rebellion that goes deep and is so deluding that it leads to dismissing all charges of wrong-doing. It is an internal sin that ultimately produces the external fruit of transgression.

There are some guilty and soon-to-be rejected ones who even profess that Jesus is the Christ. Indeed, with their marvelous powers they are thought to be leaders in the field of the miraculous. In His Name they have cast out demons and done many wonderful works.

> LAWLESSNESS
>
> ...MEANS
>
> VIOLATION OF
>
> LAW, WICKEDNESS,
>
> INIQUITY,
>
> TRANSGRESSION,
>
> AND
>
> UNRIGHTEOUSNESS

They have worked signs, wonders, miracles, and given powerful testimony. But in the end, it avails them nothing. The Lord still refuses them entry and position in His Kingdom.

---

15 *Strong's:* workers: #G2040; iniquity: #G93; lawlessness/*anomia*: #'s G458 and 459, respectively. Law: see chapter 7.

If we do not want to be counted among those who are counted out, we must ask ourselves, *"Why are they being rejected?"*

They are counted out because they refuse to recognize and obey the Commandments; they refuse YHVH's eternal Torah. They are willfully and persistently disobedient. Knowingly or unknowingly, their tongues have been channels for the "Lying Spirit." They have taught lawlessness to their own ruin and encouraged others to do the same. To be sure, they can do miracles, but that counts for nothing when weighed against their iniquity.

A terrible scene is portrayed in these verses. As we consider this deception, we ask, Who are these deceived people? What hallmarks identify them?

They are *many* and they supposedly work *miracles* for our Lord. He says, "Many will say to Me in that day, 'Lord, Lord, have we not prophesied in Your name, cast out demons in Your name, and done many wonders in Your name?" (Mat 7:21-23).

Presently, some wonder-working Christian groups might be said to fit some or all of this description and to be doing the things described in the prophecy. Some even claim such powers almost exclusively, and many claim to have a Holy Spirit baptism. In addition, many who call themselves Christian are opposed to the idea of "the Law" (as they mistakenly see it). It is taught in many churches that the Law is dead and that it does not apply to them because it was nailed to the cross. However, to the extent that we mistakenly preach and prophesy in YHVH's Name, supposedly cast out demons, or work false wonders, we run the risk of being deluded, of appearing to, at least on some level, fit the outline found in Scripture's blueprint.

EXAMINE YOURSELVES...

To maintain balance we must acknowledge that, to some extent, all of us are deluded, all have some mistaken beliefs. None of us are all-knowing. Moreover, to use the word "deluded" in this way is not to imply that *every* Believer who might be involved with a movement that misunderstands spiritual gifts is "deluded." As Believers we grow in our faith and pass from glory to glory (2 Cor 3:18). We assume that such will be the case with many who have not yet been instructed otherwise. Also, if lawlessness is key, this judgment would have to extend to all who do not truly and fully uphold YHVH's Law. And, apart from being redeemed by Messiah's grace, *all* of us "fall short of His glory" (Rom 3:23-25).

We do not point out these things to condemn anyone, but to encourage a closer following of Scripture, which tells us to "examine ourselves," to see if we are truly in the faith (2 Cor 13:5). We also point out these things with the idea that, knowledge of mistakes must *never* be used as a whip with which to beat those who need instruction. Our point is to encourage right thinking, not to condemn mistakes.

Nonetheless, we ask: What will happen to the souls who are deluded? Are they forever lost because they have been tricked by the Lying Spirit? Will all of them perish because they try to justify their anti-law doctrines, and because they base their supposed validity on experiences that are supported by supposed miracles?

No. Many will realize their error, and like King Jehoshaphat will cry out to God before it is too late (1 Ki 22:32). Many will repent and the Holy Spirit will clothe and empower them in truth, then, from the heart they will begin to obey the eternal commandments of YHVH's promised New Covenant. [16] To them, we show mercy without measure.

> KNOWLEDGE... MUST NEVER BE USED AS A WHIP WITH WHICH TO BEAT THOSE WHO NEED INSTRUCTION

However, many others, like Ahab and Jezebel, will not obey. They will continue to practice lawlessness and will perish in their sins. From them, we flee for our lives.

---

16 Jer 31:31-33; John 14:15-21; Heb 8:10; Rev 3. Law: See chapter 7.

We flee because, in the end-days, some will have "a form of godliness but deny its power." From such people, we turn away because they are always learning, but are unable to come to the knowledge of the truth" (2 Tim 2:22-3:7).

Again, we see our need to be led by the Spirit, to know whether we are to share the Good News, or flee for our lives. And we can trust that the Spirit will lead us, even as Messiah was led. He sometimes spoke to spiritual leaders, and sometimes with sinners and publicans. He always knew where to go, what to say, and how to act, because He was led by the Spirit. The same should be true for us (Mat 4:1; Luke 4:1; Rom 8:14; Gal 5:18).

Pointing out the mistakes of people who are baptized in the Spirit, but do not yet understand about keeping the Messiah's commandments, is not done to imply that all who claim to follow, or honor, or keep Torah's commandments do so from a pure heart.

Legalism and pride can quickly creep in and taint good intentions. All must seek to walk a balanced walk, like that of Messiah Yeshua: He kept all the Law, yet was grace personified.

We must seek to be like Him in every way.

THE LAW AND THE SPIRIT...

Deceptive doctrines can lead us down a deadly path. They can lead to our being deluded, and ultimately to dismissal (Isa 29:10-14).

The nature of this issue is eternal, it is a matter of life and death. So, we ask, what did Yeshua mean by "lawlessness"?

To begin, we acknowledge that the "Law of the Spirit" of life in Messiah has "set us free from the law of sin and of death." In Him, we are made "servants of a new covenant, not of the letter but of the Spirit; for the letter kills, but the Spirit gives life." In His New Covenant, the "Law" is written on our hearts, *by the Holy Spirit.* [17]

What is the "Law of the Spirit"? Did Yeshua do away with the Ten Commandments and establish a new law based on *love*?

---

[17] Jer 31:31; Luke 22:20; Rom 8:2; 1 Cor 11:25; 2 Cor 3:6; Heb 8:,13; 9:15; 12:24.

Yeshua said, "If you love Me, you will keep My commandments." He also said He is "One" with the Father, and that His words came "from the Father" (John 10:30; 14:15,24). His "words" do not oppose the Father's, but work in conjunction with them.

Thus, we cannot separate Yeshua's commandments from those of His Heavenly Father.

We will return to this subject in chapter 7 (see especially the section, "Dead to the Law— Alive to the Spirit").

For now we note that, broadly speaking, the Abrahamic and Mosaic Covenants have to do with earthly issues and the flesh man, but Yeshua's Covenant has to do with eternity and our spirit man, and it is based on "better promises." Yeshua's Kingdom "is not of this world." To participate in it, one must be born of the Spirit, and have the Spirit write the Father's Laws on our heart (John 18:36; Heb 7:22; 8:6; 12:24).

Yeshua was "full of the Holy Spirit...[and] was led by the Spirit." And, He "fulfilled" the sacrificial Laws and showed us how to walk in the Law, yet be grace personified (Luke 4:1).

Simply put, "The one who says he abides in Him ought himself to walk in the same manner as He walked" (1 John 2:6, NASB). [18]

Having addressed some of the failings of the Church, we now ask, why is it that some in the Messianic movement seem to resist the Holy Spirit?

---

18 See "Torah," page xiii; chapter 7; and the books, *Mama's Torah: The Role of Women* (2004) and *Redeemed Israel: Reunited and Restored* (2006), both by Batya Wootten, Key of David Publishing, Saint Cloud, FL.

6

LAWLESSNESS AND LEGALISM: REPENTING OF BOTH

Why is it that the Holy Spirit is not openly spoken of by some in the Messianic Movement today?

As mentioned in the Introduction to this book, many Messianic Believers, possibly even the majority of congregational members in Messianic meetings today, have their roots in the Charismatic/ Pentecostal Sunday churches. So how is it that we are now part of a movement in which some appear to resist the Holy Spirit?

How? First, many of us began to discover that we had not been told the whole story in our churches. We dug into the Word and found the truth about our Hebrew roots. We discovered the feasts of Israel. We found the many eternal truths of the Torah, and we began to study to show ourselves approved. We began to teach, preach and practice honoring Torah. Such things are desirable signs of maturity. But, along the way, some became angry, and some made mistakes concerning the uninitiated....

We point out our mistakes in hopes of encouraging Spirit-led pursuit of our heritage— while recognizing that we have not yet achieved perfection and are in need of some course correction.

For example, some have mistakenly been intellectually focused on Torah. Studying Torah is good, but it is to be written on hearts made tender toward YHVH and His people (Jer 31:31-33). As we return to Torah, we also must give proper attention to the fruits and gifts of the Spirit and emphasize both the Spirit and the Word.

We must not bicker and back-bite over non-essentials. Such as, who is or is not a biological Israelite, use and pronunciation of the Sacred Name, and which calendar to use. We want to respectfully discuss issues, but remember that in the end, *arguments* cause divisions, drive people away and quench the Holy Spirit.

Remember, wicked shepherds *divide* the flock, good shepherds *unite* them (Eze 34). We want to unite the Body of Messiah.

As we seek to find our way in our new walk, let us remember the basic requirements for fellowship outlined in Acts 15:20-21. We ask that everyone abstain from idols, fornication, things strangled, and blood; we preach and teach Moses, and allow the Holy Spirit to do His work. We also understand that every individual and congregation is not on the same page in their understanding.

In this difficult time of transition, we must allow for individual growth and not be quick to cut people off. After all, Messiah Yeshua told His followers to let the wheat and tares grow together until the reapers gather in the harvest. Only the reapers have permission to make that division. Only the Father has the right to disinherit a son (Mat 15:29-30).

Nonetheless, due to anger with the Church, tragically, some Messianics have made a conscious decision to walk away from the baptism with the Holy Spirit. Some do so because of the "crazy antics" they have seen, and some because of "knee-jerk" reactions against anything that is thought to be "of the Church." But do we thus stand guilty of erecting walls and encouraging division? If so, have we forgotten that it is through the Church that most of us initially responded to a call to faith in the Messiah, as well as a call to baptism with the Holy Spirit? In turn, this means, the greatest things that can happen to a man come to us from "the Church."

Yet, in our misguided desire to "get it right," to return to our Hebraic roots, and be united with brother Judah, some have become cruel, even merciless concerning Church mistakes. We tend to be forgiving concerning mistakes made by the Jewish people, but most do not have a similar heart of forgiveness toward the Church. We dismiss Judah's stumbling because we know that a partial hardening happened to Israel. But we have failed to see that *both* the houses of Israel were destined to *stumble* over the One who would be a *Sanctuary* to them. Both Judah and Ephraim have stumbled over the Messiah (Isa 8:13-14; John 2:19-22; Rom 11). Thus, we need to forgive Ephraim's stumbling too. We need to be people of solution and patiently instruct interested parties about a "more accurate way" (Acts 18:26).

Another reason why some resist the Holy Spirit has to do with a problem similar to that of the Corinthians of old. Paul rebuked them for wanting the "best gifts" in order to draw attention to themselves (1 Cor 12:31). Some do that today.

It is wrong to flaunt spiritual gifts as though they were merit badges. Paul exhorted us to earnestly desire/covet, the best, or greater gifts, but for the profit of all. Moreover, he said the better gift is love. We move in the Spirit out of love for Messiah's Body.

Yet, wanting to avoid errant behavior, in turn, some Messianics have become guilty of a similar type of "flaunting." Some parade their new-found understanding of their Hebrew roots and Torah obedience. Some have acted toward Christians like goose-stepping "Torah Terrorists." They have paraded around in prayer shawls and looked down their noses at anyone who celebrates Christmas or Easter or is merciful with those who do so. They have been relentless with those whom they feel do not "gather on the right day." They erect walls of separation made of derogatory and condescending rhetoric.

Our actions could lead the Messiah to conclude that they too have errantly prophesied in His name (in regard to those who belong to "the Church"). That they too have errantly sought to cast out demons in His name (especially with "Christian Paganism"). And that, they too have done many supposedly wonderful works (specifically in demanding that people "Keep Torah").

Like misuse of the Father's gifts of the Spirit, these things too can be misrepresented. So it is that some have listened to the Lying Spirit in regard to lawlessness and some in regard to legalism. There are people in both camps who stand guilty of entertaining a haughty attitude (Prov 29:23). Both camps have those who are guilty of gossip and slander via an evil tongue, or *Lashon Hara*.

Of such evils YHVH warns, "Let everyone who names the name of Messiah depart from iniquity" (2 Tim 2:19). Yeshua gave Himself that He might redeem us from "all lawlessness" (Titus 2:14). He loves righteousness and "hates lawlessness" (Heb 1:9). James warns, "The tongue is a fire, a world of iniquity... [I]t defiles the whole body...and it is set on fire by hell" (vs 3:6). We must depart from such sin, for YHVH warns in Zephaniah:

> "I will remove from your midst your proud, exulting ones, and you will never again be haughty on My holy mountain. But I will leave among you a humble and lowly people, and they will take refuge in the name of the LORD. The remnant of Israel will do no wrong and tell no lies, nor will a deceitful tongue be found in their mouths; for they will feed and lie down with no one to make them tremble" (Zep 3:11-13, NASB).

BALANCED JUDGMENT REGARDING EPHRAIM

We must judge with righteous judgment and give honor where honor is due (John 7:24; Rom 13:17; 1 Cor 6:3). In this vein we readily agree that the organized Church has made many mistakes — and that we must not continue in them. But, let us not judge unjustly. For, the righteous ones in the Church also have a record of accomplishment that is worthy of recollection. As part of the chosen people, we have been through revivals, awakenings, and outpourings of the Spirit. Most important, we have been washed by the blood of the Lamb. We have heard His voice— even caught visions imparted to us by His Spirit. He long ago put the taste of His Salvation/Yeshua in our mouths. He has allowed us to walk in times of great anointing, to even carry the news of His glorious salvation to the ends of the earth. Our gifting is powerful. It is one that our God continues to correct and perfect in this hour.

When perfected, ours is a precious and prized anointing, and it needs to be shared with brother Judah. So, let us not forget the truth of whom we are and whom we are called to be. We are sons and daughters of the Most High. He has called us to be a holy nation and chosen kings and priests (1 Pet 2:9-10; Hos 1-2). We are Ephraim, long-lost brother of Judah. [19] And we now have a job to do. Before us lies the task of becoming healers of the breach, men in whom the Holy Breath of God has breathed life, so that, in turn, we might breathe on the rest of Israel's dry bones (Isa 58; Eze 37).

Let us therefore seek to walk in the true Spirit of the Torah that the Holy Spirit is supposed to write on our hearts. Then we will be empowered to help affect the reunion of the whole house of Israel. This reunion is dear to our God, and to accomplish it He will freely arm us with the life-changing power of His Holy Spirit. With all our hearts, let us therefore seek that infilling, to be "overwhelmed" with that transforming power.

LOST YET FRUITFUL

Ephraim's name means "doubly fruitful." [20] His heirs were destined to be scattered among the nations, there to be "lost" as to their true identity as part of the people of Israel. Yet, it is there, among the nations that they were destined to begin to fulfill the

---

19 Constance Fischer, "We Are Ephrayim," One Stick Ministries, email posting 11/28/08.
20 *Strong's* # G 8669; Gen 41:52.

promises made to them by their forefather, Jacob. For Jacob said to his sons, "Gather yourselves together, that I may tell you that which shall befall you *in the last days*" (Gen 49:1). Moses likewise spoke of blessings that would be bestowed *while Israel was scattered among the nations*. Plus, Peter proclaimed that the "last days" had begun (Deu 33; Acts 2:16-17). Both houses were scattered, both made certain mistakes, yet both have been used by the Holy One, despite their shortcomings. And, it is now time for both houses to rise above their previous failings; it is time to come together and be empowered by the Father's Ruach.

While it is right for us to stand for the truth, we must not be merciless with those who do not yet understand the truths that have been granted us to see. Yah knows more than we do, and He does not treat us that way. He also tells us He desires mercy more than sacrifice, knowledge of Him more than burnt offerings, and that He came to call sinners to repentance (Hos 6:6; Mat 9:13).

Sadly, our haughtiness has driven people away from His truth. Sadder still, who will lead these people to the ancient paths of Zion if not us? We are called to work the works of Messiah in the earth. But if we are haughty with those whom He would draw near, He will surely one day tell us that our supposed righteousness is but filthy rags in His sight. So let us first be merciful, so those whom He wants to reach might be more skillfully drawn to Him.

Lawlessness or legalism, the end result is the same. Satan has deceived both the Sunday Church and Messianics, albeit in different ways, and both are rendered ineffective on many fronts.

If our earnest desire is to see the "restoration of all things" (Acts 3:20-23), we must change our behavior. We must realize that change can come to our movement, but it will only be done through an outpouring of the Ruach haKodesh. In the Spirit, we can walk in a newness of life. We can do this because the baptism with the Holy Spirit is not a one-time event in our lives. It is instead a constant infilling, as we will discover in later chapters.

We now ask, *"When, and why, will the 'fullness' of the Ruach come?"*

7

THE COMING FULLNESS OF THE RUACH: WHEN AND WHY

*N*ow *He, which established us with you in Christ, and hath anointed us, is God; Who hath also sealed us, and given the earnest of the Spirit in our hearts.... Now he that hath wrought us for the selfsame thing is God, who also hath given unto us the earnest of the Spirit (2 Cor 1:21-22; 5:5, KJV).*

The Greek word translated "earnest" is *arrhabon* and means a pledge, like earnest money or property given in advance as security on a purchase. This deposit represents Messian's promise that there is "more to come." [21] For now, we are like a betrothed bride that is given a pledge. We patiently await our beloved Bridegroom, and the fullness of all that will be ours when He returns.

For now, we have "this treasure in earthen vessels." However, like a fully dressed bride, a day is coming when our mortality will be clothed in glorious immortality (1 Cor 15:53; 2 Cor 4:7).

---

21 Ernest/Deposit: *Strong's* #'s G728 and H6162; also see Rom 8:23; Eph 1:14; 2 Tim 1:14.

The signs, wonders, miracles, and tongues that are given to us by the Spirit are like a down payment. They are treasures that seal the deal, until the contract is finalized. The Holy Spirit is given to us "without measure" (John 3:34). But, our flesh nature is hostile toward God, which makes it difficult for us to operate in the fullness of the Spirit at this time. Still, Abba allows us to have a taste of the Spirit, to hold us over until He finally and fully institutes the New Covenant with the "whole House of Israel." Until then, we await the redemption of our bodies and only have a "first fruits" deposit of the Spirit (Rom 8:23). We should always be seeking the fullness of all that is now available, yet resting in knowing that our final fulfillment will ultimately be at Messiah's second coming.

> "Behold, the days are coming, says the LORD, when I will make a new covenant with the house of Israel and with the house of Judah— not according to the covenant that I made with their fathers in the day that I took them by the hand to lead them out of the land of Egypt, My covenant which they broke, though I was a husband to them, says the LORD.
>
> "But this is the covenant that I will make with the house of Israel after those days, says the LORD: I will put My law in their minds, and write it on their hearts; and I will be their God, and they shall be My people. No more shall every man teach his neighbor, and every man his brother, saying, 'Know the LORD,' for they all shall know Me, from the least of them to the greatest of them, says the LORD. For I will forgive their iniquity, and their sin I will remember no more" (Jer 31:31-34).

THE REASON FOR GIVING THE HOLY SPIRIT

Many in the Church claim to be filled with the Spirit and to be "New Covenant" Christians. They also boldly teach that the Law is obsolete and fulfilled in the crucifixion of Jesus. But this idea hinders our ability to see the real reason for giving the Holy Spirit.

This thinking cannot be true based on Jeremiah 33:33. "But this is the covenant that I will make with the house of Israel after those days, says the LORD: I will put My law in their minds, and write it on their hearts; and I will be their God, and they shall be My people" (Jer 31:33; also see vss.31-32; Heb 8:8-13; 10:16-17).

Since evidence of the fullness of God's promised New Covenant is having His Law written on the hearts of its people, we ask: *Do we see this being fulfilled in those of Sunday Christianity?*

Yes and no. The Sunday-based Romanized Church is known for mistakenly teaching that the Law has been done away with. Yet, mistakes in understanding the Law should come as no surprise concerning the people of Ephraim, for we read of them:

> "Because Ephraim has made many altars for sin, they have become for him altars for sinning. I have written for him the great things of My law, But they were considered a strange thing" (Hosea 8:11-12).

Nonetheless, change was promised to these once wayward ones, change would come to the Israelites once destined to become a fullness of the Gentiles. Like the house of Judah, so too, would their veil be lifted from formerly blinded eyes. Then they would be able to see and would cease to stumble over their Sanctuary, Messiah Yeshua (Gen 48:19; Isa 8:13-14; John 2:19-22; Rom 11:25).

In line with this precious promise, we now see a stirring among the former Gentiles who have been brought nigh to Israel's divine commonwealth (Eph 2:11-22). They are putting off old misunderstandings about the Law and putting on the adornments that come with seeing its eternal truths. They are putting away the bondage of legalism and putting on the strength found in the wisdom of Torah's teachings (Deu 4:6; 11:8; Prov 1:8; 3:1,22; 6:20).

The NIV says Ephraim saw the Law "as something alien."

This surely describes Church attitudes. One might even say their anthem is "We are not under the Law!" But that is only *part* of the truth. And many are beginning to realize this.

The Church is right in that Believers are not "under" the Law. [22] We are called to be born of and immersed in the Holy Spirit. And, according to the Word, "If you are led by the Spirit, you are not under the Law"(Gal 5:18). However, as the late Paul Harvey always said:

"Now for the rest of the story..."

DEAD TO THE LAW– ALIVE TO THE SPIRIT

As Messiah's followers, we cannot fully keep every commandment; moreover, breaking the Law called for a sacrifice, and in many cases, being stoned to death. [23]

Since we are all guilty of breaking those laws, to live under that system and apart from Messiah's sacrifice on our behalf likens us to being "dead men walking." We have been weighed, found wanting, and are awaiting our execution date. Apart from eternal salvation in Yeshua, we are dead in our trespasses and sins, because, the wage of sin is death.

As Believers, we can only approach the precepts of Torah as those who have been tried, found guilty, and put to death for our sins. But at the same time, we have been redeemed from the curse of death that comes from breaking the Law. We who hope in Messiah Yeshua can rejoice, because in Him, we are raised in newness of life. We live in the earth, yet we live anew! In our new Spirit-led life, we choose to serve the One Who found us guilty in the first place. Paul thus writes that we "become dead to the law through the body of Christ, that you may be married to another— to Him who was raised from the dead, that we should bear fruit to God" (Rom 6:23; 7:4).

If we look to the Law for salvation, we are deceived. If we seek to establish our righteousness by keeping the Law, we must keep the whole Law and return to the Mosaic system of sacrifice.

---

22 Rom 2:12; 3:19; 1 Cor 9:20-21; Gal 3:23; 4:4-5.

23 Exo 21:12,16,17; 21:29; 22:19; 31:14,15; Lev 20:2,11,13,27; 24:16; Num 3:10; 15:35; Deu 13:10; 17:5; 21:21; 22:21; 22:24. See this list in *Mama's Torah* by Batya Wootten, page 87.

We do not want to do that. We cannot do that.

YHVH allowed the Temple to be destroyed after Yeshua paid the price for us, so we cannot offer the required animal sacrifices. Yet, we must emulate Him. And, He kept the commandments. He also explained His role concerning the Law: "Do not think that I came to abolish the law or the prophets; I did not come to abolish but to fulfill" (Mat 5:17; 1 Cor 6:19; 1 Pet 1:18-19).

What does *fulfill* mean?

Yeshua came to fulfill (satisfy) the sacrificial requirements of the Law, once and for all. [24] He came *to fully preach and perfect the Law, to give full, complete meaning to it, to personify how it is to be walked out by man*. And, "He who says he abides in Him ought himself also to walk just as He walked" (1 John 2:6).

Messiah is the pattern. We are to walk as He walked.

WISDOM IS STILL WISDOM

While Yeshua satisfied the *sacrificial* requirements of the Law, His sacrifice did not annul or abolish the *wisdom* found in Torah. Wisdom will forever be wisdom. Furthermore, YHVH's commandments bring soundness to our lives. He said of them, "Keep and do them, for that is your wisdom and your understanding in the sight of the peoples.... keep every commandment....so that you may be strong and go in and possess the land" (Deu 4:6; 11:8). We want to be both wise and strong, so we study His instructions to gain wisdom. In this way, we learn from our fathers and hopefully do not repeat their mistakes. "For whatever was written in earlier times was written for our instruction" (Rom 15:4; 2 Tim 3:16).

To know how to honor Torah, we look to Messiah Yeshua. He kept the Law yet is the epitome of grace and mercy. As born-again Believers, we are to have His Spirit write the Law on our hearts. Moreover, even though He put greater emphasis on the heart, Yeshua's Law is nonetheless based in the Father's Law, because He and the Father are "One" (John 10:30).

---

24 Fulfill: *Strong's* # G 4134. Rom 6:10; Heb 7:27; 9:12; 10:10;1 Pet 3:18; Jude 1:3.

Abba (the Father) does not want us to be obedient because we feel it is "mandated" that we do so. He is not looking for puppets or robots. He wants our obedience to be born from a heart filled with love for Him. He wants Israel to choose Him, to choose to love His ways, and to realize that His Laws better our lives (John 14:15). [25]

We must understand these crucial truths if we want the fullness of the Spirit, because the Spirit is given that He might write Father Abba's eternal Laws on our hearts. To have His Spirit dwell in us in fullness, we must be in agreement with His end purposes— which means we cannot deny the eternal wisdom of His Law.

Seeing the Glory That is to Come

For now, we dwell in corruptible bodies and we do not have, nor can we handle the fullness of the Spirit. But we are moving toward a day when our mortal bodies will put on immortality. When Yeshua comes again and we have new incorruptible bodies, then He will give us the fullness of the Ruach haKodesh. At that time, we will be able to handle all of His spiritual blessing and power. Until then, we only have an earnest deposit of the Spirit, a taste of what is to come (Rom 8:8,21,23; 1 Cor 15:50,53).

We get a glimpse of the glory to come when we examine the setting of John the Baptist. Scripture tells us that multitudes came to him to be baptized in the Jordan River. They came from every walk of life and from all directions to be buried in a watery grave and to be raised up to walk in newness of life.

John serves as a symbolic figure, as did his environment and ceremonial setting; his is another "spiritual blueprint." The reality of that shadow will be seen when Yeshua baptizes us in His River of Life. Then, our sinful, carnal nature, with all its inherent, lawless traits will be slain and forever buried. We will rise anew with minds that are fully overwritten with the eternal Law of YHVH— the Almighty God of Israel (Isa 11:9; 65:25; Joel 3:17; Rev 22:1).

---

25 See *Redeemed Israel: Reunited and Restored*, Wootten, Chapter 28, "The Law and New Covenant Believers," 2006, Key of David Publishing, St. Cloud, FL 34770.

Every Believer who enters the Kingdom of Heaven will be fully baptized in the Holy Spirit. The old carnal nature, the one that we are all born with, the nature that is inherently hostile to the commandments of our God, will be slain. In its place the Messiah will give us a mind like His own and write on it His Torah. We will then be totally obedient sons and daughters of God, not because we have to be, but instinctively, and because we want to be.

This glorious hope is guaranteed in YHVH's promise:

> "Finding fault with them, He says: 'Behold, the days are coming, says the LORD, when I will make a new covenant with the house of Israel and with the house of Judah— not according to the covenant that I made with their fathers in the day when I took them by the hand to lead them out of the land of Egypt; because they did not continue in My covenant, and I disregarded them, says the LORD. 'For this is the covenant that I will make with the house of Israel after those days, says the LORD: I will put My laws in their mind and write them on their hearts; and I will be their God, and they shall be My people. None of them shall teach his neighbor, and none his brother, saying, 'Know the LORD,' for all shall know Me, from the least of them to the greatest of them"(Heb 8:8-11; also see verse 10:16).

The above-described experience is, in fact, the climax of the New Covenant. It describes a time when the whole family of God will assemble at Mount Zion and have YHVH's Law forever and fully inscribed on the tablets of their souls. In this Covenant His commandments will be inscribed on our minds, forever etched by His divine hand into our spiritual minds. We will then be absolutely holy people in thought, word and deed (Micah 4:7; Heb 12:22; Rev 14:1). The glorious promise is that Messiah Yeshua will fully baptize us with His Ruach haKodesh.

Until that glorious day comes, we must seek Him with all our heart, each and every day of our lives.

RECEIVING THE HOLY DEPOSIT

If you have not yet asked the Messiah to fill you with His Spirit, know that He will do so if you ask. He will slay your sinful nature, which in varying degrees, is at enmity with His Torah. In the place of sinful rebellion, He will ultimately put total obedience.

When we experience the ultimate full baptism with the Ruach haKodesh, we will never sin again, then 1 John 3:9 will fully apply: "Whoever has been born of God does not sin, for His seed remains in him; and he cannot sin, because he has been born of God."

This wonderful prospect awaits every Believer who desires with all their heart to obey God and to enter His Kingdom. If the Spirit is speaking to you now about receiving this wonderful gift, do not back away: "In the day when you hear His voice, do not harden your heart" (Heb 3:8,15). Open your heart and invite Him in, now. If you have been resisting Him out of fear, ask Him to forgive you and fill you (Mat 7:9-11). Trust that He will give you good gifts, put your feet on the path of salvation, and lead you back to Zion.

Do not approach this infilling as though you will be gaining a "spiritual merit badge." Do it because your heart is truly hungry for more of the Holy One. Also, do not put the Spirit "in a box" due to preconceived ideas, but allow Him to move at will. For "the wind blows where it wishes and you hear the sound of it, but do not know where it comes from and where it is going; so is everyone who is born of the Spirit" (John 3:8). We cannot see the wind, but it is there, and it can be gentle or quite powerful.

The baptism with the Holy Spirit is given that you might have supernatural power to be Messiah's witness, and the best witness you can be is one who honors Him. That means, follow His ways, honor His Word, and love like He loved.

With the Ruach's baptism you can have awesome power today. Even though it is only a first fruits earnest deposit, just a touch, it is an awesome gift. So ask for it, now— and, begin your new walk in righteousness and obedience!

8

THE RUACH HAKODESH: BORN OF AND BAPTIZED WITH

We began by likening the baptism of repentance to a "blueprint," an illustration of that which is to come. However...

Defining the Holy Spirit is almost impossible: "The wind blows wherever it pleases. You hear its sound, but you don't know where the wind comes from or where it's going. That's the way it is with everyone born of the Spirit" (God's Word®).

Using our blueprint analogy, we know that blueprints define rooms, but rooms do not stand alone, walls are instead often shared by other rooms. So it is with the Spirit. There are various baptisms, but we should not think of them as "standing alone." Especially when dealing with a Holy Spirit that blows where *He* pleases.

John said Yeshua did so many different things, that, if they were written down in detail, the world itself would not be able to contain all the books that would have to be written (John 21:25).

So it is that we will not be able to fully define the indefinable works of the Sprit. Nonetheless, we will suggest some guidelines and address the secondary effects of Holy Spirit baptism— the *endowments* of the Ruach, the spiritual gifts and talents given that empower us to be His witnesses in righteousness and obedience.

We begin with some often asked questions about Holy Spirit baptisms, starting with some foundational verses penned by Paul. We will pose questions, but without answering them in full detail, because more detail will be given in each of the chapters about its particular manifestations (see the Index for subject listings).

Paul explains how we should operate in the gifts. He writes:

> "Now concerning spiritual gifts, brethren, I do not want you to be ignorant…. There are diversities of gifts, but the same Spirit. There are differences of ministries, but the same Lord. And there are diversities of activities, but it is the same God who works all in all. But the manifestation of the Spirit is given to each one for the profit of all, for to one is given the word of wisdom through the Spirit, to another the word of knowledge through the same Spirit, to another faith by the same Spirit, to another gifts of healings by the same Spirit, to another the working of miracles, to another prophecy, to another discerning of spirits, to another different kinds of tongues, to another the interpretation of tongues. But one and the same Spirit works all these things, distributing to each one individually as He wills. For as the body is one and has many members, but all the members of that one body, being many, are one body, so also is Christ. For by one Spirit we were all baptized into one body— whether Jews or Greeks, whether slaves or free— and have all been made to drink into one Spirit. For, in fact, the body is not one member but many. If the foot should say, 'Because I am not a hand, I am not of the body,' is it therefore not of the body?" (1 Cor 12:1,4-15).

QUESTIONS

We ask, "Is there a difference in being *born of* the Spirit and being *baptized (filled or empowered) with, or in,* the Spirit?"

We answer by noting that Yeshua said, "Do not marvel that I said to you, 'You must be born *again* [*anew,* or *from above*].'" [26]

To enter into God's kingdom, we must be "born of water and the Spirit" (John 3:5-8). Our born-anew process begins when we repent of our sins and believe in His "Only Begotten Son." It starts when we believe in our hearts that Jesus is the Christ, that Yeshua is the Messiah. [27] Such faith is an inward act of the heart, and should soon be connected to an outward water baptism— which should then be connected to, and evidenced by our beginning to, 1) *practice righteousness,* 2) *love God and our fellow man,* and, 3) *by faith, beginning to overcome the world* (1 John 2:29; 3:9; 4:7; 5:1-4,18).

We physically declare to the world and spirit realm our commitment to the Lord when we are openly baptized in water. (We may want to have two or more witnesses present to affirm our declaration since Scripture repeatedly upholds that standard [Num 35:30; Deu 19:15; John 8:17; 2 Cor 13:1].)

Before we are immersed in the waters of baptism, [28] we should determine in our hearts that our old man will be left below. We also should look forward to rising from our watery grave, by the power of the Ruach, into new obedient life, in and through Messiah. Then we will begin to continually have our mind renewed by the Holy Spirit and the Word. Our question is, will we be "baptized with the Spirit" when we rise from water baptism?

Scripture indicates that may, or may not, be the case.

---

26 *International Standard,* and, *American Standard Versions,* and *God's Word.*® Born and Anew: *gennao* and *anothen, Strong's* #'s G1080 and 509 respectively. Being born anew of water and the Spirit indicates the importance of the waters of baptism in our rebirth.

27 John 1:14,18; 3:16-18; 9:35; Acts 16:31; 1 John 3:23; 4:9; 5:1,13.

28 An immersion in water (baptism) was called a "mikveh." This word speaks of *hope,* and of *a gathering of waters.* Even so, Israel found *hope* when they crossed the *mikveh/waters* at the Red Sea. These waters speak of YHVH, who is called the "hope/mikveh of Israel," and the "fountain of living waters." See *Strong's* # H 4723. (Gen 1:10; Exo 7:19; Jer 17:13).

When Messiah Yeshua was baptized in the Jordan, as a sign of His special anointing, the Holy Spirit descended upon Him as He arose from the waters (Mat 3:16: Mk 1:10; John 1:32).

However, in Ephesus, Paul asked some disciples if they had received the Holy Spirit when they believed. They said, "We have not so much as heard whether there is a Holy Spirit." So Paul asked, "Into what then were you baptized?" They replied, "Into John's baptism."

To this, Paul replied, "John indeed baptized with a baptism of repentance, saying to the people that they should believe on Him who would come after him, that is, on Messiah Yeshua." When they heard this, they were baptized in Yeshua's name, and when Paul laid hands on them, "The Holy Spirit came upon them, and they spoke with tongues and prophesied" (see Acts 19:1-6).

Once, when Peter was preaching, the Holy Spirit fell on all who heard his word. That means, *first*, they were given the gift of the Holy Spirit, *then* Peter asked, "Can anyone forbid water, that these should not be baptized who have received the Holy Spirit just as we have?" (Acts 10:44-47).

Thus we see that Believers can experience the baptism of repentance, be born from above, yet not know of, or be immersed in, the Holy Spirit. They also can be baptized with the Holy Spirit, and *afterward*, go through the outward sign that is water baptism.

This leads us to conclude that we cannot exactly declare how our proverbial house "is to be built." We know certain "rooms" are available, meaning, the Word tells us of certain promises, but we also know that "unless the LORD builds the house, they labor in vain who build it" (Psa 127:1). We must allow the Spirit to lead, guide and build, *as He will*.

Yeshua spoke of many "rooms" being in His Father's house, and He has gone there to prepare a place for us (John 14:2). Surely the Master Carpenter will provide each of His unique children a unique custom built home.

MORE THAN ONE BAPTISM?

Is there more than one baptism?

John the Baptist said to some Sadducees and Pharisees, "I baptize you with water for repentance. But after me, will come one who is more powerful than I, whose sandals I am not fit to carry. He will baptize you with the Holy Spirit and with fire" (Mat 3:11).

> ...THERE IS A BAPTISM OF REPENTANCE, AND THERE IS A BAPTISM WITH THE HOLY SPIRIT AND FIRE

There is a baptism of repentance and a baptism with the Holy Spirit and fire. This second, *fiery baptism* must be the one John earnestly desired because he surely had been baptized in water for repentance. [29] We know he knew baptism with the Ruach haKodesh was coming because he quoted the prophet Joel:

> "And...afterward...I will pour out My Spirit on all flesh; Your sons and your daughters shall prophesy, Your old men shall dream dreams, Your young men shall see visions. And also on My menservants and on My maidservants I will pour out My Spirit in those days" (Joel 2:28-29).

These verses rank as some of the most controversial in the Church today. Do they speak of us being "filled with the Holy Spirit," as John the Baptist seems to suggest, or do they speak of us being "born of the Spirit" when we are converted? (John 3:5-8).

We assume Yeshua's disciples followed His lead in experiencing water baptism. Thus, in Acts 2 we see that the baptism with the Ruach had just been given on the feast of *Shavuot* (Pentecost). Then, Peter boldly stood up and addressed a crowd of scoffers who were questioning what was happening:

---

29 John was reluctant to baptize Messiah Yeshua. John said, "I need to be baptized by You, and are You coming to me?" But Jesus answered and said, "Permit it to be so now, for thus it is fitting for us to fulfill all righteousness." Then he allowed Him (Mat 3:14-15).

"These are not drunk, as you suppose, since it is only the third hour of the day. But this is what was spoken by the prophet Joel: 'And it shall come to pass in the last days, says God, that I will pour out of My Spirit on all flesh; Your sons and your daughters shall prophesy, your young men shall see visions, your old men shall dream dreams. And on My menservants and on My maidservants I will pour out My Spirit in those days; and they shall prophesy.... And it shall come to pass; that whosoever shall call on the name of the Lord shall be saved" (Acts 2:15-18,21).

Prior to this experience, we see that: "[Yeshua commanded His assembled disciples] "not to depart from Jerusalem, but to wait for the promise of the Father, which, He said, you have heard from Me; for John truly baptized with water, but you shall be baptized with the Holy Spirit not many days from now" (Acts 1:4-5).

We also see that James and John once asked to sit at Yeshua's left or right. In His response to them, Yeshua mentioned His particular type of baptism: "But Jesus said to them, 'You do not know what you ask. Are you able to drink the cup that I drink, and be baptized with the baptism that I am baptized with?' They said to Him, 'We are able.' So Jesus said to them, 'You will indeed drink the cup that I drink, and with the baptism I am baptized with you will be baptized'" (Mark 10:38-39).

THE BAPTISM WITH THE RUACH

The above Scriptures reveal that the baptism with the Ruach haKodesh is a definite experience, subsequent to salvation, whereby the Holy Spirit of the Godhead comes upon the Believer to anoint and energize him or her for special service. This experience is variously described in Scripture as the Holy Spirit "falling upon," "coming upon," or being "poured out upon" the yielded Believer in a sudden and supernatural manner.

Why should we receive the baptism with the Holy Spirit?

We want the baptism, or empowerment of the Spirit so we can do the works Yeshua did. He said:

> "Believe Me that I am in the Father and the Father in Me, or else believe Me for the sake of the works themselves. Most assuredly, I say to you, he who believes in Me, the works that I do he will do also; and greater works than these he will do, because I go to My Father. And whatever you ask in My name, that I will do, that the Father may be glorified in the Son" (John 14:11-13).

What are Yeshua's works?

> "That word you know, which was proclaimed throughout all Judea, and began from Galilee after the baptism which John preached: How God anointed Jesus of Nazareth with the Holy Spirit and with power, who went about doing good and healing all who were oppressed by the devil, for God was with Him" (Acts 10:37-38).

> "The blind see and the lame walk; the lepers are cleansed and the deaf hear; the dead are raised up and the poor have the gospel preached to them" (Mat 11:5).

> Yeshua said of Himself, "The Spirit of the LORD is upon Me, because He has anointed Me to preach the gospel to the poor; He has sent Me to heal the brokenhearted, to proclaim liberty to the captives and recovery of sight to the blind, to set at liberty those who are oppressed" (Luke 4:18).

> Yeshua also said, "Most assuredly, I say to you, he who believes in Me, the works that I do he will do also; and greater works than these he will do, because I go to My Father" (John 14:12).

How do we receive the baptism with the Ruach?

We simply pray and ask in faith, and we believe the Father will supply all of our needs (Acts 1:14; Phil 4:6,19; Heb 11:6).

Yeshua said, "I say to you, ask, and it will be given to you; seek, and you will find; knock, and it will be opened to you. For everyone who asks receives, and he who seeks finds, and to him who knocks it will be opened. If a son asks for bread from any father among you, will he give him a stone? Or if he asks for a fish, will he give him a serpent instead of a fish? Or if he asks for an egg, will he offer him a scorpion? If you then, being evil, know how to give good gifts to your children, how much more will your heavenly Father give the Holy Spirit to those who ask Him!" (Luke 11:9-13).

Notice in verse 9 that it says "will." When we ask for the baptism with the Spirit, we must not doubt. God will give to all who ask. We also can trust that, if we truly ask for His Spirit, He will not allow us to be given a snake. We will get the Holy Spirit.

Selah. Meditate on this point. We can trust in our God.

Is the baptism with the Holy Spirit for every Believer?

That question is answered in the Book of Acts:

"Now when they heard this, they were cut to the heart, and said to Peter and the rest of the apostles, 'Men and brethren, what shall we do?' Then Peter said to them, 'Repent, and let every one of you be baptized in the name of Jesus Christ for the remission of sins; and you shall receive the gift of the Holy Spirit. For the promise is to you and to your children, and to all who are afar off, as many as the Lord our God will call'" (Acts 2:37-39).

This second baptism, this Holy Spirit immersion, is available to all Believers. Those who ask will receive the Spirit.

However, not all Believers show up and ask...

We see a case in point in the following verses:

Paul said he delivered "all that which I also received: that Christ died for our sins according to the Scriptures, and that He was buried, and that He rose again the third day according to the Scriptures, and that He was seen by Cephas, then by the twelve. After that He was seen by over five hundred brethren at once, of whom the greater part remain to the present, but some have fallen asleep" (1 Cor 15:3-6).

Messiah spoke to more than five hundred of the disciples, yet we see a different number in attendance in the following account:

"[An account]... of all that Jesus began both to do and teach, until the day in which He was taken up, after He through the Holy Spirit had given commandments to the apostles...He also presented Himself alive after His suffering by many infallible proofs, being seen by them during forty days and speaking of the things pertaining to the kingdom of God. Being assembled together with them, He command-ed them not to depart from Jerusalem, but to wait for the Promise of the Father, 'which,' He said, 'you have heard from Me; for John truly baptized with water, but you shall be baptized with the Holy Spirit not many days from now.' Therefore, when they had come together, they asked Him, saying, 'Lord, will You at this time restore the kingdom to Israel?' And He said to them, 'It is not for you to know times or seasons which the Father has put in His own authority. But you shall receive power when the Holy Spirit has come upon you; and you shall be witnesses to Me in Jerusalem, and in all Judea and Samaria, and to the end of the earth.

"Now when He had spoken these things, while they watched, He was taken up, and a cloud received Him out of their sight. And while they looked steadfastly toward heaven as He went up, behold, two men stood by them in white apparel, who also said, 'Men of Galilee, why do you stand gazing up into heaven? This same Jesus, who was taken up from you into heaven, will so come in like manner as you saw Him go into heaven.'

"Then they returned to Jerusalem.... And when they had entered, they went up into the upper room where they were staying: Peter, James, John, and Andrew; Philip and Thomas; Bartholomew and Matthew; James the son of Alphaeus and Simon the Zealot; and Judas the son of James. These all continued with one accord in prayer and supplication, with the women and Mary the mother of Jesus, and with His brothers. And…Peter stood up in the midst of the disciples (altogether the number of names was about a hundred and twenty), and said… (Acts 1:3-16).

In the above verses, we see that Yeshua told the 500 to wait in Jerusalem for the promise— but only 120 showed up. That means 380 did not go to the Upper Room. The gift of immersion of the Holy Spirit was for the 380 as well, but they did not receive, because they did not obey the word of the Lord. This does not mean, however, that any of the 380 could not have received the baptism with the Holy Spirit at a later date. It is for *all* who ask. However, when YHVH speaks to us, if we do not want to take a chance on being left out, we need to respond immediately.

In summary, we have seen, and will continue to see that being born of/immersed in the Spirit, essentially consists of four parts:

- Repentance/conversion = being born of the Ruach
- Water baptism (outward sign of the above inward event)
- Empowered by the Ruach = receiving an earnest deposit
- Fullness of the Spirit = receiving our glorified bodies

Now we ask, what happened when the disciples were baptized with the Ruach haKodesh?

9

RECEIVING THE MARK
OF THE RUACH HAKODESH

On an eventful Pentecost day, Messiah Yeshua's disciples were gathered in an upper room. We read of that all-important meeting:

> "When the Day of Pentecost had fully come, they were all with one accord in one place. And suddenly there came a sound from heaven, as of a rushing mighty wind, and it filled the whole house where they were sitting. Then there appeared to them divided tongues, as of fire, and one sat upon each of them. And they were all filled with the Holy Spirit and began to speak with other tongues, as the Spirit gave them utterance.
>
> "And there were dwelling in Jerusalem Jews, devout men, from every nation under heaven. And when this sound occurred, the multitude came together, and were confused, because everyone heard them speak in his own language.

Then they were all amazed and marveled, saying to one another, 'Look, are not all these who speak Galileans? And how is it that we hear, each in our own language in which we were born? Parthians and Medes and Elamites, those dwelling in Mesopotamia, Judea and Cappadocia, Pontus and Asia, Phrygia and Pamphylia, Egypt and the parts of Libya adjoining Cyrene, visitors from Rome, both Jews and proselytes, Cretans and Arabs— we hear them speaking in our own tongues the wonderful works of God. So they were all amazed and perplexed, saying to one another, 'Whatever could this mean?' Others mocking said, 'They are full of new wine.'

"But Peter, standing up with the eleven, raised his voice and said to them, 'Men of Judea and all who dwell in Jerusalem, let this be known to you, and heed my words. For these are not drunk, as you suppose, since it is only the third hour of the day. But this is what was spoken by the prophet Joel'" (Acts 2:1-16).

Many things stand out when we read the account of this watershed meeting of Messiah's early disciples. To begin, 120 people who were devoted to prayer and supplication, were in an upper room that was probably located in Solomon's Portico. Then YHVH showed up and in essence gave them one of the keys to the kingdom of heaven: He gave them His Ruach, the Comforter, the Spirit of Truth, the One whom Yeshua said would "guide them in all truth." Yeshua also said of the Spirit, "He will bring glory to Me, will take what is Mine and make it known to you, and He will tell you what is yet to come" (John 16:13-16).

If we want to be guided in all truth, if we want the giftings of Messiah Yeshua, and want to understand what is yet to come, we too need this Comforter; we need the Spirit of Truth to guide us.

We see that 120 were gathered together in Yeshua's Name. Some believe Israel required a minimum membership of 120 to have a community with its own "governing council." (Stressing this number would indicate the congregation's legitimacy.) [30]

In our day and according to Jewish tradition, one must have ten followers present, a *minyon*, to carry out certain traditions.

Messiah Yeshua had 120 disciples present, with a tithe of them being in leadership: 120 disciples, 12 apostles. The number also equals a *minyon* for each of the twelve tribes: 10x12=120.

Could it be that the Messiah of Israel was sending a message to the people of Israel with this particular number of attendees?

We do know that He told the chief priests and the elders of Israel, "The kingdom of God will be taken from you and given to a nation bearing the fruits of it" (Mat 21:43). He also said that His kingdom was not of this world, and that He conferred His kingdom on His disciples (Luke 12:32; 22:30; Dan 7:9-22; Acts 1:6).

Regardless of numbers and potentially symbolic meanings, the important point is that Messiah Yeshua was establishing His congregation of firstborn ones and wanted its members to be marked with and led by His Ruach haKodesh (1 Cor 15:20-23; Heb 12:23).

FIRE AND ITS SYMBOLISM

John said he baptized people in water for repentance, but the Messiah would baptize them "with the Holy Spirit and fire" (Luke 3:16). When the disciples were baptized in the Spirit and began to speak in other tongues, they saw divided tongues, as of fire, resting on their heads. But what does that fire represent?

Our God "is a consuming fire." He speaks "from the midst of the fire" and thus shows His "greatness." He goes before us as a consuming pillar of fire and defeats our enemies. When Moses was with YHVH on Mount Horeb, He "wrote on the tablets the words of the covenant, the Ten Commandments [Ten Words]." In the "midst of fire" He wrote them. [31]

---

30 *The Book of Acts in Its Graeco-Roman Setting* by David W. Gill, Wm. B. Eerdmans Publishing, 1994, page 131. http://books.google.com/books?id=W-L1DA1ptKQC

31 Exo 13:21; 34:28; Deu 4:24,33; 5:24-26; 9:10;10:4,13. Words: *Strong's* # H1697. The Ten Words are His "Covenant" (Deu 4:13); those Commandments/Laws will be in effect forever.

Brother Judah's tradition says that YHVH gave the Ten Commandments to the children of Israel on *Shavuot*, or *Pentecost*. Scripture tells us that on a Shavuot day, centuries later, the Ruach haKodesh was poured out on Yeshua's disciples as they expectantly gathered together in prayer. With this outpouring, the Law that was once written on tablets of stone by the fiery finger of God began to be written with fire on hearts of flesh by the Spirit of God. [32]

Fire purifies. The trials and fires of life forge spiritual character.

When we follow the Lamb of God, we are tested, purified by, and baptized in fire. "Those whom the LORD loves He disciplines, and He scourges every son whom He receives" (Mal 3:3-4; Zec 13:9; James 1:12; 1 Pet 1:7; Heb 12:6; Rev 3:18, NASB).

CLOVEN TONGUES OF FIRE

We read that when the disciples were filled with the Holy Spirit, they saw what seemed to be tongues of fire that separated and came to rest on each of them. According to the King James, "There appeared unto them *cloven tongues like as of fire*, and it sat upon each of them" (Acts 2:3, KJV).

The NIV speaks of "tongues of fire that *separated*." The King James interprets it as "*cloven* tongues of fire." The word in question is *diamerizo*, which means to partition, divide, or part. [33]

What sort of mark was the Messiah putting on His people? Could it be that just as He was establishing an official congregation in Israel, He was likewise officially marking His followers with a fire that has hidden meaning?

While it cannot be proven, there is an interesting explanation as to what the disciples might have seen....

---

32 Israel came to Mount Sinai on the third day of the third month, and Yah visited the people three days later (Exo 19:1,10-17). This is thought to have happened 50 days after they crossed the Red Sea, on the day that came to be known as the feast of Shavuot. See, Exo 19:9-20:21; Jer 31:31-33; Acts 2:1-4; 2 Cor 3:3; Heb 8:8-13; 10:16-17.

33 *Strong's* # G1266; to partition thoroughly (lit. in distribution, fig. in dissension): cloven, divide, part.

We know a day is coming when Believers who follow the Lamb — like the High Priests of old— will have "His Father's name written on their foreheads" (Exo 28:38; Rev 7:2-4; 14:1; 22:4).

Could the cloven tongues of fire represent a similar mark? Could it even represent the *initial* of the Almighty?

In Hebrew, God Almighty is *El Shaddai*. He is known in Jewish circles by this name and the first Hebrew letter in the name *Shaddai* (Almighty), is *sheen* (ש). This letter is likened in Hebraic thought to His *initial* and is often used to represent Him.

El Shaddai— His Mark

Hebrew Sheen

The name, *El Shaddai*, means "The Power," or "The God that cannot be obstructed." Thus the common translation, the *Almighty*.

In Hebrew, *Shaddai* is written with the letters, *sheen, dalet, yod*. We see the first letter, the sheen, in the box, above right, "Hebrew Sheen." Below it, we see a stylized "Flaming Sheen."

Flaming Sheen

Finally, we see a Disciple with what might appear to Hebrew speaking people as a *flaming sheen*, a sign that the Almighty is putting His mark, His *initial*, on one of His chosen people.

Again, regardless of numbers and fire shapes, we do know that, on a Shavuot day long ago, the disciples who were gathered in the Upper Room had "cloven tongues of fire" fall on them. *El Shaddai* poured out His Spirit on them and they were forever changed. Divinely marked, they were thereafter empowered by the Holy One of Israel.

Disciple receiving the mark of the Sheen— the mark of the Holy Spirit

We who love the God of Israel and follow His Messiah should, of all people, be so marked. Like Peter and the disciples of old, we too need to have the same life-changing power fall on us.

Solomon's "Upper Room"

Some believe that in Solomon's Colonnade was a place known as the "Upper Room," and that Rabbis would often go there in order to instruct their flocks. We suggest the Pentecost events only makes sense if the location of the upper room was very close to the Temple Mount.

We say this for the following reasons:

- According to Scripture, Peter spoke with power, and about three thousand souls were immediately baptized (Acts 2:41). This makes sense if they were gathered in an upper room in Solomon's Colonnade. There, they would only have to go a few steps out the triple gate stairway to the southern stairway (the Hulda Steps), where they had many *mikvot* (plural for baths wherein people were ritually immersed in water: see footnote 25). Today, about 300 yards away from this assumed upper room location, we find an ancient and very large public mikvot.

- According to Luke's record, when the disciples were filled with the Holy Spirit, they began to worship God in foreign languages which the disciples themselves apparently did not know, yet these languages were spoken and understood by the Jewish pilgrims who had journeyed to Jerusalem to keep the feast (Acts 2:2-12). This great number of worshipers were gathered around the Temple area that they might celebrate the feast of Shavuot.

Ezekiel and the "Upper Room"

On this particular day of Pentecost in question there was such a loud noise accompanying the experience of Messiah's disciples that it attracted the attention of the Jewish visitors, and they soon went to see what the commotion was all about.

At the time of the 9:00 AM (morning) sacrifice, the Holy Spirit was being poured out upon and received by the 120 disciples. At the same time, the High Priest of the Temple would have been reciting passages of Scripture.

Many believe that on this prophetic day, he would have been reading out of the book of Ezekiel. These same scriptures are read to this very day in every Jewish synagogue on the day of Pentecost. If so, this is what the priest was reading:

> "Now it came to pass in the thirtieth year, in the fourth month, on the fifth day of the month, as I was among the captives by the River Chebar, that the heavens were opened and I saw visions of God. On the fifth day of the month, which was in the fifth year of King Jehoiachin's captivity, the word of the LORD came expressly to Ezekiel the priest, the son of Buzi, in the land of the Chaldeans by the River Chebar; and the hand of the LORD was upon him there.
>
> "Then I looked, and behold, a whirlwind was coming out of the north, a great cloud with raging fire engulfing itself; and brightness was all around it and radiating out of its midst like the color of amber, out of the midst of the fire. Also from within it came the likeness of four living creatures" (Eze 1:1-5).

The priest would then read the rest of chapter one, which describes the *Shekhinah* glory of God, and His angelic hosts. [34]

Concerning this description, we see in verse 1:27 that Ezekiel said,

> "From the appearance of His waist and upward I saw, as it were, the color of amber with the appearance of fire all around within it; and from the appearance of His waist and downward I saw, as it were, the appearance of fire with brightness all around."

---

[34] *Shekhinah*: A feminine Hebrew word that means the dwelling or settling. Used to denote the dwelling or settling presence of God (His divine presence), especially in the Temple in Jerusalem. See: http://en.wikipedia.org/wiki/Shekhinah

The High Priest would also read, "Then the Spirit lifted me up, and I heard behind me a great thunderous voice: 'Blessed is the glory of the LORD from His place!'" (see Eze 3:4-12).

In that year, as the High Priest was reading these verses from the prophet Ezekiel, what he described would have been actually happening a few hundred feet away. And...

The event was causing quite a stir on this particular Pentecost morning. As curious Jews approached the room in Solomon's Colonnade, which is where they thought the noise was coming from, something incredible happened. They heard the disciples worshiping God in various languages— yet the disciples' words were understood by the various Jews who were present as being spoken in their native tongue. The Jews were from different countries and spoke different languages, yet each one understood the worship of the disciples as being spoken in their own native tongue. It must have been an incredible experience!

Peter then preached a bold sermon to the crowd, possibly in Aramaic or Greek, and, about three thousand souls responded to his sermon that day. They accepted Yeshua as their Messiah and Lord and were baptized in the adjacent mikveh (see footnote 28).

This outpouring of the Holy Spirit took place on the very day the Jewish people were offering to God the required two wave loaves (Lev 23:17). It happened on the day that Israel had been celebrating the Feast of Pentecost for almost 1,500 years.

These two often-overlooked loaves symbolized Israel's utter dependence on YHVH— they spoke of His abundant provision. These symbolic loaves also depicted the condition of the people, for they were baked with *leaven*, a symbol of sin. One loaf represented the Jewish people (Judah), who, although they were sinners, would receive the power of God in their lives as they acknowledged Yeshua as Lord (He is represented by the fine flour in the loaves). The other loaf represented the lost sheep of the House Israel who would also receive this blessing from God— even though, they too, were sinners (Hos 1-2).

When Peter preached his sermon that day, he said the promise of the Father (baptism with the Holy Spirit) was for *everyone* who would acknowledge Yeshua as their Lord (Acts 2:39). [35]

Later, we see that there was a Gentile by the name of Cornelius who was seeking God with all his heart. An angel then spoke to him in a vision and instructed him to send for Peter who would come and preach to him and his friends. And...

> "While Peter was still speaking these words, the Holy Spirit fell upon all those who heard the word. And those of the circumcision who believed were astonished, as many as came with Peter, because the gift of the Holy Spirit had been poured out on the Gentiles also. For they heard them speak with tongues and magnify God. Then Peter said, 'Can anyone forbid water, that these should not be baptized who have received the Holy Spirit just as we have?'" (Acts 10:44-47).

Peter later shared what happened at that meeting with his Jewish brethren, saying, "As I began to speak, the Holy Spirit fell upon them, as upon us at the beginning. Then I remembered the word of the Lord, how He said, 'John indeed baptized with water, but you shall be baptized with the Holy Spirit'" (Acts 11:15-16).

In this inclusion of the non-Jewish Believers, we begin to see the significance of the fine flour and the two leavened loaves:

Messiah was perfectly righteous and without sin. But, the two wave loaves—Judah and Ephraim—have the leaven of sin in their camps. Yet... in Messiah, both can receive Holy Spirit power that will help them overcome their sin (Gen 4:7). In Messiah, they become acceptable as a first fruit wave offering to the Almighty (Lev 23:17). In Him, they know that one day, like their Messiah, they too will be resurrected from the dead (1Cor 15:20). [36]

---

35 *Israel's Feasts and their Fullness: Expanded Edition*, Batya Ruth Wootten, chapter 23, "Shavuot – In Scripture and Tradition," (2008, Key of David Publishing, Saint Cloud, FL).
36 *Ibid.*

A RECAP

To review, we note that a partial hardening happened to all Israel— both houses were blinded, but in different ways. For a season Judah would be unable to see that Yeshua is the Messiah.

Ephraim was destined to be scattered among the nations and there, to lose touch with his own Hebraic heritage. However, he also was destined to be doubly fruitful, to even learn certain things.

It is *imperative* that we see that, in his return, Ephraim must not leave behind the idea of being empowered by the Holy Spirit. For, prodigal Ephraim is destined to be used to encourage Holy Spirit led celebration of Israel's eternal feasts. Like the returning prodigal son, Ephraim is now being called to return home and celebrate with His Heavenly Father (Jer 31:18-21; Luke 15:11). He is being called to learn to delight in Israel's Shabbat (Isa 58:13). Israel's eternal feasts need to be celebrated *in the Spirit*. [37]

It is in being empowered and inspired by the Ruach haKodesh, that redeemed Israel will finally be fully restored. Thus, the call is for us, even as it was in Messiah's day:

> *"Go therefore and make disciples of all the nations, baptizing them in the name of the Father and of the Son and of the Holy Spirit"* (Mat 28:19).

PRODIGAL EPHRAIM IS DESTINED TO BE USED TO ENCOURAGE HOLY SPIRIT LED CELEBRATION OF ISRAEL'S ETERNAL FEASTS. LIKE THE RETURNING PRODIGAL SON, EPHRAIM IS NOW BEING CALLED TO RETURN HOME AND CELEBRATE...

---

37 *Ibid*, chapter 5, "Repentance and Rehearsals."

IO

THE BAPTISM: IT IS CONTINUAL— AND IT IS FOR EVERYONE

Peter did not say the experience of the disciples was the fulfillment of Joel's prophecy, as in, *it happened and is now history*. He did not say that because, the baptism with the Spirit is not a one-time event, but something that goes on. It is continual.

"'And it shall come to pass in the last days,' says God, 'That I will pour out of My Spirit on all flesh; Your sons and your daughters shall prophesy, Your young men shall see visions, Your old men shall dream dreams. And on My menservants and on My maidservants I will pour out My Spirit in those days; And they shall prophesy. I will show wonders in heaven above And signs in the earth beneath: Blood and fire and vapor of smoke. The sun shall be turned into darkness, And the moon into blood, Before the coming of the great and awesome day of the LORD. And it shall come to pass That whoever calls on the name of the LORD Shall be saved.'

"Men of Israel, hear these words: Jesus of Nazareth, a Man attested by God to you by miracles, wonders, and signs ...being delivered by the determined purpose and fore-knowledge of God, you have taken by lawless hands, have crucified, and put to death; whom God raised up, having loosed the pains of death, because it was not possible that He should be held by it. For David says concerning Him: 'I foresaw the LORD always before my face.... Therefore my heart rejoiced, and my tongue was glad; Moreover my flesh also will rest in hope. For You will not leave my soul in Hades, Nor will You allow Your Holy One to see corruption. You have made known to me the ways of life; You will make me full of joy in Your presence.'

"Brethren...David...is dead and buried...[but God swore] ...that... He would raise up the Christ... [and David,] fore-seeing this, spoke concerning the resurrection... that His soul was not left in Hades, nor did His flesh see corruption. This Jesus God has raised up, of which we are all witnesses. And being exalted to the right hand of God, and having received from the Father the promise of the Holy Spirit, He poured out this which you now see and hear....Therefore let all the house of Israel know assuredly that God has made this Jesus, whom you crucified, both Lord and Christ.

"Now when they heard this, they were cut to the heart, and said to Peter and the rest of the apostles, 'Men and brethren, what shall we do?' Then Peter said to them, 'Repent, and let every one of you be baptized in the name of Jesus Christ for the remission of sins; and you shall receive the gift of the Holy Spirit. For the promise is to you and to your children, and to all who are afar off, as many as the Lord our God will call. And with many other words he testified.... Then those who gladly received his word were baptized; and that day about three thousand souls were added to them" (Acts 2:17-41).

Peter preached with boldness a Spirit-inspired sermon and 3,000 souls were added to the faith (vss. 14, 41). Conversely, when Moses brought the Law down from Mt. Sinai, 3,000 people perished (Exo 32:25-28). In these depictions, we see that the Law identified sin in the flesh and thus brought death, but the Spirit writes the Law on the heart and thus brings new life.

The Spirit also brings *empowerment*. Eight weeks before Peter preached his life-transforming message, as Messiah prophesied, three times, Peter denied that he even knew Him (Mat 26:34; John 18:27). Peter denied Him because of fear of the religious leaders. But, on Pentecost, he preached to them with incredible boldness. His daring exemplifies the power that was promised in Acts 1:8: "But you shall receive *power* when the Holy Spirit has come upon you; and you shall be witnesses to Me in Jerusalem, and in all Judea and Samaria, and to the end of the earth."

Can we expect to receive similar empowering when we receive the Spirit? Yes. Peter said, "The promise is to you and to your children, and to all who are afar off, as many as the Lord our God will call" (Acts 2:39). If we have been called by the Almighty, this promise is for us.

Peter said this empowerment is for those who live in the last days. And, a "day" is said to be as a thousand years (2 Pet 3:8). On one level, the "last days" began with Peter, and *it ends with us.*

Hosea the prophet said:

> "Come, let us return to the LORD, for He has torn us, but He will heal us; He has wounded us, but He will bandage us. He will revive us after two days; *He will raise us up on the third day, that we may live before Him.* So let us know, let us press on to know the LORD. His going forth is as certain as the dawn; and He will come to us like the rain, like the spring rain watering the earth" (Hos 6:1-3, NASB).

Two thousand years later, we live in the beginning of the third, thousand-year-long-day since Peter's "day." *The promise is for us, too!*

Is being filled with the Spirit a one-time event?

In Acts we read of the Spirit being "poured out," and of disciples being "filled" with the Spirit (vss. 2:4; 4:8,17,31; 10:45). In Ephesians 5:18 we are told to "be filled with the Spirit." And, in Acts 13:52 we see that "the disciples were *continually filled* with joy and with the Holy Spirit" (NASB).

Filled is here translated from the Greek, *pleroo* (play-ro'-o), which is a *present imperative*, meaning, it is "a command to do something ...and involves continuous or repeated action." [38]

Being filled with the Spirit is not a one time event. When we need to be especially empowered, we remember that the Father is ever saying, "Open your mouth, and I will fill it" (Psa 81:10).

We want to be continually filled and empowered!

THE HOLY SPIRIT: POURED OUT ON GENTILES!?

Again, while Peter was giving his powerful message, the Holy Spirit came on all who heard him.

Moreover, the circumcised Believers were astonished that the gift of the Spirit was being poured out on the "Gentiles." For, they heard them, too, "speaking in tongues and praising God."

Seeing this was the case, Peter said, "'Can anyone forbid water, that these should not be baptized who have received the Holy Spirit just as we have?' And he commanded them to be baptized in the name of the Lord" (Acts 10:44-48).

If we have received the baptism of repentance, and been born of the Spirit, we also need to, should want to, be baptized with the Holy Spirit.

The Holy Spirit became the signature sign that the God of Israel was again on the move. He was moving powerfully among those who were former "Gentiles." He was moving and drawing them, by His Spirit, into the commonwealth of Israel (Eph 2:11-22).

---

38 *Strong's* # G4137; "Grammatical Notations," *The Hebrew-Greek Key Word Study Bible*, © 1984, 1990, AMG International, Inc., pg. 1703. (Note: In English, verb tenses generally denote the *time* of action. In Greek, verb tenses generally denote the *kind* of action.

II

HOLY COMMUNICATION
TONGUES AND THEIR TYPES

Speaking in languages one did not naturally learn has caused much controversy among Believers— especially in our day. We will not make excuses for abuses, but suggest that it is very important that we put the phenomenon in proper perspective.

To begin, we need to realize the importance of speech in the economy of our God. Speech began with Him. He spoke and the world was created. His words are both holy, and filled with creative power. That is how we, too, should regard speech. We need to have proper regard for the place YHVH gives speech. We especially need to have high regard for the idea of Him communicating with us. In fact, we cannot overemphasize the importance of us learning to hear the voice of the Almighty— especially in the difficult days in which we now live. We cannot overstate the role intimate communication, via the Holy Spirit, should play in our day-to-day, earthly walk.

When Adam and Eve were in the Garden, the Holy One walked and talked with them, in the *cool* of the evening (Gen 3:8-9). The Hebrew word translated "cool" is rooted in the word for *ruach*, as in Ruach haKodesh, The Holy Spirit. [39] Adam and Eve walked in the Garden, *in the Ruach*, with YHVH Elohim. We need to do likewise. [40]

(We will return to this subject in the next chapter.)

We also must walk in holy fear (reverence) as we attempt to examine the truth about Holy Spirit inspired speech. We must not misrepresent, in any way, the Spirit Most Holy. Messiah Yeshua warns that, those who speak against the Spirit will not be forgiven, in this age or in the age to come (Mat 12:31-32). So, our speech about the Holy Spirit, should be just that: Holy. With that idea in mind, we present our opinions about the works of the Spirit with great humility. Ours are but the suggestions of mere mortals.

KNOWN AND UNKNOWN TONGUES

As for languages, each of them is derived from a supernatural act of the Almighty. With tongues, it appears that once more, YHVH is acting in a supernatural way in regard to man's speech.

All people of the earth at one time spoke the same language (Gen 11:1). At the Tower of Babel the Holy One confounded man's language and the people scattered. Then they began to gather in groups based on their common language, which is the ability to understand and be understood by others.

To give us a new language would be a simple thing for our God to do. Moreover, if confounding our languages played a part in our being scattered, perhaps language likewise plays a part in our being regathered. Perhaps we begin our restoration by speaking in tongues, "not to men, but unto God" (1 Cor 14:2).

---

39 *Strong's #* H 7307.

40 We recommend the book, *The Voice... Hearing the Almighty* by Batya Wootten (2009, Key of David Publishing). It is a "companion" volume to this work. In it, Batya shows how our patriarchs heard the voice of the Almighty. She also shows the meaning, and place of "the voice" in Scripture, and she explains the importance of our learning to hear the voice of the Almighty for ourselves.

As for the terms, *known* and *unknown* languages, we note that there is said to be some 3000-7000 earthly languages and dialects in the earth (there is disagreement as to how to count dialects). And, it is highly doubtful that anyone on earth has the capacity to be familiar with all of these languages. Beyond this, we ask, how many once "known" tongues have come and gone during man's sojourn here on earth? Use of these terms can therefore be misleading when describing the phenomenon of speaking in tongues. The tongue is "unknown" to its user, but, who can know for certain whether it is "known or unknown" in the earth?

Some claim that tongues are ecstatic utterances that are not known in any country on earth. But again, who can know that for certain? The point cannot be proven, and thus should not be argued, for or against. Besides, Paul speaks of there being "many kinds of languages in the world" (1 Cor 14:10). This indicates that he thought the tongues being spoken were earthly languages. More importantly, the point in speaking in tongues is not so that man can speak to man, but so man can speak to YHVH, and thus be built up in his faith. So the question is, does YHVH understand?

Also, we see that in Scripture, the six uses of the term "unknown" to describe *glossa*, or "tongues" (1 Cor 14:2-27), is *italicized*, which signifies that it is not in the Greek manuscripts but was added for clarification purposes by translators. [41]

Glossa appears in the New Testament fifty times and means a language, except in three cases: Once it refers to the physical tongue (James 3:5), once to say, "My tongue (speech) was glad [joyous]" (Acts 2:26), and once to refer to the flames of fire shaped like tongues that appeared over the disciples (Acts 2:3).

DO ALL SPEAK IN TONGUES?

In 1 Corinthians 12:30 Paul asks, "Do all speak with tongues?" Some say the fact that the question is asked proves that all do not speak in tongues. However, the question is asked in regard to

---

41 *Strong's* # G1100; tongue; a language not acquired in a natural manner.

"tongues and interpretation." Thus, it should be applied to this dual-gift (see next page), and, it is true that not all operate in it. The verse should therefore not be applied to the idea of speaking in a prayer language, or praying in the spirit.

In Mark 16:17 we read, "These signs will follow those who believe: In My name they will cast out demons; they will speak with new tongues." Many feel Mark 16:9-20 should not be included in Scripture because the verses are not found in the oldest manuscripts (Codex Sinaiticus and Codex Vaticanus). We do not suggest building doctrine on these verses, but do note that they are found in all later manuscripts, thus proving it is not a "new doctrine." Plus, every time Scripture speaks of an outpouring of the Spirit, the event is evidenced by the companion gifts of Believers speaking in tongues and prophesying (Acts 2:4-11; 10:43-48; 11:1-18; 15:5-9; 19:6). [42]

Now, we move to an overview of the different types of tongues we see in Scripture.

DIFFERENT KINDS OF TONGUES

1 Corinthians 12:28 reveals that there are different kinds of tongues (*glossolalia*). While this term applies to man's various languages, we suggest it also applies to the idea of various types, or *categories* of Spirit-inspired speech. [43] We also suggest that there *may possibly* be five types. We will address each one, and call them:

- Un-interpreted but Understood Tongues (Acts 2:4-6)
- Tongues and Interpretation (1 Cor 12:10,30; 14:5,13,27)
- Private Tongues (Rom 8:26-27; 1 Cor 14:18; Eph 6:18)
- Groaning in the Spirit (Rom 8:23-27; 2 Cor 5:2,4)
- Singing in the Spirit (1 Cor 14:15)

---

42 Mark 16:18 speaks of *taking up serpents*. This is a *metaphor*, like *pluck out an offending eye*. Snakes depict evil and demons. Woman's seed, meaning the Messiah, would one day bruise/overwhelm the serpent. The disciples were given protection from and authority over them (Gen 3:14-15; Psa 91:1-16; Mat 18:9; 23:33; Luke 10:17-20; 2 Cor 11:3; Rev 12:9).

43 *Tongues/Glossolalia*: *Strong's* # G1100 (a language not naturally acquired).
 Diverse: *Strong's* # G1085.

We *tentatively* suggest that there are five types, because, like dialects of the same tongue, we are unsure as to how to categorize the last two types. So to speak, both may be "dialects," or different forms of private prayer. And/or, singing in the spirit may be a form of prophetic utterance or it may fit with any of the first three types.

UN-INTERPRETED BUT UNDERSTOOD TONGUES

In Acts 2:4-6 we read that, on Shavuot the disciples "were all filled with the Holy Spirit and began to speak with other tongues, as the Spirit gave them utterance. And there were dwelling in Jerusalem Jews, devout men, from every nation under heaven. When this sound occurred, the multitude came together, and were confused, because everyone heard them speak in his own language" (NASB). Here we see that the Spirit gave the disciples an "ability," they spoke, and through this particular "gift of tongues" the Spirit communicated a message that was understood by the listeners in their own earthly language. In this case, there was no "interpreter" involved. The disciples spoke and were understood, without outside help, by people who spoke other languages. This miracle is said to have bewildered and amazed the hearers. There is no mention of an "interpreter" who translated in this case (the hearers understood on their own). So, we will call this unique gifting *un-interpreted but understood tongues*.

TONGUES AND INTERPRETATION

In Paul's letter to the Corinthians, we see a different type of *gift/ charisma* of tongues. It is only to be used *in connection with* the *gift/ charisma* of interpretation. [44] In this case, in an open meeting, a message was spoken that *had to be interpreted* for others. This dual-gift of *tongues and interpretation* is said to be equal to the one gift of *prophecy* (1 Cor 12:10; 14:3). In addition, such messages are given for the purpose of edification, encouragement, and comfort of the Body. We call this prophetic dual gift *tongues and interpretation*.

---

[44] *Strong's # G 5486, from G5483: a divine gratuity, spiritual endowment, free gift.

PRIVATE TONGUES

A third type of tongue is seen in connection to praying "in the spirit." To understand this gift, we note that we are told to pray "always with all prayer and supplication in the Spirit" (Eph 6:18). And that, "the Spirit helps in our weaknesses. For we do not know what we should pray for as we ought, but the Spirit Himself makes intercession for us [and]... for the saints according to the will of God" (Rom 8:26-27). (These verses also speak of "groanings," which we will address later.) Intercession suggests Spirit-led personal prayer. This type of prayer happens especially when we feel we do not know how to pray as we should. The Spirit then graciously leads us in intercession and we pray a perfect prayer concerning a situation we do not understand.

Although prayer sometimes needs to be communal (James 5:14), it most often consists of private communication with the Almighty:

> "When you pray, you shall not be like the hypocrites. They love to pray standing in the synagogues and on the corners of the streets, that they may be seen by men. Assuredly, I say to you, they have their reward. But you, when you pray, go into your room, and when you have shut your door, pray to your Father who is in the secret place; and your Father who sees in secret will reward you openly" (Mat 6:5-6).

With this idea in mind, a careful reading of 1 Corinthians 14 reveals a difference in the two types of tongues mentioned there.

> "Pursue love, and desire spiritual gifts, but especially that you may prophesy. For he who speaks in a tongue does not speak to men but to God, for no one understands him; however, in the spirit he speaks mysteries.
>
> "But he who prophesies speaks edification and exhortation and comfort to men. He who speaks in a tongue edifies himself, but he who prophesies edifies the church. I wish you all spoke with tongues, but even more that you

prophesied; for he who prophesies is greater than he who speaks with tongues, unless indeed he interprets, that the church may receive edification" (1 Cor 14:1-5).

Paul first mentions speaking in a tongue, not to men but to God, of uttering mysteries in the Spirit, of not being understood by others, and, he says the one who is praying is edified, built up.

This description appears to refer to a personal prayer language. Otherwise, it does not fit Paul's instructions about a tongue that is to be interpreted and understood, so *everyone* would be edified.

PRAYING IN THE HOLY SPIRIT

Some dismiss the idea of praying in tongues and think the idea is rooted Corinthian paganism. But, Paul spoke in tongues, and he would not have participated in pagan practices. He said, "I thank God, I speak in tongues more than you all." Paul spoke in a tongue that was not understood by others and was grateful that he could do so (see vss. 14:14-20).

So, what was the real issue in Corinth?

Paul was establishing order in the congregation. He wanted the people to learn to pray with their *understanding* (vss. 13-18). He did not want them to "camp" around the idea of being able to speak or pray in tongues, but instead wanted them to put the gift in its proper perspective.

PRAYING WITH "UNDERSTANDING"

Paul wrote to the Corinthians:

"Let him who speaks in a tongue pray that he may interpret. For if I pray in a tongue, my spirit prays, but my understanding is unfruitful. What is the conclusion then? I will pray with the spirit, and I will also pray with the understanding. I will sing with the spirit, and I will also sing with the understanding. Otherwise, if you bless with the spirit, how will he who occupies the place of the uninformed say

"Amen" at your giving of thanks, since he does not understand what you say? For you indeed give thanks well, but
the other is not edified. I thank my God I speak with tongues
more than you all; yet in the church I would rather speak five
words with my understanding, that I may teach others also,
than ten thousand words in a tongue" (1 Cor 14:13-18). [45]

Paul was not speaking against praying in tongues, but for
seeking greater *understanding* of what is being said (1 Cor 14:19). As
stated earlier, tongues should not be viewed as an end result. It is
a sign that points to something greater; it is given to point to, help
lead us to, personal transformation by the Spirit.

How do we grow in our *understanding*?

YHVH said of His commandments, "Keep and do them, for that
is your wisdom and your understanding in the sight of the peoples."
Honoring them also makes us "strong" (Deu 4:6; 5:29; 11:8).

We are not supposed to stop growing when, as new Believers,
we begin to speak in tongues. Instead, we are to learn and grow in
Abba's eternal wisdom, which is found in His commandments.

We see this in that the early disciples decided that new
Believers would be accepted *if* they immediately began to observe
certain "minimal" standards of behavior. *However...* Their acceptance was connected to a conditional statement. To paraphrase, we
note that James said, "Brethren, it is not necessary that these new
followers begin to immediately observe, understand, and follow all
the ordinances of Israel. We should not suddenly put Torah teachings before them as a stumbling block. Rather, let us write to them
outlining certain minimal standards for them to follow. *If* they
agree to abide by these minimal behavior modification standards
we can receive these people into our sect of Judaism— *for*— in
every town, ever since the earliest times, there have been those who
teach the law of Moses" (see Acts 15:1-21).

---

[45] Note that two different Greek words are used in verses 13-14: "Let him who *speaks*
in a tongue...," and, "If I *pray* in a tongue..." (*Strong's* #'s G 2980 and 4336 respectively).

The apostles agreed. The new Believers would become part of "The Way," go to the synagogues and the Temple, and, *in Messiah,* they would learn of the wisdom found in the Law of Moses.

"Amen," they all said. And the matter was settled. [46]

Hearing the eternal truths of Torah helps us to grow in our understanding of YHVH and His ways.

THE MENORAH OF UNDERSTANDING, WISDOM, AND STRENGTH

Isaiah speaks of "The Spirit of wisdom and of understanding, the Spirit of counsel and of power, the Spirit of knowledge and of the fear of YHVH" (Isa 11:2, NIV).

These facets of our God can be seen in the menorah diagram at the end of this chapter (page 86). There, we see a man with a candlestick, or *menorah* in the center of his being, and a menorah-like pattern above it, with the facets of the Spirit as listed by Isaiah. If we read the matching branches in Hebraic form, which is from right to left, we find that:

- When we Fear/Revere YHVH, we gain Understanding
- When we have Knowledge of the Word (Yeshua), we gain Wisdom
- When we receive the Counsel of the Ruach, we gain Strength

In this way we also see Father, Son, and Holy Spirit.

We also read in Isaiah: "They also that erred in spirit shall come to understanding, and they that murmured shall learn doctrine" (Isa 29:24). We have surely labored under the burden of unsound doctrine and have erred in "spirit" when it comes to the Holy Spirit. But now is the time for us to learn a better way. It is now time for us to grow, in the Spirit, and in wisdom and understanding.

---

46 See *Redeemed Israel: Reunited and Restored*, Batya Wootten, Chapter 23, "New Kingdom— New Rules," 2006, Key of David Publishing, Saint Cloud, FL 34770.

BEING BUILT UP IN THE SPIRIT

Paul spoke of praying in an unknown tongue that edifies the one who is praying. Jude similarly mentions "building yourselves up on your most holy faith, praying in the Holy Spirit" (Jude 1:20). Elsewhere, Paul encourages us to "pray always with all prayer and supplication in the Spirit" (Eph 6:18).

Such prayer must either be silent or private, because, to have everyone always praying aloud would cause chaos in public.

Also, this is not just called "prayer," but prayer "in the Spirit."

Again, prophecy "edifies the church." Public tongues are to be interpreted (so the people will be edified), these two giftings equal a prophecy. Yet, a private prayer tongue is not understood by others and it builds up the faith of the individual.

From the above cited verses we conclude that we have thus far seen three *primary* types of tongues:

- *Un-interpreted* tongues (as in the Book of Acts)
- Tongues and interpretation (*prophetic, public tongues*)
- Praying in the Spirit (*private prayer tongues*)

TONGUES OF ANGELS

In 1 Corinthians 13:1, Paul speaks of "the tongues of men and of angels." He mentions speaking to God, and of man not understanding the speech. So we ask, are private prayer tongues "a heavenly language"? Are they a "tongue of angels"?

Again, we cannot know the answer for certain. If man does not understand the tongue, then we cannot know for certain what type of tongue is being spoken. However, we do know that the Almighty understands the one who is speaking to Him. Again, Paul speaks of there being "many kinds of languages in the world" (1 Cor 14:10). So it appears that his appraisal is that the tongues being spoken are earthly languages.

(As an aside, we note that YHVH does sometimes give a Believer a private utterance that is then interpreted in a known language. However, we must not allow "personal experience" to set our standards. Our definitions must be Scriptural. One answer to this situation could be that this type of spiritual manifestation falls into the category of prophecy— wherein the tongue is supposed to be interpreted.)

OUR FOURTH CATEGORY: GROANINGS

We read that the Spirit helps our weakness when we do not know how to properly pray. And, He "intercedes for us with *groanings* too deep for words" (Rom 8:26, NASB).

The word translated *groanings* is *stenazo*. It means to be in difficult straits, thus to sigh, to pray inaudibly or with grief. [47]

Sometimes, words simply will not express the depths of our emotions, so we groan and cry out. We travail in prayer until that which the Father would have "birthed" in the earth comes forth (Gal 4:19). We read of this type of prayer: We, having the first fruits of the Spirit, "groan within ourselves, waiting eagerly for our adoption as sons [which is]... the redemption of our body. [48] ... Indeed in this house [body] we groan, longing to be clothed with our dwelling from heaven.... In this tent [body], we groan, being burdened, because we do not want to be unclothed but to be clothed, so that what is mortal will be swallowed up by life" (Rom 8:23; 2 Cor 5:2,4, NASB).

Also, we see that when Yeshua saw Mary weeping over the death of her brother, Lazarus, He "groaned in the spirit, and was troubled." He then asked where they had laid him. Then, Yeshua *"wept"* (John 11:33-35). Here again we see grief that surpasses the limits of words. The Greek word translated *wept*, can mean to snort with anger; to have indignation, to sigh, enjoin, or groan. [49]

---

47 *Strong's* #'s G4726 and 4727. Note: Different aspects of a subject might be addressed in various chapters. Please check the Index for the particular subject of interest.

48 Our "adoption" has to do with our full redemption, with becoming sons of the Living God and calling Him, "Father" (see Romans 8:15,16,23; 9:4; Gal 4:5; Eph 1:5).

49 *Strong's* #'s G 1690 and 1722.

Here, we must issue a warning: *Groanings must not be conjured up to try to attain an imagined new plateau in one's prayer life.* They are instead the true fruit of an existing condition. They are born of true concern for a matter. Yeshua's groaning was a result of the intense grief that He felt. It was not groaning for the sake of groaning.

Truly understanding this type of prayer is especially important for those who long for Israel's restoration. For, Zephaniah 3:18 speaks of Believers, who, in the last days, *grieve over*, or long for the restoration of Israel's feasts: "I will gather those who grieve about the appointed feasts — They came from you, O Zion; the reproach of exile is a burden on them" (NASB).

Soncino Books of the Bible, The Twelve Prophets, translates the verse, "I will gather them that are far from the appointed season, who are of thee, that hast borne the burden of reproach." [50]

Jeremiah likewise speaks of us grieving because we are far from the feasts:

> "The ways of Zion do *mourn*, because none come to the solemn feasts [*mo'edim*]: all her gates are desolate: her priests *sigh*, her virgins are afflicted, and she is in bitterness.... the LORD has caused her grief because of the multitude of her transgressions; Her little ones have gone away as captives before the adversary. All her majesty has departed.... Jerusalem remembers all her precious things that were from the days of old" (Lam 1:4-7).

Deliverance came to the children of Israel when YHVH heard their *cry*: "Their cry for help because of their bondage rose up to the LORD." He heard their *groaning*, then He remembered His covenant with their fathers and took notice of their plight (Exo 2:23-25). Crying out is key. If we *sincerely* call on the Holy One in true repentance, He will take notice and deliver us. He said He would be like a lion to us, tearing us, *until* we acknowledge our guilt and seek His face. We must therefore, readily admit our sin

---

50 London, Soncino, 1980, p. 251.

and cry out for deliverance from the Egypt that binds us. Like Daniel, we must accept that we have sinned and repent, then Abba will take notice and redeem us (Hos 5:14-15; 9:5-15; Mat 6:5-18). [51]

OUR FIFTH CATEGORY: SINGING IN THE SPIRIT

Our final category is "singing in the Spirit." Paul said he would "sing with the spirit" *and* with "understanding" (1 Cor 14:15).

The difference in these two types of song is uncertain. Paul may be speaking of Believers collectively and harmoniously singing in "unknown" tongues. Or, it may mean that, he was seeking interpretation of what was being sung (in order to grow in his understanding). And/or, it may mean that there is this type of singing, and, there is singing led by Spirit in which Believers collectively sing a new song in a language that they understand.

This much we do know: Scripture repeatedly speaks of saints learning to sing a "new song" (Psa 33:3; Rev 5:9; 14:3). One of the Psalms says, YHVH "put a new song in my mouth, a song of praise to our God." David also said, the meadows and valleys "sing" (Psa 40:3; 65:13). When Yeshua's disciples broke out in shouts of praise, others told Him to rebuke them. But, He said that if He did, the "stones" would cry out (Luke 19:40). [52]

Mankind can cause glasses and bells to "sing," and we now know that there is a song that can be heard in the expanse of the Universe. We can hear and enjoy such songs, yet their sounds are "unintelligible." So, should we arbitrarily dismiss beautiful songs in the Spirit if we do not understand the words?

If they give glory to our God, edify and lift us up, perhaps we should ask Abba to allow us to join in the singing.

We will address this subject in further detail in the chapter, "Prophetic Singing in the Spirit."

---

51 *Israel's Feasts*, chaps. 29; 36, "Ten Days of Prayer," "Restoring David's Fallen Tabernacle." *The Voice... Hearing the Almighty* by Batya Wootten, 2009, Key of David Publishing.
52 See also, Psa 40:3; 96:1; 98:1; 144:9; 149:1; Isa 42:10-11.

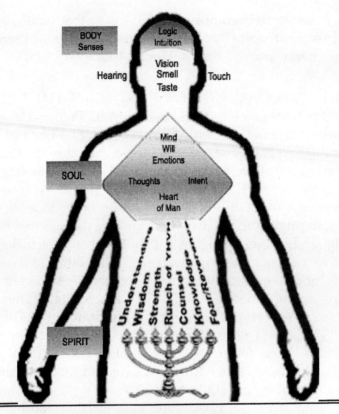

Knowing YHVH

*We do not want to focus on the things of the world
but on the things of the Spirit. We want to put away the
cares of this world and have our hearts filled with the purposes
of the Holy One of Israel. We want to be led by His sevenfold Spirit
(as outlined in Isa 11:2).
When we follow that menorah-like pattern and read the matching branches
first right, then left, then right again, and left..., we find:
When we fear/revere YHVH, we gain understanding.
When we have knowledge of the Word (Yeshua), we gain wisdom.
When we receive the counsel of the Ruach, we gain strength.
Thus we see Father, Son, and Holy Spirit in Isaiah 11:2.
Chart by Batya Ruth Wootten. Graphic and idea from the book, "Sons to
Glory" by Paul Jablonowski: www.sonstoglory.com.*
Used with Permission.

12

COMING FULL CIRCLE

W hen we were in the Garden, Adam walked and talked with YHVH in the *cool* of the day (Gen 3:8-9). Again, the Hebrew word translated "cool" is rooted in the word for *ruach*, as in *Ruach haKodesh*. Moreover, Yeshua said, "True worshipers will worship the Father in spirit and truth." This means, we need to come full-circle— we need to return to the language of the Garden. We also need to be on the way to Heavenly Zion. So it is that, those who worship the God of Israel, must learn to worship Him *"in the Spirit/Ruach"* (John 4:23; 17:17).

However...

We have a problem in that, many who seek to worship the Father "in the Spirit," leave out the "truth" of the matter. And, we must worship "in spirit *and* truth." Yeshua defined truth when He said to the Father, "Your word is truth" (John 17:17). Unfortunately, many who claim to worship in the Spirit rely only on the words found in Matthew to Revelation. They essentially dismiss the earlier books as though they were of no consequence.

But King David said, "The entirety of Your word is truth, and every one of Your righteous judgments endures forever" (Psa 119:160). The *entirety*, the *sum* of our Father's Word will endure forever: Genesis to Revelation. Man cannot have the truth of the Spirit apart from the truths of the Torah. It takes both. We need to worship in spirit and truth; "for the Father is seeking such to worship Him" (John 4:23). That is what He wants, and we need to be the people who give it to Him.

We do not want to be a people who embrace Torah yet do not realize that Our God is able to do a "new thing"— and that His mercies are "new every morning." We must realize that He has promised, and begun to give us a "new and better covenant." Surely, He will not change, yet, by His Spirit, He is a God Who is ever teaching His children to "sing a new song." [53]

To appreciate the role of spiritual communication in our faith, we note that biting into forbidden fruit was not the first sin. We first missed the mark by *not listening* to the voice of the Almighty. We cannot overstate this vital point. We failed to listen, and then to obey, and ever since, our testing has been about whether or not we will listen to, and obey His voice. [54] Therefore, if Abba has now chosen to open lines of private communication with His children, so they might learn to better hear and understand Him, and mortal men do not understand the words being spoken, we must not be so highhanded as to dismiss such speech as "gibberish." Who are we to say YHVH does not understand what is being said?

We must put the gift in perspective: Its purpose is, to help us by-pass limited understanding, to pray perfect prayers, to speak of the mysteries of the Almighty, and thereby, to be built up in our faith. It is a tool, an aid, a gift that helps us in our walk. It is a sign that points to and helps us arrive at something greater: Righteous living in the Kingdom. We do not want to boast about or camp around the gift, but to move on, using it to gain understanding.

---

53 Exo 15:1; Lam 3:22-23; Jer 31:22-33; Mal 3:6; Heb 7:21-22 ; 8:6; 12:24-25; Rev 5:9; 15:3.
54 See the book, *The Voice... Hearing the Almighty* by Batya Wootten.

WHAT IS THE LANGUAGE OF THE GARDEN?

James, the Lord's brother, said of man's tongue, and his words:

> "No one can tame the tongue; it is a restless evil and full of
> deadly poison. With it we bless our Lord and Father, and ...
> curse men, who have been made in the likeness of God; from
> the same mouth come both blessing and cursing....these
> things ought not to be this way. Does a fountain send out
> from the same opening both fresh and bitter water? Can a fig
> tree, my brethren, produce olives, or a vine produce figs?
> Nor can salt water produce fresh" (James 3:8-12).

In YHVH's eyes, speech is a holy and creative thing. So we ask,
Did YHVH preserve His language in some way after man sinned?
Adam began his descent by disrespecting YHVH's spoken
command. Did this thereafter affect Adam's ability to properly hear
YHVH? Could it be that, when sin entered into man, the voice of
the Holy One departed from within Adam's being? Is that what
Adam meant when he was frightened, and said in Genesis 3:8 that
he heard the Father's voice "in the garden"?

We suggest the answer is "Yes," and that our sojourn here on
earth is about learning to hear and obey that voice. [55] Moreover,
"tongues are for a sign" (1 Cor 14:22). So, does that sign point
toward a coming aspect of our full restoration? Could it be that a
pure language lies ahead for us? Will we again speak in Heaven's
tongue? Will we once more speak in a language that mankind has
not been allowed to contaminate? We suggest the answer to each
of these questions might well be "Yes." For, Paul said:

> "I know a man in Christ who fourteen years ago—
> whether in the body [or]...out of the body I do not know...
> such a one was caught up to the third heaven.... into
> Paradise and heard inexpressible words, which it is not
> lawful for a man to utter" (2 Cor 12:2-4).

---

[55] See the book, *The Voice... Hearing the Almighty*, by Batya Wootten (2009, Key of
David Publishing, Saint Cloud, FL).

Paul heard inexpressible words that man is not permitted to speak. This suggests a divine tongue that man has not been allowed to corrupt. Perhaps Paul heard and knew a "tongue of angels," yet could not repeat it. While we cannot know this for certain, the above verses indicate that we are not being permitted to speak the language of the holy and eternal Kingdom that is yet to come.

So, what is this "forbidden language"? Could the answer be ....

SPIRIT TO SPIRIT COMMUNICATION?

All earthly languages are filtered through the human mind. Man often says one thing with his tongue, yet thinks something else within himself. But an evil or lying tongue is an abomination to YHVH (Pro 6:16-17; Jer 9:8). A picture is painted of its sin in that, leprosy is a contagious disease associated with a wayward tongue. Lepers had to cover their mouths. Being healed of the disease spoke of absolution of sin. This depicts the truth that lying tongues breed disease. The Father instead wants Israelites in whom there is no guile. He wants us to speak the truth in love (Num 12:1,10; Lev 15:8; 13:45; Isa 6:7; John 1:47; Rom 10:10; Eph 4:15; Rev 21:27).

One day, we will "know, even as we are fully known" (1 Cor 13:12). Could it be that in the Kingdom, even as in the Garden, we will once again communicate "spirit-to-spirit"? Could it be that there will be no place for dishonesty in eternity, because the truth of what lies within us will be made manifest to all?

To this end, the Psalmists prays, "Deliver my soul, O LORD, from lying lips, from a deceitful tongue." He tells us to guard our tongue. We are told to put away a "deceitful mouth" and "devious speech" (Psa 39:1; 120:2; Pro 4:24). For, YHVH has sworn that, "The remnant of Israel will do no wrong and tell no lies, nor will a deceitful tongue be found in their mouths" (Zep 3:13, NASB).

WHY PRAY IN THE SPIRIT?

Having briefly outlined the varieties of communication in and by the Holy Spirit, we now ask "why?"

Why should we pray in a Spirit-given language? What, if any, are the benefits?

We pray in the Spirit because our physical mind cannot fully comprehend the things of our God (Job 37:5; 1 Cor 2:9-11). When we pray in the Spirit and give ourselves over to His leading, we are not limited by our human understanding. Our spirit prays according to His truth. We allow the Spirit of God that dwells in us, to speak with God, to pray for us according to His will. We allow the Spirit to pray in an unfettered way, and He always seeks what is best for us. Such prayer cannot be corrupted— or used to our disadvantage. Our carnal mind, which is not able to truly comprehend the things of God, does not get in the way, so it cannot bear its corrupt earthly fruit. Instead, the Spirit brings forth eternal fruit, words that are in accord with the Spirit, words that will bear good fruit in our lives.

We also pray in the spirit because it is written:

> "Eye has not seen, nor ear heard, Nor have entered into the heart of man The things which God has prepared for those who love Him. But God has revealed them to us through His Spirit. For the Spirit searches all things, yes, the deep things of God. For what man knows the things of a man except the spirit of the man which is in him? Even so no one knows the things of God except the Spirit of God. Now we have received, not the spirit of the world, but the Spirit who is from God, that we might know the things that have been freely given to us by God" (1 Cor 2:9-12).

We pray in the spirit because, "The hour is coming, and now is, when the true worshipers will worship the Father in spirit and truth; for the Father is seeking such to worship Him. God is Spirit, and those who worship Him must worship in spirit and truth" (John 4:23-24). We are equipped to do this via Messiah's New and "better" Covenant (Heb 7:22; 8:6). In Him, pure communication is being restored.

Finally, we note that, the various gifts of the Spirit were manifested in the Hebrew Scriptures (Old Testament), all except for the gift of speaking in tongues. Moreover, in every place in Scripture where we see the baptism of the Spirit, it is evidenced by speaking in tongues. [56]

So it is that intimate communication is part of our renewal and restoration. We do not want to resist or abuse this gift, and we want to keep it in perspective. Paul said he would rather speak five words with understanding, than ten thousand words in a tongue (1 Cor 14:19). Tongues indicate a level of spiritual understanding, but arriving there with the whole man is more important.

The Spirit teaches us the mysteries of the kingdom of heaven (Mat 13:11; John 14:26; Eph 3:16). The tongue of 1 Corinthians 14:2 is a private endowment that helps us to be edified and to properly speak to our God when we do not understand His way in a matter.

Some say Satan cannot understand our private prayer language. Whether true or not, we do know that YHVH understands us, and that this gift is a potent weapon in our fight against the forces of evil. When we are led by the Spirit, He intercedes for us based on what is best for us, He leads us to pray in accord with Abba's will. Prayers that originate with Him are perfect and without mistakes. Having the Spirit help us in prayer is like having a powerful sword that we can readily wield. Let us take up that sword (Eph 6:17).

We pray in the spirit because it is a gift from our Beloved. We gratefully receive, and put to good use, every gift He gives us. But again, we must keep it in perspective: It's all about arriving at true understanding of our Father's Holy Word and Ways.

We must not be contentious nor divisive over speaking in tongues. Instead, we close with Paul's conclusion in the matter: *"Therefore, brethren, desire earnestly to prophesy, and do not forbid to speak with tongues" (1 Cor 14:39).*

Next, we will examine a key component that has to do with *how* the gifts of the Spirit should work within the Body of Messiah.

---

56 Acts 2:4, 11; 10:43-48; 11:1-18; 15:5-9; 19:6.

13

THE LOVE CONNECTION

I f we want to operate in, and understand the gifts of the Holy Spirit, we first must make "The Love Connection."

To make sense of the gifts of the Spirit, we first need to see that, 1 Corinthians, chapters 12 through 14, should be viewed as one continuous block.

Many mistakenly think a natural chapter division is found at chapter 13 (often called the "Love Chapter"). This imagined division causes us to approach each chapter as if they were new topics—but they are not. Collectively, the three chapters are Paul's treatises on spiritual endowments, and they should be treated as one unit of thought.

Paul begins by outlining the gifts, then explains that they are to be crowned by love, then explains how we are to operate in them. He emphasizes the importance of prophecy, but then says, even if we do have that important gift, if we do not have love, it profits us nothing. Paul explains that love is more important than *any* of the gifts. We might even call it the *"gift of gifts."*

At the risk of using a sorely overworked cliché word, we say: Whatever the answer may be to our many questions about spiritual giftings and their operation, "*love*" is the answer. Love must be behind it. Otherwise, our words and teachings are no more than a "sounding brass or a clanging cymbal" (1 Cor 13:1).

Love is the answer.

Lots of people have been saying this for a long time.

The problem is that true love is not about having a mushy, "anything goes," attitude toward people and their wrong actions.

True love speaks the truth.

Truth sets people free.

On the other hand, the truth is that true love, will always first be born of mercy for the one who needs to hear the truth.

Love and truth do not give license for meanness or mush.

To love someone is to have true affection for them.

True love will always want the best for others.

True love also will always be confirmed in the Word of our God. He is "love" (1 John 4:8,16). From the beginning, He taught His people to love (Exo 20:6; Lev 19:18,34; Deu 5:10; Luke 10:27).

Paul said of love:

> "Though I speak with the tongues of men and of angels, but have not love, I have become sounding brass or a clanging cymbal. And though I have the gift of prophecy, and understand all mysteries and all knowledge, and though I have all faith, so that I could remove mountains, but have not love, I am nothing. And though I bestow all my goods to feed the poor, and though I give my body to be burned, but have not love, it profits me nothing.
>
> "Love suffers long and is kind; love does not envy; love does not parade itself, is not puffed up; does not behave rudely, does not seek its own, is not provoked, thinks no evil; does not rejoice in iniquity, but rejoices in the truth; bears all things, believes all things, hopes all things, endures all things.

"Love never fails [becomes of none effect]. But whether there are prophecies, they will fail [cease, become unnecessary]; [57] whether there are tongues, they will cease [same word: cease, become unnecessary]; whether there is knowledge, it will vanish away.

"For we know in part and we prophesy in part. But when that which is perfect has come, then that which is in part will be done away.

"When I was a child, I spoke as a child, I understood as a child, I thought as a child; but when I became a man, I put away childish things. For now we see in a mirror, dimly, but then face to face. Now I know in part, but then I shall know just as I also am known.

"And now abide faith, hope, love, these three; but the greatest of these is love" (1 Cor 13:1-13).

Paul is telling us that love endures forever. But, prophecies, tongues, and words of knowledge will not be necessary when we are in the Kingdom. Then, we will see face to face. We will know even as we are known. Our knowledge will no more be in part.

For now, we are like little children who seek to enter into the Father's Kingdom (Mat 18:3). Once we fully enter into that Kingdom, we will be matured "sons of the living God."

For now, the lost sheep of the house of Israel have been given certain gifts of the Spirit that will help them find their way back home to Zion. On this path, there are many children, and they are in many different places in their singular journey home. As we individually walk this journey, we must not be contentious with each other about fleeting things that are destined to pass away. We should instead prefer to abide with one another in faith and hope— and especially in love.

---

57 Two different words are here translated "fails." See *Strong's* #'s G 1601 and 2673.

Love never fails (# 1601 becomes inefficient or, of none effect). However, tongues, prophecies, and words of knowledge all "cease" (word # 2673), because they are no longer necessary.

Love—
The Identifying Fruit of a Believer

The Word tells us that "the fruit of the Spirit is love, joy, peace, longsuffering, kindness, goodness, faithfulness, gentleness, self-control" (Gal 5:22-23).

Love is a fruit of the Spirit. It is an outgrowth of true life in Messiah. Only when we abide in Him can we bear the fruits of the Spirit. By these fruits, we prove to the world that we are His disciples (John 15:2-17).

The trees on which such fruits grow are best fertilized by the death of self (John 12:24; Rom 7:4).

We need to pray that our fruits might be ever increased: "Ask that you may be filled with the knowledge of His will in all wisdom and spiritual understanding; that you may walk worthy of the Lord, fully pleasing Him, being fruitful in every good work and increasing in the knowledge of God; strengthened with all might, according to His glorious power" (Col 1:6-11).

The goal of our instruction must always be love from a pure heart, a good conscience, and a sincere faith. And, we must always avoid fruitless discussion (1 Tim 1:5-8). "The wisdom from above is first pure, then peaceable, gentle, reasonable, full of mercy and good fruits, unwavering, without hypocrisy." And, "the seed whose fruit is righteousness is sown in peace by those who make peace" (James 3:17-18, NASB).

We must not be contentious about these things.

Again, love is the answer. It is the beginning of the fruits of the Spirit. Out of it, all of the other fruits will grow straight and tall.

14

TAKING, KEEPING, AND YIELDING CONTROL

We can receive a new language when baptized with the Holy Spirit. However, we also can refuse to speak out the words we are given. If we refuse to utter the sounds, the Father will not force us to speak; we are in control of the privilege being given, but it will not become evident if we do not allow it to happen.

Pastor Jack Hayford, prolific author and president of "The International Church of the Foursquare Gospel," testified in his book, *The Beauty of Spiritual Language,* [58] that, he received his spiritual "tongue" when he earnestly asked Yeshua for the baptism with the Holy Spirit. He received a word in his mind, but did not speak it out verbally for four years. When the situation and circumstances were right and agreeable to him, he spoke his one word, and a Native American Indian interpreted it. Then, more words came to Jack's mind, and he freely spoke them out.

---

58 1996. Thomas Nelson, Inc. Nashville, TN. ISBN 0-7852-7268-2

(Note: We can hear words in our mind and then speak them or we can speak words and hear them as we speak.)

Hayford's example proves that God is very patient with us. It also depicts the truth that His gift to us calls for our cooperation if it is to be utilized. Our God will do His part, then we must do our part. Acts Chapter 2 says "they" spoke, meaning, 1) they were willing, and 2) they used their voice. They employed their vocal cords, with air, and were not in any sort of trance.

The Word says "the spirits of the prophets are subject to the prophets" (1 Cor 14:32). Restated, Ruach-filled Believers must "control themselves" (God's Word®).

This means, YHVH respects our free will and will not interfere with it. He says to us, "I know the plans that I have for you… plans for welfare [*shalom*] and not for calamity to give you a future and a hope" (Jer 29:11, NASB). However, conversely, Satan wants control of our minds and bodies so he can destroy us. He wants the opposite of what YHVH wants for us. Satan also wants to cause us to misunderstand, or not use, and/or misuse, the gifts of the Holy Spirit. Thus, the Father wants us to keep them under control, and away from evil. But again, He will not override our free will. And, we are always in charge.

With this understanding in mind, we see that, so to speak, we are to yield control to YHVH and no other.

We must choose to *yield* to Him because He will not *take* control. We need to *keep* control, yet willingly and voluntarily *yield* control to the Ruach. We yield to Him because He wants to lead us into righteousness. Yet, when we do yield control, we will not be in a trance, and without control. We are instead allowing the Holy Spirit to help us. That is why He is called the "Helper." He teaches us, brings to remembrance Messiah's teachings, and helps us to effectively testify about Him (John 14:16,26; 15:26; 16:7).

The Ruach will not lead us to behave in an unrighteous or inappropriate manner, nor will He lead us to oppose Scripture in any way.

Yet, to be candid, some have behaved with the gifts in an unseemly way. In turn, their behavior has served to turn some Believers away. They simply do not want the craziness they have seen exhibited by some, in the name of the "Holy Spirit."

That is beyond sad.

It is sad in that, some miss out on awesome blessings, because some misunderstand, and/or misuse wonderful gifts that our Father wants to bestow on us. However, just as Torah has been misrepresented by many, yet is not to be thrown out, so it is that the gifts of the Spirit should not be thrown out either. We instead need to embrace the truth about them at this time.

Concerning spiritual gifts, we are first and foremost to seek to operate in love for the whole Body of Messiah. With this idea firmly implanted in our minds, we return to our study of the various gifts of the Spirit.

1 CORINTHIANS 14:
THE "HOW IT WORKS" CHAPTER

In 1 Corinthians 14:1-28 Paul essentially explains the following:

- We are to pursue love, and desire spiritual gifts, but especially that we may prophesy.
- He who speaks in a tongue is not speaking to men but to God, generally, no one understands him, and in the spirit, he speaks mysteries. He who speaks in this type of private tongue also does so to edify himself.
- Prophecies are given to *edify, exhort* and *comfort* the Body.
- Paul wished that all spoke with personal tongues, and thus would be edified in their inner man, but even more so, he wanted us to be able to prophesy—because prophecies are given to build up the congregation. It is deemed to be a "greater" gift because *it lifts up many.*
- Prophecy is the greater gift, but public tongues followed by interpretation is equal to it and it edifies the congregation.

- We are not to speak indistinct sounds to the congregation (which is what our private language sounds like to others), because they will not understand us. We will be unintelligible to them, our words will seem "foreign." Instead, we clearly share with the Body understandable words of knowledge, prophesying, and teaching.
- We are to be zealous for spiritual gifts— for the express purpose of edification of the Body. In this way, the uninformed will be able to say "Amen" to our giving of thanks and be encouraged by the things they learn.
- When we come together, whether we have a psalm, a teaching, a tongue, a revelation, or an interpretation, all things are to be done for "edification."
- Paul is addressing *proper order*, saying, "If anyone speaks in a tongue, let there be two or at the most three, each in turn and let one interpret. But if there is no interpreter, let him keep silent in church, and let him speak to himself and to God. Let two or three prophets speak, and let the others judge. But if anything is revealed to another who sits by, let the first keep silent. For you can all prophesy one by one, that all may learn and all may be encouraged. And the spirits of the prophets are subject to the prophets. For God is not the author of confusion but of peace, as in all the churches of the saints"(1 Cor 14:26-30).

Paul is establishing guidelines for order in this chapter (14).

He specifically speaks of some women who were not behaving properly. We suggest he was not saying women could not "speak" in churches, but that they should not "chatter," [59] as though they were not "subject" to the teachings.

If they did not understand a matter, they were not to disrupt the teaching with endless questions but were to inquire of their husband at home. This must be his meaning, because, three

---

[59] *Strong's* word # G4601.

chapters earlier, Paul affirmed that women could "pray and prophesy" in meetings (vss. 11:5-6).

The women in question probably were former worshipers of Dionysus— the god of wine and madness. His female followers were known as maenads, or mad ones, because, their loud, frenzied shouting at ceremonial events often resulted in riots. The Greek verb translated "remain silent" in essence means to keep your peace, to control yourself, to refrain from speaking out of respect, just as we do not talk during prayer or a performance.

There are proper times and places for questions, and Paul's point is that they should not be asked when it will disrupt everything for many. He was explaining when to speak and when to defer to others in a meeting (verse 14:40). These women were not addressing the assembly as leaders— but were instead chattering during the service and disturbing others. So Paul told them to be quiet and maintain congregational order. [60]

In summary, our private prayer language is given to us that we might speak and pray mysteries to our God and be built up in our inner man. And, at times we may privately intercede with prayerful, grief-filled sighs, groanings, and moanings (Rom 8:26-27). [61]

Public tongues, when they are accompanied by the gift of interpretation, are equal to a prophecy, and together are given for the sake of building up the congregation, by means of human understanding of what is being spoken.

The point behind our public meetings should be to build up the Body and to teach the uninitiated. However, this will not be accomplished without proper order. Let us, therefore, ask the Holy One of Israel to bestow on us His gifts, and to empower us to lovingly use them according to His scripturally stated purposes, and in His proper order.

---

60 From *Mama's Torah: The Role of Women* by Batya Ruth Wootten, 2004, Key of David Publishing, Saint Cloud, FL.

61 *Strong's* word #'s G4726 and 4727.

15

A More Excellent Way

Thus far we have laid groundwork concerning speaking in tongues, discovered its many advantages (especially regarding prayer), recounted what happened when the Ruach fell on the disciples, and seen that those who are baptized with the Ruach can receive a spiritual language, and, they can hold it back. We saw that when Peter was speaking, the Spirit fell on all who heard him, astonishing the circumcised Believers, because the Spirit was poured out on the Gentiles, which was unheard of. They knew this was so because they heard them speaking with tongues and magnifying God. So Peter determined that no one should forbid them a mikveh, because they had received the Spirit just as had the Jewish Believers (Acts 10:44-47: see footnote 28). And, Paul, having come to Ephesus, asked some disciples if they had received the Spirit when they believed. When they said, they only knew of John's baptism of repentance, he laid hands on them, the Spirit came upon them, and they spoke in other tongues and prophesied (Acts 19:1-6).

Moving forward, we see that concerning spiritual "gifts," as Scripture sometimes calls them, Paul tells us not to "be ignorant."

To avoid misunderstanding, we note that the word *"gifts"* is not found in the original text of 1 Corinthians 12:1. It was added for clarification, and is thus *italicized*. The Greek word for "gift," *dorea* (used in Acts 2:38 to speak of "the *gift* of the Holy Spirit"), is not present here. [62]

Translating the word used as "gifts" does not clarify the matter but tends to confuse the issue. The English word *spiritual* is translated from the Greek *pneumatikos* (*pnyoo-mat-ik-os*), meaning, non-carnal, ethereal, a spirit, divinely supernatural. [63] Thus, a better rendering of this text might be, "Concerning *spirituals* brethren, I do not want you to be ignorant." Or, "Concerning the *supernatural*, brethren, I do not want you to be ignorant."

To see the verse in context, we read:

> "You know that you were Gentiles, carried away to these dumb idols, however you were led. Therefore I make known to you that no one speaking by the Spirit of God calls Jesus accursed, and no one can say that Jesus is Lord except by the Holy Spirit. There are diversities of [spirituals] gifts, but the same Spirit. There are differences of ministries, but the same Lord. And there are diversities of activities, but it is the same God who works all in all. But the manifestation of the Spirit is given to each one for the profit of all: for to one is given the word of wisdom through the Spirit, to another the word of knowledge through the same Spirit, to another faith by the same Spirit, to another gifts of healings by the same Spirit, to another the working of miracles, to another prophecy, to another discerning of spirits, to another different kinds of tongues, to another the interpretation of tongues. But one and the same Spirit works all these things, distributing to each

---

62 *Strong's* # G1431; from G1435; a gratuity, gift.
63 *Strong's* # G4152; from # G4151.

one individually as He wills. For as the body is one and has many members, but all the members…being many, are one body, so also is Christ. For by one Spirit we were all baptized into one body— whether Jews or Greeks, slaves or free— and have all been made to drink into one Spirit…. the body is not one member but many. If the foot should say, 'Because I am not a hand, I am not of the body,' is it therefore not of the body? If the ear should say, 'Because I am not an eye, I am not of the body,' is it therefore not of the body? If the whole body were an eye, where would be the hearing? If the whole were hearing, where would be the smelling? But now God has set the members, each one of them, in the body just as He pleased. And if they were all one member, where would the body be? But now indeed there are many members, yet one body. The eye cannot say to the hand, 'I have no need of you'; nor again the head to the feet, 'I have no need of you.' No, much rather, those members of the body which seem to be weaker are necessary. Those members of the body which we think to be less honorable, on these we bestow greater honor; and our unpresentable parts have greater modesty, but our presentable parts have no need. But God composed the body, having given greater honor to that part which lacks it, that there should be no schism in the body, but that the members should have the same care for one another. And if one member suffers, all the members suffer with it; or if one member is honored, all the members rejoice with it. Now you are the body of Christ, and members individually. And God has appointed these in the church: first apostles, second prophets, third teachers, after that miracles, then gifts of healings, helps, administrations, varieties of tongues. Are all apostles? Are all prophets? Are all teachers? Are all workers of miracles? Do all have gifts of healings? Do all speak with tongues? Do all interpret? But earnestly desire the best gifts. And yet I show you a more excellent way" (1 Cor 12:2-31).

In Acts 10 we see the Apostle Peter in Caesarea, ministering to the centurion Cornelius and his household. The Jewish Believers who accompanied Peter were astounded that YHVH would pour out the Ruach on those who were thought to be "heathen," yet were convinced that Cornelius and company had been baptized with the Holy Spirit— as evidenced by their speaking in tongues.

In Acts 19 we see Paul in Ephesus with a congregation of new Believers who were never taught of things concerning the baptism with the Ruach. After their instructions, these Ephesians freely received the Spirit, again evidenced by their speaking in tongues and praising God.

The Corinthian church was well acquainted with the baptism with the Holy Spirit as we can conclude from 1 Corinthians 12. It would appear that they were so acquainted that various abuses of the manifestations soon raised their ugly heads. Thus, Paul was addressing the misuse of *"spirituals"* in his letter. It is a reprimand and exhortation, and in that context, we now reexamine verse 31.

Earnestly Desiring "Spirituals"

In verse 31 Paul makes a critical statement. He quotes back to the Corinthians concerning the very thing they were boasting about. The NKJV renders the verse: "But earnestly desire the *best* gifts. And yet I show you a more excellent way." The NIV reads: "But eagerly desire the *greater* gifts. [64] And now I will show you the most excellent way."

These translations do not fully fit the context of what Paul was expressing in chapter 12. If we think he was rebuking the Corinthians for their abuse of spiritual manifestations, and simply telling them to "desire the greater, stronger, or best gifts"— if we do not see the connection to chapter 13— we miss his point.

The NIV footnote shows an alternate translation, which well fits with the overall context of Paul's letter. It says, "but you are eagerly

---

[64] Best/Greater: *Strong's* # G2909. *kreitton*: stronger, better, nobler.

desiring." The Lutheran translation, God's Word,® says: "You want the better gifts, but I will show you the best thing to do." *Life Application Notes* point out this problem as well. We read in its footnote for the verse, "Paul has already made it clear that one gift is not superior to another, but he urges the Believers to discover how they can serve Christ's body with the gifts God has given them. Spiritual gifts are not for your own self-advancement. They were given to you for serving God and enhancing the spiritual growth of the body of Believers." [65]

The Corinthians may have been into self-promotion. They may have seen spiritual endowments as "merit badges" and then fell into the trap of ranking them. In this case, man would tend to put greater emphasis on the vocal manifestations. They may have done this because they are the most prevalent, being "freely given," and due to human frailty, vocal manifestations bring more attention to the speaker (1 Cor 2:12).

We must not think of spiritual gifts as being something we can rank, own, or control. Instead, we are but holders of them: "We have this treasure in earthen vessels, so that the surpassing greatness of the power will be of God and not from ourselves" (2 Cor 4:7, NASB).

If we rank the gifts, our focus will tend to move toward the gift and away from the Gift Giver. Moreover, this wrong attitude can encourage self-centered individuals to get puffed up and be carried away by pride because of "their" high-ranking gifts.

As for gifts, the Holy Spirit is the "Gift" (Acts 2:38). When we ask for the Spirit, we get all of Him that is available at this time. Then, as He sees fit, He imparts to us the supernatural endowment(s) we need in a given situation. Thus, Scripture encourages us to continually seek a "renewing of our mind," to be ever growing into greater depths of maturity and spiritual giftings:

65 *God's Word*, 2003, Baker Books, Ada, MI. ISBN 978-1-932587-08-1; and, *Life Application Notes*, 1988, Tyndale House Publishers, Inc., Wheaton IL.

"Do not be conformed to this world, but be transformed by the renewing of your mind, that you may prove what is that good and acceptable and perfect will of God." For, "We all, with unveiled face, beholding as in a mirror the glory of the Lord, are being transformed into the same image from glory to glory, by the Spirit of the Lord." It is the Holy Spirit of our LORD "who will transform our lowly body that it may be conformed to His glorious body, according to the working by which He is able even to subdue all things to Himself" (Rom 12:2; 2 Cor 3:18; Phil 3:21).

Paul did not reprimand his readers without steering them on to the right path. He even said, "And now I will show you the most excellent way." That most excellent way is "love." The Spirit is the Gift. Love is the channel for the flow of His *supernatural expressions*.

Having explained this, Paul then penned the next 13 verses as the suggested avenue of correction. As stated earlier, a chapter division (at chapter 13) is unfortunate. Its existence implies that the verses pertain to a new topic, which couldn't be further from the truth. To see Paul's correction in context, we need to consecutively read 1 Corinthians 12 through 14. Then the subject comes alive. Then we see the depths of Paul's inspired instruction.

Once we see this connection as it was originally intended, we need to pray for an infilling of love and compassion, so the Spirit will feel free to manifest Himself through us. We pray knowing, when we ask YHVH to baptize us, we receive the gift of the Holy Spirit. He can give us many spiritual endowments, or He may choose to give us one particular spiritual expression/endowment at a time.

Nine gifts of the Spirit are listed. Some list them in categories:

1) Wisdom, knowledge, and discernment.
2) Faith, healing, and working of miracles.
3) Prophecy, tongues, and interpretation of tongues

(See 1 Corinthians 12:8-10, and the *Nine Gifts Chart*, page 116.)

In addition, we see that there are various ministries:

> "He Himself gave some to be apostles, some prophets, some evangelists, and some pastors and teachers, for the equipping of the saints for the work of ministry, for the edifying of the body of Messiah, till we all come to the unity of the faith and of the knowledge of the Son of God, to a perfect man, to the measure of the stature of the fullness of Messiah" (Eph 4:11-13).

These particular callings are given to *some:* "Some" are apostles, some are prophets, evangelists, pastors, teachers. In other words, not all operate in these particular callings.

As for the nine gifts of the Spirit, Paul compares them to parts of the human body and points out their different functions:

> "We have many members in one body, but all members do not have the same function, so we, being many, are one body in Messiah, and individually members of one another. Having then gifts differing according to the grace that is given to us, let us use them: if prophecy, let us prophesy in proportion to our faith; or ministry, let us use it in our ministering; he who teaches, in teaching; he who exhorts, in exhortation; he who gives, with liberality; he who leads, with diligence; he who shows mercy, with cheerfulness" (Rom 12:4-8).

We want to balance Paul's analogy with the fact that he also spoke of us being constantly transformed by having our minds renewed, and of us moving "from glory to glory" by the Spirit (Rom 12:1-3; 2 Cor 3:18). Thus we suggest that, rather than thinking in terms of receiving only *one* of the above listed "nine gifts" of the Spirit, we need to think in terms of receiving all of the Holy Spirit that is available to us at this time. Grace can increase in our lives. Peter even tells us to "grow in it." However, the gifts of the Spirit cannot be "earned" (John 1:16; 1 Cor 4:7; 2 Pet 3:18).

When we receive the Spirit, we will tend to walk as individuals with various propensities and interests. For example, compassionate people will gravitate toward the sick and probably have the gifts of healings or miracles manifested in their lives. But, we must not limit the idea of our empowerment. We must not think, *"That person needs a word of wisdom, but that is not my gift."* If someone has a need, it can *possibly* be filled through us. The Holy Spirit will surely equip us to handle any opportunities that He presents to us. He will surely give us the tools we need to do the job (1 Cor 12:11; 2 Tim 3:17; Heb 13:21).

When we are filled with Yah's Spirit and seek to minister in loving compassion, we can trust that, whatever the need might be, the necessary spiritual giftings to accomplish the Father's will, will be there. He will surely equip us to do the job at hand, to minister to the one whom He wants us to minister. Again, our focus should be on having all of the Spirit and not just a singular "gift."

PARTICIPATION AND SPIRITUALS

To review, we have seen tongues to be a spiritual endowment that enables us to speak in a language that comes from our spirit. It is one that we have not formally learned or understand in the natural, yet, it is perfect in dialect and pronunciation. We also have seen that when the Day of Pentecost had fully come, the disciples were gathered together, were in one accord, and there suddenly came a sound from heaven, like a mighty wind, and it filled the whole house. Over each one appeared divided-tongues, as of fire, and they were all filled with the Holy Spirit and began to speak with other tongues, as the Spirit gave them utterance (Acts 2:1-4).

From this description, we glean two important points: First, they began to "speak." This indicates *participation*. The Holy Spirit does not take over our voice, and we do not go into a trance. We will be in control, yet under the control of the Holy Spirit. Secondly, we see that they spoke as the Spirit gave them utterance. So we now ask, "What is Spirit-inspired 'utterance'?"

Utterance is ultimately referring to something that comes from the speech center of our brain. Tongues is not a vocal miracle; it is a mental miracle manifested through our voice. All speech starts at a certain point in our brain. We'll call it the speech center.

To demonstrate this point, the following little exercise will help put us in touch with the speech center of our brain.

First, we choose a language spoken in the world today, but one that we have not studied and do not speak (although we may know a few of its scattered words). Having made our choice, we next translate the following phrase into that language:

"Hello, how are you." And we then speak it out loud.

If we chose French, it would be: *Bonjour comment vas-tu?* If we chose Spanish, it would be: *Hola cómo estás.* In Italian: *Ciao come stai?*

Whatever language we chose, since it was foreign to us *we had to think about speaking in it*— and this thought process put us in touch with the *speech center* of our brain. We thought about the phrase before speaking it.

How It Works...

When we ask and are baptized with the Ruach, YHVH, through His Spirit, will put a word, or words, into our speech center. We may hear a particular word (or sound) in our mind, and we may have to think about it before uttering it. Yes, it will be foreign to us and we will not understand it. We may hear it in our mind, and in our own voice, as though we were talking to ourselves. Our job is to speak what we hear, whether it is a word, phrase, or sentence. When we hear or imagine the words, we must cooperate with the Ruach and speak them out. The point is not so much the above process, as it is the idea of needing to speak what we feel we hear. Some may simply vocalize the words given by the Spirit without "thinking" about them. However our infilling happens, we will find ourselves manifesting the act of speaking in tongues.

Once we experience this high with the Holy Spirit, the odds are that the Devil will soon show up to drag us down.

When we ask YHVH to baptize us with the Holy Spirit and speak our first word or words in our new spiritual language (because it has happened to so many), we know something that will very likely follow: We will most likely get a thought in our mind, such as, *"You made this up."* Or, *"That was only baby talk or gibberish."*

This occurs more often than not and the reason for it is simple: the enemy of our soul is attempting to kill, steal and destroy us (John 10:10). Satan absolutely does not want us armed with our most lethal weapon against him, it being our spiritual language.

Satan will do anything and everything to keep us from using our new gift. He does not want us to be able to speak in an unfettered fashion to the Holy One. Let us therefore be wise enough to reject any doubts about our experience and instead learn to rejoice in the glory of YHVH. Again, "He who speaks in a tongue does not speak to men but to God, for no one understands him; however, in the spirit he speaks mysteries. But he who prophecies, speaks edification and exhortation and comfort to men. He who speaks in a tongue edifies himself" (1 Cor 14:2-4).

When our mortal language fails us, when our human reasoning comes to an end, we find that a divinely imparted tongue will be right there for us. It will aid us in times of need because it is designed to be a language of prayer. By it, we bypass the limits of our human reasoning and offer a perfect prayer to our God, one that the enemy of our soul cannot fight against. It may be a tongue of angels, or a known tongue, whatever it is, it is given to us for private use, because our God wants to speak to us— privately.

And now we move to a subject that has precious little Scriptural instruction given concerning how it is to be applied...

CONTROLLING PUBLIC TONGUES

As for public tongues, Paul says, "If anyone speaks in a tongue, let there be two or at the most three, each in turn, and let one interpret. But if there is no interpreter, let him keep silent in church, and let him speak to himself and to God"(1 Cor 14:27-28).

If a tongue is manifested in an open meeting (and there is nothing that says it has to happen), it should be two or three at most, and an interpreter must be present. (This indicates that those in the assembly should be closely knit together and thus know whom within the congregation operates in this gift.) Again, chapter 14 focuses on *order* in the assemblies; thus Paul instructs us, if an interpreter is not present, we are to keep silent, to speak only to ourselves and to God. We also can pray: "Let him who speaks in a tongue pray that he may interpret" (1 Cor 14:13).

If the Ruach gives us a message in a tongue, we first say it silently to ourselves and then pray for its interpretation. If the interpretation comes, we know we have the freedom to present the tongue at an appropriate time in the meeting. However, *out of respect for the congregation and its leadership,* we should first inquire of their elders (Rom 13:1-7; Titus 3:1; 1 Pet 2:13).

We should not "blurt it out" at some pause in the meeting—while the speaker takes a breath, nor try to slip it in between two songs. Such behavior is an abuse. We have all seen people waiting for that one silent moment to *jump in there.* This is out of order and disrupts the service. To be candid, it also means we are not being considerate of others. When the appropriate time is granted by the leadership, we should present the tongue and wait for an interpretation. If no one else interprets, then the eldership should direct us to do so.

If we receive a message in tongues, pray for an interpretation, but do not receive one, what do we do? Again, *out of respect,* we take it to the leaders and ask them to privately direct us to someone present that God has used to interpret tongues. We submit our tongue to them and see if they have an interpretation. We allow them to determine when the time is right. These two gifts then equal a prophecy. This same suggested order applies to the presentation of words of wisdom or words of knowledge. We "honor" leadership and let them decide appropriate times so as to maintain order (Rom 13:7; 1 Cor 14:29-33).

Speaking in a spiritual language is an utterance; it is a pronouncement of God's will and purpose. It is a wonderful work of God, and therefore, when we speak in a tongue, it is a wonder. Our spiritual language is a work of praise to Him. We are speaking a mystery, which has been hidden from man, but is being made known in Messiah Yeshua. We are speaking that which is being revealed for the moment. Tongues are a language of praise and prayer. It is truly a gift to be treasured.

TONGUES AND DIVINE REVELATION

The Apostle Paul used his new language extensively. In 1 Corinthians 14:18 he said he spoke in tongues more than they did. But he did it in private.

Paul made other revealing statements about tongues that apply to us as well: via his spiritual language Paul was receiving in his spirit understanding of new concepts; he was getting glimpses of mysteries, things that had once been hidden but were being brought forth in Yeshua. The Lord was revealing in Paul's spirit the "wonderful works of God." YHVH was showing Paul the continual revelation that is found in His eternal purposes in Messiah Yeshua (2 Cor 12:2-7; 1 Cor 14:2; Psa 145:5).

Paul was praying in his spiritual language, realizing that the understanding was only in his spirit and not in his mind. Therefore, he prayed for interpretation of the things that were being revealed to his spirit, which would then be revealed in his mind, so he could gain true godly understanding (1 Cor 2:10; Eph 3:5).

Paul also shared in the public square the things that were being made known to him. He was ever gaining new understanding, however, his understanding would always be confirmed in the Word. In this way, he was empowered to teach those of the nations about where they were in regard to the divine purpose of God.

In his spiritual language, Paul was caught up into the realm of the Holy Spirit (2 Cor 12:4). Did YHVH use such experiences to inspire Paul to pen most of the Apostolic Scriptures? We cannot know for certain, and will have to ask Paul these things when we see him in eternity. For now, each of us can likewise experience "true Word-based revelation" by the power of the Holy Spirit. By the Spirit, we can bypass our corrupted pea-sized brains and enter into infinity. We can pray in our new spiritual language and ask our God for the interpretation.

A Warning

By way of caution, we also note that Paul said, "I went up by revelation, and communicated unto them that gospel which I preach among the Gentiles, but privately to them which were of reputation, lest by any means I should run, or had run, in vain" (Gal 2:2). Paul did this because he wanted to have the things he received in the spirit confirmed by the Word and by the brethren. He knew very well that we need to fear being vainly puffed up by our fleshly minds; we need to beware being carried away by strange teachings or being enticed by our own fleshly lusts for fame, position, or power.

If we receive revelation from the Father of lights, there will be no variation or shifting shadow in it. It will line up with His Word. Period. Anything less will give birth to sin and ultimately will bring forth death. For that reason, we seek the council of the brethren: "Without counsel, plans go awry, But in the multitude of counselors they are established" (Pro 15:22).

All errant actions of the flesh make us part of the problem. So let us ask the Father to protect us, to keep us from misusing, in any way, any of His gifts. Let us ask Him to help us fix our eyes on Messiah, to help us run our race in purity, and run in a way that we might win the prize (Col 2:18; Heb 13:9; James 1:14-17; Heb 12:1-2).

Let us ask Him to protect us from all deception, and to reveal His mighty truths to us.

The Nine Gifts of The Spirit

Paul lists nine supernatural endowments, or "gifts of the Spirit" in 1 Corinthians 12:4-11.
These nine gifts are often divided into three groups:

Revelation Gifts
These Empower us to Know Supernaturally:

1. *Wisdom (vs. 8)*
2. *Knowledge (vs. 8)*
3. *Discernment of Spirits (vs. 10)*

Power Gifts
These empower us to Act Supernaturally:

4. *Faith (vs. 9)*
5. *Healing (vs. 9)*
6. *Working of Miracles (vs. 9)*

Prophetic Gifts
These empower us to Speak with Supernatural Inspiration:

7. *Prophecy (vs. 10)*
8. *Tongues (vs. 10)*
9. *Interpretation of Tongues (vs. 10)*

These endowments are supernaturally, even spontaneously, imparted by the Holy Spirit. Apart from our "personal tongue," which is always with us— we do not own, possess, or control these gifts, and we cannot call them into operation at will.
The Ruach works through Spirit-filled vessels to distribute these giftings— as He will. These giftings belong to the Spirit, not to man, and they are given for the good of Body. When in operation His gifts will always edify, exhort and comfort YHVH's people.

16

PROPHECY— THEN AND NOW

Pursue love, and desire spiritual gifts but especially that you may prophesy. For he who speaks in a tongue does not speak to men but to God, for no one understands him; however, in the spirit he speaks mysteries. But he who prophesies speaks edification and exhortation and comfort to men (1 Cor 14:1-3).

Prophecy is a gift, a "spiritual" (see pp. 104-106), one that we are to desire above all others. However, prophecy is not greater than the other gifts. To help us put it in perspective, we will examine it as it is presented in Paul's first letter to the Corinthians.

Again, the context in which this verse was given was in regard to "love." The point being that we should prefer others ahead of ourselves, and that prophecy is to be given for the strengthening, encouragement and comfort of Messiah's Body. When we examine in context each of the spiritual manifestations Paul listed, we see that they all flow from the loving and finished work of Messiah. They are given to us because:

- He died
- He arose
- He ascended into Heaven
- He sent us His Ruach haKodesh

The Ruach is sent to reveal to us, to remind us of, to teach us the truth about, the finished work of Yeshua our Messiah.

While we do want to pray with our understanding, we also want to pray and even sing in the spirit (1 Cor 14:15).

We might say tongues are given to us because our brains are too corrupted and prejudiced to be able to perfectly communicate with the living God. So He equips us. To give us greater understanding of His ways, He gives us His Ruach— He places His Spirit within us. Then, by His Spirit, we speak to Him concerning His mysteries (1 Cor 2:6-10; 14:2).

In 1 Corinthians 14, prophecy is ranked higher than the other spirituals, above tongues, unless the tongue is accompanied by interpretation, which then makes it equal to prophecy. So exactly what is this elevated gift that is prophecy? What purpose is it meant to serve in our lives?

WHAT PROPHECY IS— AND WHAT IT IS NOT

We begin by pointing out that after Yeshua's crucifixion, resurrection, and ascension, prophecy began to play a different role than it did in the First, or "Old" Covenant. And in our day, many are dangerously obsessed with foretelling the future, especially in regard to the perilous times in which we now live. Thus, we note some of the dangers associated with "prophecy."

Wondering what the future will bring, people sometimes mistakenly resort to things like astrology, tarot cards, horoscopes, etc. But the Word warns concerning these things:

> "You shall not ...use enchantment, nor observe times.... Give no regard to mediums and familiar spirits; do not seek after them, to be defiled by them: I am the LORD your God.

... The person who turns to mediums and familiar spirits, to prostitute himself with them, I will set My face against that person and cut him off from his people.... A man or a woman who is a medium, or who has familiar spirits, shall surely be put to death; they shall stone them with stones. Their blood shall be upon them. ... There shall not be found among you anyone who makes his son or his daughter pass through the fire, or one who practices witchcraft, or a soothsayer, or one who interprets omens, or a sorcerer, or one who conjures spells, or a medium, or a spiritist, or one who calls up the dead. For all who do these things are an abomination to the LORD, and because of these abominations the LORD your God drives them out from before you" (Lev 19:26,31; 20:6,27; Deu 18:10-12).

We need to have a healthy respect for, even a fear of, the idea of seeking out details concerning the future— because misuse of such knowledge, real or imagined, can lead to death.

Many blame the Devil when people succumb to the above devices, but the Bible says that sorcery is primarily a work of the flesh: "Now the works of the flesh are evident, which are: adultery, fornication, uncleanness, lewdness, idolatry, sorcery, hatred, contentions, jealousies, outbursts of wrath, selfish ambitions, dissensions, heresies" (Gal 5:19-20).

What kind of flesh is described in Galatians; what failing of the flesh leads to sorcery?

It is born of curiosity, of our desire to know, to taste. Curiosity got us in serious trouble in the Garden. To this day we need to beware being enticed to eat from the Tree of the Knowledge of Good and Evil. We instead want to eat only from the Tree of Life.

Some are curious to know the future because they crave the power that comes with appearing to know what the future holds. They want to have power over others. Such supposed knowing also can bring financial gain. But the funds garnered by leading the beguiled astray will prove to be of little help to them in eternity.

Prophecy is not given that man might gather wealth or power. Prophecy is not given for the sake of man foretelling the future. Prophecy is given that it might bring glory to the Holy One.

To keep things in perspective, we need to understand the purpose of prophecy itself. Sir Isaac Newton once gave a telling insight into its end purpose:

> The Almighty gave "the Prophecies of the Old Testaments, not to gratify men's curiosities by enabling them to foreknow things, but that after they were fulfilled they might be interpreted by the event; and his own Providence, not the Interpreters, be then manifested thereby to the world. For the event of things predicted many ages before, will then be a convincing argument that the world is governed by Providence." [66]

If we approach prophecies with the idea that "we" are going to figure it all out, we risk trying to take the glory of the Almighty to ourselves. Instead, prophecy must always be kept in perspective. Its purpose, first and foremost, is to bring glory to "Providence." And, we again note that in our day, prophecy plays a different role than it did before Yeshua's First Advent...

THE PROPHETS OF OLD

In the Apostolic Scriptures, commonly called the New Testament, a prophet or prophecy is not the same as in the Hebrew Scriptures, or in what is commonly called the Old Testament. Furthermore, the last Old Testament prophet was John the Baptist. The first was Moses, and he spoke of others to follow.

These prophets spoke infallibly. They prefaced their words with, *"Thus sayith the LORD."* When they spoke, they stepped out of themselves and would say, *"I say unto you."* Yet, everyone that

---

66 Gleick, James, *Isaac Newton*, New York: Pantheon Book, 2003, pp 244-245. www.johnpratt.com Newton.

heard their words knew, without a shadow of doubt, that it was God speaking through them. They were God's mouthpieces.

One could not challenge a true Old Testament prophet, or at least one did so at their own peril. When these prophets spoke, they added to Scripture. When Moses spoke, his words ultimately filled the Torah (the first five books of the Bible). Similarly, Samuel gave us the Books of Samuel, Ezekiel the Book of Ezekiel, etc.

Each prophet gave to Israel the piece of the puzzle given to him by the Almighty. And all of them were waiting for the final Word of God. They brought forth the words of God; they had a message from Him. And they all pointed forward— to the Final Word— toward Messiah Yeshua. When He came, He was called "The Word," and "The Prophet" (John 1:14; 6:14). He was the final speaking forth, or prophesying in this vein.

The Hebrew prophets often are called "the Prophets of Old." They had a message, but Yeshua was *the* central figure of that message. With Him, the Final Prophet had come. So to speak, we no longer look for "similar eternal words" from God, because *The Word* has come in the flesh:

> "God, who at various times and in various ways spoke in time past to the fathers by the prophets, has in these last days spoken to us by His Son, whom He has appointed heir of all things, through whom also He made the worlds; who being the brightness of His glory and the express image of His person, and upholding all things by the word of His power, when He had by Himself purged our sins, sat down at the right hand of the Majesty on high, having become so much better than the angels, as He has by inheritance obtained a more excellent name than they" (Heb 1:1-4).

We might say that in earlier times God spoke "prophet language," and now He speaks "the language of the Son." In other words, Yeshua is the final language of God. YHVH has spoken. His final Word is found in His Son.

The prophetic point in time at which we now find ourselves is much like the dark of night. During the night, we're glad when the moon is shining, but when the day comes, the light of the sun swallows up the moon— which got its light from the sun in the first place. Similarly, the prophets got their light from the Son of Righteousness, who was about to rise. Like the moon, they saw Him, and reflected His light, but many of the people on earth did not see Him. The prophets of old spoke of Him and thus, were like a light in the darkness. When the Son of Righteousness rose from the grave and ascended to the Father, the Hebrew prophets were proven right. They got their glory from Him and were then swallowed up by His "greater light." The whole story of Scripture is the whole story of Yeshua. Hebrew History is "His Story." With His coming, with the telling of His Story, the word *prophet* took on a new meaning, because there was essentially nothing new left to say. While true that there are prophecies that have yet to be made manifest, they nonetheless have to do with His Story.

THE APOSTOLIC PROPHETS AND THE GOSPELS

The writings of Matthew, Mark, Luke and John hold a unique position in Scripture. Their writings are affirmed in Torah itself. We see this in that the Father said to Moses:

> "I will raise up for them a Prophet like you from among their brethren, and will put My words in His mouth, and He shall speak to them all that I command Him. And it shall be that whoever will not hear My words, which He speaks in My name, I will require it of him" (Deu 18:18-19).

Messiah Yeshua is that Prophet. He claimed to have given His promised words to His disciples. He said to the Father, "I have given to them the words which You have given Me; and they have received them, and have known surely that I came forth from You; and they have believed that You sent Me" (John 17:8).

THE WRITINGS OF MATTHEW, MARK, LUKE AND JOHN... ARE AFFIRMED IN TORAH ITSELF... (DEU 18:18-19)

In turn, they told of the coming of this One who is deemed to be "worthy of greater honor than Moses" (Heb 3:3). They told of His life, affirmed His establishment of Israel's New Covenant, recounted His death, burial and resurrection. They beheld the Son. Unlike those who foretold His coming, they looked full in His face. Then they told His Story.

Some make the mistake of thinking less of the Gospels than they do of "Torah," and that is a tragedy. For the Torah is like a foundation upon which we build our understanding— and so to speak, the roof, the Gospels, must fit within its initial form. To dismiss the Gospels because they came "later" is foolishness. They came later because Yeshua's coming happened later in Israel's history. But that does not make the story of His coming any less worthy of being guarded by the Holy One.

We must trust that the Holy One is the final author of Scripture, and that He guards the Word He gave to us— from Genesis to Revelation. Men may try to mess with translations, but in the end, the Holy One is able to feed His hungry children with His pure unadulterated Word.

The position in history of Yeshua's apostles and their account of His life differs in style and purpose from that of the prophets of old. However, their writings are no less valid. Their words were even foretold, promised in Torah. Their writings recount the story of the very One to whom all of the promises of Torah, the Prophets, and the Writings point (John 5:46-47; 8:28; 12:49-50; 17:8,17-21).

We read of our patriarchs, "These were all commended for their faith, yet none of them received what had been promised... [for] only together with us would they be made *perfect*" (Heb 11:39-40, NIV). They did not complete, accomplish, finish, nor fulfill all that was promised to them. Without *us*, their blessing is *imperfect*. It is *incomplete*. [67] It was further revealed to them that "they were not serving themselves, but *you*, in these things which now have been announced to *you* through those who preached the gospel by the Holy Spirit sent from heaven" (1 Pet 1:10-12, NASB).

As we seek to return to the truth of Torah, let us not follow in the mistaken footsteps of those who detract from the account of Him who is "The Living Torah."

Having made this point, we return to our examination of change in the role of "prophets" before and after Yeshua's finished work.

A PARADIGM SHIFT

When the final word has been spoken, we can't add to it. It is finished. In the Apostolic Scriptures, Matthew, Mark, Luke and John speak of beholding the Promised One: Yeshua. In this way, YHVH's Scriptures keep building and building. Throughout them, we see that He first chooses a people, scatters them, promises to regather them and give them a New and better covenant, then sends His Son to institute it at His Passover table and through His death on the Tree. Paul then comes along and through him, a mystery is revealed, it being the Scriptural truth that believing "Gentiles are fellow heirs" (Eph 1:9; 3:3-7; 6:19; Col 1:27).

Then the paradigm shifts, and we thereafter look back. Even for details regarding the future second coming of Messiah Yeshua, we have to look back. To see that He now has His resurrected body, now sits at the right hand of the Father, and is coming soon to wrap up all time— we look back to that which was once foretold.

In the Hebrew Scriptures, prophecy was a matter of *fore-telling*, of *predicting*, the coming of Messiah. Once He came, once His Gospel was told, once His Story began to go forth to the Nations, so to speak, prophecies became a matter of *forth-telling* things that have to do with YHVH's glory.

---

67 Perfect: *Strong's* # G 5048.

> WE NOW
> FORTH-TELL,
> OR BRING
> INTO VIEW,
> MATTERS THAT
> WERE ONCE
> FORE-TOLD,
> OR PROPHESIED

In our day, a prophecy has to do with bringing forth, recounting and reminding people of the promises of our God. We now *forth-tell*, or *bring into view*, matters that were once *fore-told*, or *prophesied*.

Restated, we do not add to YHVH's Word, lest He reprove us: "Do not add to His words, Lest He rebuke you, and you be found a liar" (Prov 30:6).

This ancient principle is true even in regard to Yeshua's return and the promises once made in relation to that return. We must look back to that which was once spoken by the prophets of old. There, we see eternal truths that tell of His coming glory.

Today, since we "forth-tell" the Word of God, we must judge the prophet. Our foundation for this judgement can be non other than the Holy Scriptures.

1Corinthians 14:29: "Let two or three prophets speak, and let the others judge."

In this vein, we see that the role of the prophet and prophecy, is now different.

17

PROPHETIC DO'S AND DON'TS

S urely the Lord GOD does nothing unless He reveals His secret counsel to His servants the prophets (Amos 3:7).

In our day, YHVH Elohim continues to reveal His counsel to His servants. However, He also warns us, "Beloved, do not believe every spirit, but test the spirits, whether they are of God; because many false prophets have gone out into the world" (1 John 4:1).

We have to test the prophets of our day, and our standard of measure is Scripture. We must always ask ourselves, "Is the prophecy 'Scriptural'?" However, while Scripture is our standard, we must balance this truth with the idea that our Messiah did not say to us, "Behold, I go to the Father, but I will leave you with a Holy Book to guide you." No. He said He would not leave us as "orphans," but would instead "send the Comforter," meaning the Holy Spirit. And that He, "will not speak on His own initiative, but whatever He hears, He will speak; and He will disclose to you what is to come. He will glorify Me, for He will take of Mine and

PROPHECY MUST NEVER CONTRADICT SCRIPTURE

will disclose it to you." Yeshua also said, "All things that the Father has are Mine. Therefore I said that He will take of Mine and declare it to you" (John 14:18; 16:7-15, NASB). Our Messiah is One with the Father, and He said the Holy Spirit, the Spirit of truth, "will guide us into all truth," and that He "will show us things to come" (John 10:30; 16:13).

This, then, leaves us in the place of being able to hear truth from the Spirit of Truth, yet, knowing that all truth must line up with the Book of Truth: Scripture— Genesis to Revelation.

PROPHECY AND PREDICTIONS

Prophecy must never contradict Scripture. According to *Strong's Exhaustive Concordance*, the Hebrew word for *prophecy* is *nabiy'* (naw-bee'). It speaks of the words of a prophet, an inspired man. In Greek, the word is *propheteia* (prof- ay-ti'-ah), which speaks of a prediction (scriptural or otherwise), of prophesying, and it comes from a word that means, fore-teller or inspired speaker. [68]

The idea of prophecy meaning "prediction" has grown over the years, especially as the Church separated itself from Israel and tried to find its future role. In our day, prophecy is usually seen as having to do with the future, which concept is capitalized on by some "prophetic" books. This "prediction only" idea can be dangerous because *prophecy* also means a message of divine will and purpose.

A fuller definition of the Greek words for prophecy, prophesy, and prophesying is provided in *Vines Expository Dictionary Of Old And New Testament Words*. It says it has to do with "speaking forth of the mind and counsel of God." It also says, "Though much of OT prophecy was purely predictive… prophecy is not necessarily, nor even primarily, fore-telling. It is the declaration of that which

---

68 *Strong's* # H5030 and G4394, from G4396: *prophetes* (from G4253 and G5346).

cannot be known by natural means… it is the forth-telling of the will of God, whether with reference to the past, the present, or the future." *Vine's* also points out that the purpose of prophetic ministry is "to edify, to comfort, and encourage the believers…" And that its "effect upon unbelievers was to show that the secrets of a man's heart are known to God, to convict of sin, and to constrain to worship." [69]

With the completion of the Canon of Scripture, prophecy changed. In our day, it is especially gathered from, or at the very least, is not to be opposed to, the "completed revelation" contained in Scripture. To be a prophet, to prophesy, now carries with it the primary meaning of telling forth the Divine counsels. [70] In this vein we "foretell the future." [71]

When Paul encouraged us to "desire earnestly to prophesy," his was not a clarion call for us to seek to "predict the future," but to sincerely desire to be divinely inspired to deliver the Gospel of the Kingdom (1 Cor 14:39). Again, prophesy is not fore-telling, but forth-telling. The point is to teach and expound on the Word, to direct people to the path and ways of Yah. It is to admonish, guide and instruct them, to help bring them to a place of repentance and thus to return to Yah. The purpose of all prophetic ministering should be to edify, comfort, and encourage Believers. Prophecy is not to be used to bring power or glory to mortal man. We do not predict the future so we will be promoted by mortals.

DARING TO PROPHESY…

We must have a healthy respect for the fact that all true prophecy will be just that: True.

We must have a healthy fear of daring to prophesy. We must fear saying something has been given to us by the Almighty if, in truth, it is a product of our flesh.

---

69 See *Notes on Thessalonians* by Hogg and Vine, pp. 196,197. Also see 1 Cor 14:3,24-25.
70 Mat 7:22; 26:68; 1 Cor 11:4,5; 13:9; 14:1,3-5,24,31,39; Rev 11:3.
71 Mat 15:7; John 11:51; 1 Pet 1:10; Jude 1:14.

As children we are taught to guard the family name and not to do anything that will bring disgrace to the family. So it should be. In the same way, if we say something is from our Father, and it is not, we bring disgrace to Him. Others will use our mistake as an excuse not to believe Him or to dismiss one of the gifts He wants to give. While we need freedom to "grow" in our gifting, we want to balance our freedom with a healthy fear of bringing any form of shame to the family name of Israel.

We instead want to walk in a way that brings honor to the people and God of Israel. For He speaks of a day when prophets will be ashamed of their false prophecies. He has sworn that He will remove from our midst all idols, false prophets and unclean spirits. Those who tried to deceive in this way will meet with His justice. Those who are truly repentant and humbled will say of themselves, "I am not a prophet; I am a tiller of the ground, for a man sold me as a slave in my youth" (Zec 13:2-5).

We are but bond-slaves to the Holy One and must beware taking the title of prophet unto ourselves. Titles are something He should impart to us. It is for Him to declare what role He thinks we are walking in. If we dare take a title to ourselves *when He did not give it*, we will one day be made very ashamed of our actions.

We also want to beware supposed prophetic insights and scenarios that separate Believers from being part of the eternal commonwealth of Israel (Eph 2:11-22). Because, we simply cannot understand the latter-day game plan if we do not understand who are the players. Knowing who are the players is foundational to gaining insights into the game plan.

A PROPHETIC KEY
To keep Biblical prophecy in perspective, we would do well to understand Romans 11:25: "For I do not desire, brethren, that you should be ignorant of this mystery, lest you should be wise in your own opinion, that blindness in part has happened to Israel until the fullness of the Gentiles has come in."

To begin, Paul said he was explaining a "mystery," and that, not understanding this mystery could lead us to be "wise in our own opinion." He said the mystery is, "blindness in part has happened to Israel." Important to our understanding is the fact that this "blindness" would not be ended "until" after the "fullness of the Gentiles has come in." When we examine this mystery in detail, we see that Paul was actually outlining a mystery that would not be fully understood for almost two thousand years!

Jacob said those of Ephraim (the Northern Kingdom of Israel) would become "*a melo hagoyim/fullness of the Gentiles*" (Gen 48:19). [72]

Paul said "blindness in part/*meros* has happened to Israel." Restated, Israel is "*partially* blinded." [73]

Christianity has long seen that the people of Judah are "blind to the truth of the Messiah," but they have failed to note that Israel was long ago divided into two houses by the Almighty (1 Ki 12:15, 24; 2 Chr 11:4). And, one of the two houses, one of His two chosen families, is Joseph/ Ephraim/Israel (Jer 33:23-26; 1 Pet 1:1; 2:9-10). Moreover, Isaiah said "*both* the houses of Israel" would "stumble over the Sanctuary." The Sanctuary, or Temple, is Messiah Yeshua (Isa 8:13-14; John 2:19-22). [74] He is YHVH come to dwell among men (John 1). Israel was divided into two houses, and in different ways, both have stumbled over the One Who would be a Sanctuary to them. Our body is now His "Temple." And, concerning prophecies, we stumble when we fail to see this pivotal, all-important truth. [75]

---

72 The *ArtScroll Tenach Series, Genesis*, Vol. 6 (1982, Mesorah, NY NY), says *m'loh* means a "fullness" and "Connotes abundance...meaning: His seed will become the abundance of the nations ....They will have to inhabit lands of other nations" (p 2121). Also see *Strong's* #'s H 4393 and 1471. Note that Psalm 24:1 uses the word *melo*, which King James translates as, "The earth is the LORD's and the fulness thereof." Also, according to *Gesenius'* (Hendrickson, p 163a, word # 1471), *goyim* is "specially used of the (other) nations besides Israel."

73 Part: *Strong's* # G 3313.

74 We are "the temple of the living God," even as we also are Messiah Yeshua's "Body" (2 Cor 6:16-19; Eph 1:22-23; 5:30; Col 1:24).

75 From *Redeemed Israel — Reunited and Restored,* Batya Ruth Wootten, especially chapter 13, "Israel: A Mystery Until..."

Having missed this foundational truth, many have thus invented prophetic and eschatological theories that are rooted in separating the Church (here meaning the true Believers in Messiah) from the called-out people of Israel. But the truth is, apart from the Covenant given to the sons of Israel, there is no New Covenant. We are thus part of the people of Israel, or we have no Covenant (Jer 31:31-33; Heb 8:8-10).

So it is that many are turning from the errant and flawed theories presently being put forth. They are hearing and turning toward a roar from the Lion of Judah. It is a call to repent and return to Zion (Hosea 11:10; Jer 31:18-21). The problem is, in their desire to turn from past mistakes, some are making a different mistake; they are turning away from anything they perceive might have to do with the Church's misguided interpretations. And in turn, they are missing out on a true blessing...

PROPHESYING IN PART
PUZZLE PIECES AND PRIVATE INTERPRETATION

> "We know in part and we prophesy in part. But when that which is perfect has come, then that which is in part will be done away.... For now we see in a mirror, dimly, but then face to face. Now I know in part, but then I shall know just as I also am known" (1 Cor 13:9-12).

We are only capable of knowing a small part of the vast universe that is Yah's truth. Thus, Paul comforts us with the promise that when "that which is *perfect/complete/teleios* has come," our partial knowledge will be ended. [76] When all that the prophets have prophesied is fulfilled, all will be complete, and we will know even as we are known. Paul uses the mirror of his day to amplify his point. In antiquity, mirrors were small pieces of metal or brass, slightly distorted, and they offered a limited reflection.

---

76 *Strong's* # G5046. *Young's Literal Translation* says "in part we know...in part we prophesy."

In this same vein, our God might be compared to the Pacific Ocean while we are but a puddle. Little puddles cannot contain all that is in the Great Pacific. Yet, even with our limited capacity, our God graciously grants those who seek Him pieces of His great puzzle. When we gather together, if we lay out our collective pieces and properly fit them together, we gain new insights. Each one has a piece, or pieces; each has insights, and collectively we grow together. Even so, Scripture is comprised of progressive revelation. Each inspired writer added their piece, but none of them were given the whole picture.

We cannot know all, yet we must be diligent to present ourselves approved to God, a worker who does not need to be ashamed, rightly dividing the word of truth (2 Tim 2:15). We must seek Him and His ways with every fiber of our being, knowing that He will show us great and mighty things that we do not know (Jer 33:3).

The Word furthermore warns concerning prophecies:

> "We have the prophetic word confirmed, which you do well to heed as a light that shines in a dark place, until the day dawns and the morning star rises in your hearts; knowing this first, that no prophecy of Scripture is of any private interpretation" (2 Pet 1:19-20).

Through compilation of Scriptures we can gain glimpses into coming glory. But these glimpses should always bring glory to the confirmed prophetic Word, the Morning Star, Yeshua (Rev 22:16).

Prophetic glimpses can be like the breaking of dawn, which comes in stages, light adding to light. We can add "light to light," or Scripture to Scripture, and have the compilation, the sum total of the verses, provide new insights about the Lord, His ways, and His plans for His people. [77]

---

77 For example, in Leviticus we see the principle that, if the Almighty seeks to correct us, but we do not turn from our sinful ways and begin to obey Him, He will then punish us "sevenfold" for our sins (Lev 26:18, 27-28). In Ezekiel we see that both Ephraim and Judah were given certain punishments for their idolatry. And, in addition to her 40 years, Judah
(continued...)

PROPHECY AND ORDER

1 Corinthians 14:31 says, "You may all prophesy one by one, that all may learn, and all may be comforted." 1 Corinthians 14:3 says, he that prophesies speaks for the purposes of "edification, and exhortation, and comfort" (KJV).

Prophecy is given that we might learn, be edified, instructed and built up. It is given that we might be exhorted, or comforted (*parakaleo:* par-ak-al-eh'-o), called near, feel invited, invoked, implored, beseeched by the Almighty. He especially wants us to be encouraged, consoled, and comforted. He wants to instruct us in His Word, that we might draw nearer unto Him. Comfort, or *parakaleo* carries with it the idea of being an *advocate*. A prophet, therefore, is someone speaking forth on behalf of God words of exhortation, edification, and comfort. [78]

- Edify is a construction term. From it we get the English term "edifice," meaning to *build up.*
- Exhort means to *call after* someone, as a shepherd calls his sheep. The Good Shepherd is ever calling to His people.
- Comfort is a compound word, meaning *come*, as in come along side, and as in helping to bear the burden, much like a bellboy that picks up our suitcase for us. (Within this

---

[77] (...continued)
also had to "drink her sister's cup" for an additional 390-year penalty. This gave Judah a total of 430 years of punishment, which began when their capital, Jerusalem, became a vassal city of Babylon. Judah lost political control around 595 B.C., and their punishment came to an end in 166 B.C., when the Temple was cleansed by the Maccabees. However, Ephraim did not repent of her idolatries, so her 390-year punishment was increased sevenfold, resulting in a total of 2730 years in which she would be "Not a people" (Hosea 1-2). Her cities became vassals of conquering Assyria starting in 734 B.C. She lost her capital, Samaria, and went into captivity in 722 B.C. If we use the prophetic, 360 day calendar, we see the 2730 years ended around 1967, the year Jerusalem was reclaimed as modern Israel's capital (see Gen 7:11,24; 8:3-4; 5-14; Rev 11:2-3; 12:6,14; 13:5). If we use a solar calendar, we see the punishment ending around 1996, and no later than 2008. In our day Ephraim continues to be restored to her Israelite roots and heritage. (See *Restoring Israel's Kingdom* by Angus Wootten, 2000, Key of David Publishing, Saint Cloud, FL, p 131.)

[78] *Strong's* #'s G3619; 3874 and 3870; 3889 and 3888; 3844 and 2564.

word we also see the word *fort,* indicating *protection.*)

The Word tells us to "Let two or three prophets speak, and let the others judge" (1 Cor 14:29).

Here, the word, *judge,* is from *diakrino* (dee-ak-ree"-no); meaning to separate thoroughly, withdraw from, or oppose; to discriminate, to decide, contend, discern. It comes from two Greek words, *dia* (dee-ah'), a preposition that denotes "the channel," and *krino* (kree'-no), which means to distinguish, decide (mentally or judicially); to try, condemn, decree, determine, ordain, or call in question. [79]

In our day, a prophet is especially to be *judged.* For, "no prophecy of Scripture is of private interpretation" (2 Pet 1:20). The New International Version interprets this verse, "No prophecy of Scripture came about by the prophet's own interpretation" (NIV). The New American Standard reads, no prophetic utterance is a matter of "one's own interpretation." Whether past or present prophecies, this verse can be applied to both.

THUS SAITH WHO?

Because prophecy needs to be reviewed, Believers should beware prefacing a prophetic utterance with the phrase, *"Thus saith the LORD..."*

Wisdom dictates that others should decide from whom the message originates. Nonetheless, many do begin their utterance with, *"Thus saith the LORD..."* Then, they deliver their "word" in old King James language. Such methods are often used, but the truth is that our God can speak in modern English. If a prophetic word is given for the purpose of revelation, we should ask, "How can people be edified, comforted or exhorted if they cannot understand what is being said?"

Sad to say, speakers who utilize this style, sometimes, whether realized or not, are trying to draw attention to self.

---

79 *Strong's #'s* G1252; 1223 and 2919.

Another reason why "Thus saith the LORD" is theologically dangerous is that we are not to question a direct word from God, yet we are told that we must judge prophecy. Everyone who prophesies in our day must be ready to be questioned.

Another point about prophesying is that it might be said to be "preaching beyond self." We are given revelations that impresses even the giver. That is a good indicator that the word is coming down from above. That is why prophecy can occur even while having coffee with someone at a restaurant. Speaking to someone about the Lord and having words flow out of our mouth that astound even us is prophecy in a pure form.

PROPHETIC DIRECTION AND OTHERS

Sometimes a Believer who operates in prophetic utterances will be asked, *"Do you have a word from the Lord for me?"*

The answer should always be, *"No. You need to read your Bible for yourself and seek direction from the Ruach."*

Such inquirers are looking for "direction," but we must be cautious about offering prophecies and words of wisdom and knowledge that offer *new* direction to people. The veil is rent. The Holy One wants to speak to each of us, face to face. We can be used by the Almighty to affirm direction for another, but we should beware being their mediator, "For there is one God and one Mediator between God and men, the Man Christ Jesus" (1 Tim 2:5).

Abba may at times use people to suggest direction, because the individual is not hearing what He wants to say to them, but overall, giving direction to others is not His best plan for the individual. If, for example, someone comes to us and says we are being called to "be a missionary in Brazil," and we have never thought of such a thing, the odds are that they do not understand spiritual manifestations.

Prophecy should not *direct* others. Abba wants our direction to come from within— from Him. He wants to speak to us. He uses others to affirm His voice.

We see a case in point in Acts chapters 20 and 21. All around the Aegean Sea, prophets were telling Paul that bonds and chains were waiting for him in Jerusalem. Finally, Agabus took Paul's belt and used it to dramatically bind his own hands. Then Agabus said the owner of the belt would be thus bound in Jerusalem.

Paul then walked across the peninsula (instead of taking the boat), and when he met his friends on the other side, he said he would nonetheless go to Jerusalem— even if it meant his death. The point is that they did not tell Paul what to do— they only told him what would happen. Remember, our God does not violate our free will, and He personally leads us from within.

In Acts chapter 13, Paul and Barnabas left Antioch, being sent forth by the church and the Ruach. But Paul and Barnabas knew about their trip several years earlier. The Word says: "As they ministered to the Lord and fasted, the Holy Spirit said, 'Now separate to Me Barnabas and Saul for the work to which I have [already] called them'" (Acts 13:2). This "word" was not direction, but confirmation. Paul and Barnabas already knew where they were going; their previous decision was being confirmed.

PROPHESYING ACCORDING TO OUR FAITH

In Psalm 81:10 we read, "I, the LORD, am your God, Who brought you up from the land of Egypt; Open your mouth wide and I will fill it" (NASB).

Some take this verse out of context. We open our mouths, yes, but our heart should first be full of our Father's Word. As Jeremiah said, "Your words were found, and I ate them, and Your word was to me the joy and rejoicing of my heart; for I am called by Your name, O LORD God of hosts" (Jer 15:16).

In saying this, we recognize that there are degrees of prophecy. Romans 12:6 tells us to "prophesy according to the proportion of your faith." New Believers can be used to prophesy, but older Believers are more likely to speak in greater depth. However, for young and old alike, the more we eat of the Word, the more sure, the more accurate will be the prophetic words we are used to bring forth. Even so, we see that "solid food belongs to those who are of full age, that is, those who by reason of use have their senses exercised to discern both good and evil" (Heb 5:14). Scripture speaks of those "who because of practice have their senses trained" (NASB); it refers to "mature" Believers who, "by constant use have trained themselves to distinguish good from evil" (NIV).

> WE NEED TO BECOME MATURE PEOPLE WHO ALLOW THE RUACH TO TRAIN OUR SENSES TO DISCERN BOTH GOOD AND EVIL

It is the Word of God that helps us to discern the difference between good and evil, between that which is true, and that which is untrue. Therefore, we need a steady diet of the Word.

We need both "Spirit and Truth." We need to hear the voice of the Spirit and to have it confirmed in the Word of Truth.

In summary, we need to become mature people who allow the Ruach to train our senses to discern both good and evil. And we will not get there if we simply walk away from prophetic utterances. Abba intended that His gifts might be used to comfort us, to build us up, to encourage us in the faith. Let us therefore ask Him to lead and guide us in proper use of His spiritual blessings.

18

PROPHETIC SINGING IN THE SPIRIT

Before addressing the subject of singing in the Spirit, we want to point out a few things. We do so, not to condemn anyone, but to encourage us to seek the right direction.

For instance, spiritual manifestations often operate in unison. We cannot isolate them. At times, a word of prophecy will operate in conjunction with a word of knowledge, which can speak to a person's future (but not as in giving "new direction"). However, prophecy that emotionally moves people to the feet of Messiah does not necessarily have to come as a climax to a period of singing; it does not have to immediately follow worship— which pattern is promoted in some movements. Also, some, probably in ignorance, use worship to work people up, rather than simply worshiping the Lord and allowing the Holy Spirit to lead us. Perhaps they do this because, Satan was once Heaven's master musician, and since his fall, he has encouraged man to misuse music (Isa 14; Eze 28:12-19). Even so, we note that some use multiple repetitions that almost feel like the mantras Hindu mystics use for self hypnosis.

When worship is misused in this way, those who feel they cannot enter in, or have a check in their spirit, often feel condemnation for a lack of spirituality— when in truth, they are discerning error.

Some, whether realized or not, put on an act so as to appear to be "entering in" and thus be accepted. As we seek a true move of the Holy Spirit, let us beware all contrived emotional manipulation. Let us remember, too, that the worship leader may not realize they are being used in this way, but the truth is, music can "mesmerize" people— which word comes from the man Mesmer— a hypnotist.

Music can control the mind much like drugs. Tribal warriors use a repetitive 2x2 beat to get hyped up for battle. We need to beware mesmerizing music, as well as worship music that does not focus on our God. Again, Satan was in charge of music, and we do not want him nor his music in our worship settings.

This is not to imply that God cannot work through repeating a song, but prophetic words do not always have to follow a time of worship. They often develop through study and prayer. Our heart and head should first be filled with the Word. When that is the case, suddenly (there usually is an element of suddenness) the Spirit puts thoughts together deep in our being. Suddenly, we see, suddenly we've got it, and a word comes forth. Such words will usually have a level of premeditation, meaning the word, the thought, has been in our heart; then it becomes rich with meaning and God puts it all together. The result is the freshness of the Ruach and the Word coming together.

When the Holy Spirit puts thoughts together so perfectly, we know deep in our being that we did not do it. We may have been in prayer and meditation prior to that point, but it was the Spirit of God that gave our meditations life and meaning.

The experience can be much like the historic Quaker services. They sat in silence, sometimes for hours on end, but through their individual prayer and meditation throughout the week, YHVH put it all together at the meeting when one would stand to speak and others would then follow.

Now we move on to another type of prophetic utterance.

In regard to how the gifts are supposed to work together, we first note that Paul said of them:

> "Tongues are for a sign, not to those who believe but to unbelievers; but prophesying is not for unbelievers but for those who believe. Therefore if the whole church comes together in one place, and all speak with tongues, and there come in those who are uninformed or unbelievers, will they not say that you are out of your mind? But if all prophesy, and an unbeliever or an uninformed person comes in, he is convinced by all, he is convicted by all. And thus the secrets of his heart are revealed; and so, falling down on his face, he will worship God and report that God is truly among you. How is it then, brethren? Whenever you come together, each of you has a psalm, has a teaching, has a tongue, has a revelation, has an interpretation. Let all things be done for edification. If anyone speaks in a tongue, let there be two or at the most three, each in turn, and let one interpret. But if there is no interpreter, let him keep silent in church, and let him speak to himself and to God. Let two or three prophets speak, and let the others judge. But if anything is revealed to another who sits by, let the first keep silent. For you can all prophesy one by one, that all may learn and all may be encouraged. And the spirits of the prophets are subject to the prophets. For God is not the author of confusion but of peace, as in all the churches of the saints" (1 Cor 14:22-33).

If all speak in tongues in an open meeting and an unbeliever walks in, he would likely think the congregation is "nuts." (Such abuse is prevalent in some churches.) However, verse 24 reveals that if this same unbeliever comes into the meeting and "all are prophesying, he is convinced by all, and he is convicted by all." To see how both statements may be true, we now look to Malcolm Smith's insights as to what it might mean to have *all prophesying.*

We first see a manifestation of people being led by the Ruach haKodesh in the Torah. There we see that Moses had gathered the elders around the Tabernacle and...

> "Then the LORD came down in the cloud, and spoke to him, and took of the Spirit that was upon him, and placed the same upon the seventy elders; and it happened, when the Spirit rested upon them, that they prophesied, although they never did so again" (Num 11:25).

The Spirit that was on Moses was put on the seventy elders, and we read that they *prophesied together*. "Prophesied" is taken from *naba'* (naw-baw'), meaning to prophesy, speak, or *to sing by inspiration*.

A problem is found in the interpretation, "they never did so again," because the statement is rooted in the word *yacaph* (yaw-saf), and, it can be translated as *cease*, but it is more often used to mean add to, augment, continue to do a thing, increase, do more, prolong, and do again. [80] With this idea in mind, we see that Scripture may actually be telling of a *prolonged period of singing in the Spirit*. Even so, the King James (and others) read: "The spirit rested upon them, they prophesied, and *did not cease*."

We see more *prophesying together* in 1 Samuel:

> "After that you shall come to the hill of God where the Philistine garrison is. And it will happen, when you have come there to the city, that you will meet a group of prophets coming down from the high place with a stringed instrument, a tambourine, a flute, and a harp before them; and they will be prophesying" (1 Sam 10:5). And, "Then Saul sent messengers to take David. And when they saw the group of prophets prophesying, and Samuel standing as leader over them, the Spirit of God came upon the messengers of Saul, and *they also prophesied*" (1 Sam 19:20).

---

80 *Strong's* #'s H5012 and 3254.

Samuel was the leader of these prophets. And Saul's men, who were not very spiritual, being trained soldiers in the art of killing, also were swept up in this "prophecy." Another example of prophetic singing involves beloved David and musical instruments:

"David and the captains of the army separated for the service some of the sons of Asaph, of Heman, and of Jeduthun, who should prophesy with harps, stringed instruments, and cymbals. And the number of the skilled men performing their service was: Of the sons of Asaph: Zaccur, Joseph, Nethaniah, and Asharelah; the sons of Asaph were under the direction of Asaph, who prophesied according to the order of the king. Of Jeduthun, the sons of Jeduthun... six, under the direction of their father Jeduthun, who prophesied with a harp to give thanks and to praise the LORD" (1Chr 25:1-3).

To this idea of prophetic singing, we see the addition of music played by skilled musicians. The Word says, they prophesied with harps, stringed instruments, and cymbals, and that, *skilled men* were performing this service.

Now we connect this ancient form of prophetic singing with Paul's teachings. He spoke of "speaking to one another in psalms and hymns and spiritual songs, singing and making melody in your heart to the Lord" (Eph 5:19). He said we were to "Let the word of Christ dwell in... [us] richly in all wisdom, teaching and admonishing one another in psalms and hymns and spiritual songs, singing with grace in your hearts to the Lord" (Col 3:16).

So, what is this type of prophecy?

The Bible calls it *prophesying*, but we call it *"Singing in the Spirit."* And if an unbeliever walks into this, they know that God is with us— because it is a beautiful thing to hear, and it is something that is divinely orchestrated by the Ruach haKodesh. [81]

---

81 A Personal Testimony from Pastor Wally Smith:

(continued...)

The liturgical churches in their chants (such as the Gregorian type of chant), could have its roots in this type of meeting.

Although they are not said to be prophetic, we do know that "Songs of Ascent" played a role in celebrating the feasts of Israel (see Psa 120-134). Singing also seems to have accompanied the sacrificial offerings (2 Chr 29:27-28; Ezra 3:1-6; Neh 7:73-8:13). [82]

The prophets tell of the returning Daughter of Zion singing aloud, even shouting: "The redeemed of the LORD shall return [*shoov*], [83] and come with singing unto Zion; everlasting joy shall be upon their head..." (Isa 51:11, KJV; Zep 3:14-18).

Concerning repentance and returning (*teshuvah*), Rabbi Simon Jacobson writes in his book, *60 Days: A Spiritual Guide to the High Holidays*:

> "Before you can embrace the right path, you must leave the wrong path; you must regret having taken it and you must go away from it." The idea of teshuvah is not just repenting, but also includes the idea of returning..... It's not just damage control, it is returning to the essence that was always pure— it is returning to G-d." [84]

As we seek to return to our God and to His eternal truths, may He protect, lead and guide us in the way He wants us to worship. May we be open to His move of the Ruach haKodesh in our congregations and gatherings.

---

81 (...continued)

Many years ago I was present at a pastors' meeting at Phoenix First Assembly, under Pastor Tommy Barnett. At this gathering we had a time of prayer that lasted well over an hour. This kind of prophecy suddenly broke out like fans engaged in "a wave" at a football game. No one led it. No one stopped it. It happened and stopped as if it was choreographed. This is a clear manifestation of the Ruach and it definitely left the hearers with "spirit bumps."

82 Songs: See 2 Ch 7:3; 20:21; 23:18; Psa 89:15; 136:1 137:3,4; Rev 5:9; 14:3; 15:3.

83 *Strong's* #H7725, "to turn back."

84 *60 Days: A Spiritual Guide to the High Holidays, First Edition*, Simon Jacobson, Brooklyn, NY, 2003, Kiyum Press., p 48.

19

WORD OF WISDOM—
WORD OF KNOWLEDGE
LIGHTS AND PERFECTIONS

*N*ow concerning spiritual gifts, brethren, I do not want you to be ignorant…. Therefore I make known to you that…. There are diversities of gifts, but the same Spirit. There are differences of ministries, but the same Lord. And there are diversities of activities, but it is the same God who works all in all. But the manifestation of the Spirit is given to each one for the profit of all: for to one is given the word of wisdom through the Spirit, to another the word of knowledge through the same Spirit, to another faith by the same Spirit, to another gifts of healings by the same Spirit, to another the working of miracles, to another prophecy, to another discerning of spirits, to another different kinds of tongues, to another the interpretation of tongues. But one and the same Spirit works all these things, distributing to each one individually as He wills (1 Cor 12:1-11).*

"To one is given a word of wisdom, to another, a word of knowledge..." (verse 12:8).

A central truth found in the Apostolic Scriptures is that the Ruach will lead us into all truth and reveal to us the full knowledge of Messiah. Concerning this subject Paul prayed that the Father of glory might give us "the spirit of wisdom and revelation in the knowledge of Him." Paul wanted the eyes of our understanding, the eyes of our heart, to be "enlightened," so we might know what is the hope of Yah's calling, and the riches of the glory of His inheritance in the saints. Paul wanted us to know the exceeding greatness of His power toward us who believe, according to the working of His mighty power (Eph 1:18-20).

Spiritual endowments, such as the word of wisdom and the word of knowledge, are of supreme importance in our walk. They help us to better know the things Paul prayed that we might know. When we come to wisdom and knowledge, we come to the God that Yeshua, through His finished work, has reintroduced to us. He is the God who knows all things; He is God omniscient, all knowing. He has all knowledge and all truth:

> "For the eyes of the LORD run to and fro throughout the whole earth, to show Himself strong on behalf of those whose heart is loyal to Him" (2 Chr 16:9). And, "Known to God from eternity are all His works" (Acts 15:18). And, "There is no creature hidden from His sight, but all things are naked and open to the eyes of Him to whom we must give account" (Heb 4:13).

God knows absolutely everything. His knowledge is limitless.

Human beings find limitlessness hard to understand, because we try to understand it with a limited mind. Thus, if we feel we fully understand a matter, we have probably lost it, because we have limited our understanding of limitlessness understanding.

In the knowledge of God we find infinite knowledge. He knows Himself completely; He is "the" infinite God and infinitely knows

His infinite self. However, we do not know Him outside of what He has chosen to reveal to us of Himself. Our Bibles reveal all the knowledge of Him that we need for this life. But, in the next life or dimension, we will know YHVH in a far greater way than we can ever imagine while here on this earth.

God knows all things that are, that ever were, that ever will be, and He knows them perfectly and instantly so that He doesn't have to search through His knowledge to find an answer. He also knows all peoples, completely, and all our past, present, and future. He knows our every thought, desire, and action, and He knows it instantly, without anyone having to teach Him.

He has always known these things and that boggles the mind. To think that He knows the same thing about everyone, at the same time, further boggles our minds. He knows the same thing about every person that ever was, is, and will be, and He knows it instantly, completely, perfectly. That is infinite knowledge.

He knows every spirit. He knows all angels and all demons. He knows all of heaven, all of hell and all of earth. He is never amazed or surprised. He never discovers anything. He knows all and is filled with infinite wisdom. He is not only the all-knowing God, He is the all-wise God. Wisdom is achieving the most perfect end in the most perfect way, and that is the way of our God.

We can have a lot of knowledge in a matter, but unless it is coupled with wisdom, it is useless. It is much like a student fresh out of college who knows enough to have earned his degree, but due to inexperience is a bit useless on the job.

God's wisdom is so vast that He not only knows all things that were in the past but He knows all things that might have been but did not come to fruition. He not only knows what now is, He also knows what could be, what isn't, and what will never be. In other words, God knows our futures, not only what will be but what could have been.

So it is that we need to be directed by His knowledge and by His wisdom.

DEFINING WORDS OF KNOWLEDGE AND WISDOM

A word of knowledge consists of God's making known to us certain truths by the Ruach. By the Spirit, we receive knowledge beyond our understanding— but not by natural means.

Knowledge is the state of knowing, feeling, or perceiving something. It speaks of familiarity, awareness, of understanding of what has been perceived, discovered, or learned; it is specific information about something.

Wisdom is the ability to discern or judge what is true, right, or lasting; to have wisdom is to have the insight, common sense, and good judgment to know what to do with knowledge. Wisdom offers a wise outlook, plan, or course of action in a matter. A word of wisdom is spiritual insight as to *how* the Ruach would have us apply the knowledge given to us. We can "know something in our inner man," but wisdom tells us what to do with that knowledge. Thus, we are encouraged to love wisdom above gold (Prov 16:16).

> A WORD OF KNOWLEDGE HELPS US TO KNOW SOMETHING, A WORD OF WISDOM HELPS US TO KNOW HOW TO WISELY APPLY THAT KNOWLEDGE

A word of knowledge helps us to know something, a word wisdom helps us to know how to wisely apply that knowledge.

Words of knowledge and wisdom are powerful aids that help Believers in their walk. However, they are not simply New Covenant giftings. YHVH has always sought to direct His people with these outstanding gifts.

THE URIM AND THUMMIM

In Exodus chapter 25, YHVH told Moses that He would commune with him over the top of the Ark of the Covenant. YHVH said, "There I will meet with you, and I will speak with you from above the mercy seat, from between the two cherubim which are on the ark of the Testimony, about everything which I will give you in commandment to the children of Israel" (Exo 25:22).

Levi by Spencer Williams
www.jesuspaintings.com

Over the Mercy Seat, there was a supernatural light called the *Shekhinah Glory*. Moses could go before that *Shekhinah* light and know that God Himself was speaking to him.

The High Priest, when in full robes, wore an *ephod* (see above right). In the back of his ephod were two pockets, which held two stones called the *Urim* (*oo reem*) and the *Thummim* (*toom meem*). Not much is known about these two stones, but Scripture does reveal that, in some fashion, YHVH spoke to the people through them. He used them to reveal His will. No one knows exactly how they worked, but Scripture records that such revelations did occur, and that the results, the truths made known through these enigmatic stones, were used to settle matters among His people.

Urim means *lights*. *Strong's Dictionary* says the word speaks of the oracular item in the high-priest's breastplate, of its brilliance, and that it is rooted in a word that speaks of a luminous flame. *Thummim* means *perfections*. This word speaks of an emblem of complete Truth. When we combine their descriptions, in these two objects we find *lights and perfections*. [85] Concerning these objects that helped Israel in their walk, we see that when Moses blessed each of the twelve tribes, he said of the tribe of Levi:

> "Let Your Thummim and Your Urim be with Your holy one [Levi], Whom You tested at Massah, and with whom You contended at the waters of Meribah, Who says of his father and mother, 'I have not seen them'; nor did he acknowledge his brothers, or know his own children; for

---

85 *Strong's* Urim: #'s H224, from 217 and 215. Thummim: #'s H8550 and 8537.

they have observed Your word and kept Your covenant. They shall teach Jacob Your judgments, and Israel Your law. They shall put incense before You, and a whole burnt sacrifice on Your altar" (Deu 33:8-10).

To understand what these stones foreshadowed, we note that to give light means to "make clear," to make something visible, evident, manifest, unclouded or transparent. It is to make everything easy to see. Seeing can cause us to stand back and say *"Ahhh!"*

The Urim and Thummim speak of instructing and teaching the purposes of God in truth. Centered in those two stones was the ability to take away the veil or cloud before our eyes. Their purpose was to help us understand the Holy One and His ways.

Throughout the Psalms YHVH instructed His people and made His truth known to them. For example: "Good and upright is the LORD; therefore He teaches sinners in the way." And, "Teach me Your way, O LORD, and lead me in a smooth path, because of my enemies." However, the sons of Israel "soon forgot His works; and did not wait for His counsel" (Psa 25:8; 27:11; 106:13).

Most translators interpret the word *etsah* as "counsel," saying, YHVH reprimanded the Israelites because they "did not wait for His *counsel.*" Even so, the Hebrew word "etsah" means prudence, advice, advisement, counsel, and purpose. However, it is derived from the primary root *ya'ats*, which means to deliberate or *resolve.* If we apply this stronger meaning, we see that the Psalmist is saying that Israel did not wait for YHVH's "resolve" or result in the matter. [86]

Concerning the Urim and Thummim, the Israelites would use them to inquire of God. Through the stones they received an answer, a way to resolve the matter, a way to arrive at a good result. Through them, they knew how to proceed.

The "brilliance" aspect of the Urim depicts the idea that Godly knowledge comes to us by revelation, thus lighting the way.

---

86 *Strong's #'s* H6098; 3289.

We see these stones in use in the story of Saul, when he butchered the city of the priests. Not only did he kill all the people but all the animals as well. Abiathar, son of a High Priest, was not in the city at the time and so was spared. Because Abiathar was the High Priest, he ran and got the ephod from the Tabernacle and took it to David. In the pockets of the ephod were the Urim and Thummim, and through their use, he was able to give to David wise counsel about how to handle the matter (1 Sam 23).

When David wanted to make a wise move, he would "inquire of the Lord." For an Israelite, that meant he went to the one who wore the ephod. The High Priest, using his enigmatic stones, could tell the Israelite what was the will or mind of God in the matter. Then the Israelite would know what to do or what not to do.

We see another example of the use of these stones in the Book of Joshua. The story is sometimes called the "Gibeonite Deception" (see Joshua 9). There we see the men of Israel took some of their provisions, but they "did *not* ask counsel of the LORD" (Josh 9:14). And when Joshua and the Israelites did not inquire of YHVH, they got into trouble— lots of it. They had difficulty because they relied on their own mind; they trusted in what they could see with their eyes. But, the Word tells us, "Trust in the LORD with all your heart, and lean not on your own understanding." We are told to acknowledge Him in all of our ways, then, He will "direct our paths." We also are warned, "Do not be wise in your own eyes" (Pro 3:5-7).

Had the Israelites consulted with the High Priest and the Urim and Thummim, they would have been empowered to go beyond human vision; they could have had knowledge that was rooted in Godly revelation; a resolution could have been imparted to them.

Again, Thummim means *perfections*, which English word comes from *perfect*, but in Scripture, *perfect* has greater meaning; in Hebrew it means complete, mature, whole, entire, unblemished, innocence, integrity, perfect, and upright. (Like an apple in season, whole and wholesome, without spot or blemish, it is perfect.)

The idea behind *Thummim/perfection* is that of being true, whole, and complete. To grasp its high standard we note that, "The law appoints as high priests men who have weakness, but the word of the oath, which came after the law, appoints the Son who has been *perfected* forever" (Heb 7:28). Yeshua is true perfection.

Another word sometimes used to reflect the meaning of Thummim is *prosperous*. Unfortunately, this English word is often associated with having money. But money is not the main Hebrew emphasis. Instead, the word speaks of innocence, integrity, perfect, simplicity, of being upright. It means to be totally whole, as in having your life together. The Hebrew greeting, "shalom" or "peace" speaks of this same type of wholeness. If we put the meanings of the Urim and Thummim together, we have:

- *Urim:* Knowledge, walking in revelation and light
- *Thummim:* Having wisdom, by which we walk in perfect truth, in wholeness and togetherness, living a life that is prosperous and having the true peace of our God.

CLEANSING BY WISDOM AND KNOWLEDGE

In Psalm 51 David appears to be speaking of his sin with Bathsheba and of killing her husband Uriah. So it is that ultimately, a repentant and humbled king composes one of the most beautiful prayers ever prayed by man. In it, we see the cleansing properties of the Urim and Thummim, the restorative nature of walking in wisdom and truth:

"Have mercy upon me, O God, according to Your loving-kindness; according to the multitude of Your tender mercies, blot out my transgressions. Wash me thoroughly from my iniquity, and cleanse me from my sin. For I acknowledge my transgressions, and my sin is always before me. Against You, You only, have I sinned, and done this evil in Your sight— that You may be found just when You speak, and blameless when You judge. Behold, I was brought forth in iniquity, and in sin my mother conceived me. Behold, You desire truth in the inward parts, and in the hidden part You will make me to know wisdom. Purge me with hyssop, and I shall be clean; wash me, and I shall be whiter than snow. Make me hear joy and gladness, that the bones You have broken may rejoice. Hide Your face from my sins, and blot out all my iniquities. Create in me a clean heart, O God, and renew a steadfast spirit within me. Do not cast me away from Your presence, and do not take Your Holy Spirit from me. Restore to me the joy of Your salvation [Yeshua], and uphold me by Your generous Spirit. Then I will teach transgressors Your ways, and sinners shall be converted to You. Deliver me from the guilt of bloodshed, O God, the God of my salvation, and my tongue shall sing aloud of Your righteousness. O Lord, open my lips, and my mouth shall show forth Your praise. For You do not desire sacrifice, or else I would give it; You do not delight in burnt offering. The sacrifices of God are a broken spirit, a broken and a contrite heart— these, O God, You will not despise" (Psa 51:1-17).

David said, "Behold, You desire *truth* in the inward parts, and in the hidden part You will make me to know *wisdom*" (Psa 51:6).

We find yet other examples of a word of knowledge in 1 Samuel 9, when Saul went to Samuel to find out where his donkeys were, God gave him the answer.

We also see Naaman being healed of leprosy. Told to dip himself seven times in the Jordan River, Naaman was totally healed. He then offered Elijah a good sum of money, clothing, etc. But Elijah refused and said the gifts of God are free. Elijah's assistant, however, Gahaziah, thought his master was crazy for letting lots of loot slip through his fingers. So he ran after Naaman and told him that his master had changed his mind and would take some of the goods he offered. Later, Elijah called Gahaziah to account and told him, "My heart went with you." And Gahaziah then contracted the leprosy that Naaman had.

The Holy Spirit revealed the truth to Elijah.

We see Messiah Yeshua operating in a word of knowledge in Mark 2:8. There we see that He "perceived in His spirit" regarding how His detractors were reasoning, and He asked them a telling question, "Why reason ye these things in your hearts?" (KJV).

Paul had a word of knowledge when he said of a pending voyage, "Men, I perceive that the voyage will certainly be with damage and great loss, not only of the cargo and the ship, but also of our lives" (Acts 27:9-10, NASB).

Similarly, the Book of Proverbs is filled with God's wisdom. In it, we see that a word of wisdom from the Almighty can be rather terse, to the point, and thus hard to forget. But terse or not, we need all the divinely revealed truth and wisdom we can get. [87]

Malachi 3:1-3 speaks of the coming of YHVH's "Messenger, " meaning, the Messiah. Malachi likens Him, and His coming, to a "refiner's fire." And, in His coming, the Messiah especially purifies "the sons of Levi," so they can "present to the LORD offerings in righteousness."

As Messiah's followers, we are called to be a holy nation, a kingdom of priests, a people who proclaim the excellencies of our God to the world (Exo 19:6; 1 Pet 2:9-10; Hos 1-2; Rev 1:6; 5:10).

So it is that He wants to purify us, and He wants to give us good gifts that will help us in that process.

Let us therefore ask the Father to bestow on us these most important gifts, and to help us to know how to properly use them, that we might serve Him with excellence.

---

87 We again wish to acknowledge the Malcolm Smith Tapes Series, "Lights and Perfections" for insights gleaned from them. http://www.malcolmsmith.org/home.asp

20

MESSIAH YESHUA AND THE URIM AND THUMMIM

Messiah Yeshua is all and in all. He is the final Wisdom and the final Knowledge. He is the cosmic Messiah; everything is being summed up in Him. He is the true Light that gives light to every man that comes into the world (Col 2:9, John 1:18, Heb 1:1-2; John 1:9). He is the true meaning of the light that is the Urim. He is the ultimate perfection of the Thummim. He is the final stones, the ultimate answer, the revelation, the truth, the light. Apart from Him, "No one has seen God at any time. The only begotten Son, who is in the bosom of the Father, He has declared Him" (John 1:18). The stones were kept in the pocket of the High Priest's ephod, which he wore on his chest or *bosom*. Yeshua is "The only begotten Son, who is in the *bosom* of the Father," and "He [Yeshua] has declared Him [the Father]" (John 1:18). Yeshua is the Urim and the Thummim, He brings wisdom from the bosom of the Father; He reveals the Father's truth to us.

PARABLES AND GLEANING WISDOM

Yeshua exhibited wisdom and knowledge throughout His earthly ministry, yet He often spoke in parables. Even so, it was prophesied of Him:

> "Give ear, O my people, to my law; incline your ears to the words of my mouth. I will open my mouth in a parable; I will utter dark sayings of old, which we have heard and known, and our fathers have told us. We will not hide them from their children, telling to the generation to come the praises of the LORD, and His strength and His wonderful works that He has done" (Psa 78:1-5).

> It also is written, "All these things Yeshua spoke to the multitude in parables; and without a parable He did not speak to them, that it might be fulfilled which was spoken by the prophet, saying: 'I will open My mouth in parables; I will utter things kept secret from the foundation of the world'" (Mat 13:34-35).

When His disciples asked Him, "*Why* do You speak to them in parables?", He answered and said to them:

> "Because it has been given to you to know the mysteries of the kingdom of heaven, but to them it has not been given. For whoever has, to him more will be given, and he will have abundance; but whoever does not have, even what he has will be taken away from him. Therefore I speak to them in parables, because seeing they do not see, and hearing they do not hear, nor do they understand. And in them the prophecy of Isaiah is fulfilled, which says: 'Hearing you will hear and shall not understand, and seeing you will see and not perceive; for the hearts of this people have grown dull. Their ears are hard of hearing, and their eyes they have closed, lest they should see with their eyes and hear with their ears, lest they should understand with their hearts and

turn, so that I should heal them. But blessed are your eyes for they see, and your ears for they hear; for assuredly, I say to you that many prophets and righteous men desired to see what you see, and did not see it, and to hear what you hear, and did not hear it'" (Mat 13:10-17).

Parables have the ability, by the power of the Spirit, to reveal secrets from the Almighty. They are teaching tools that contain wisdom from on High (Mat 24:32; Mark 4:2). However, if you do not have ears to hear, you can easily miss their point. Parables also are usually based on earthly events that could actually have happened; they are stories of every day, ordinary situations.

Examples of Yeshua's parables are: the enemy sowing tares among the wheat, the widow's lost coin, and the story about the divided house (He also taught using the example of the widow's mite: Mat 12:25-29; 13:24-30; ; Mark 12:40-44; Luke 15:8-10).

Yeshua described events like these, and those who had ears to hear gained knowledge and wisdom through the word pictures they painted. The stories were somewhat abstract, yet alive with meaning. So it is that parables reveal another aspect of God's character; they show Him bestowing wisdom on His children through the telling of simple stories.

GIFTS OF KNOWLEDGE

Nathaniel was the hardheaded disciple. Philip ran up to him and said, "We have found the Messiah." But Nathaniel responded, "Can anything good come out of Nazareth?"

Nonetheless, Nathaniel did go and see Yeshua, and when he met Him, Yeshua said to him, "When you were under the fig tree, I saw you." Yeshua was operating in the gift of knowledge. He saw what human eyes could not see. He was demonstrating that which only God could have known.

Also, in Yeshua's encounter with the Samaritan woman at the well, He said she had, had five husbands, and that the man she was currently with was not her husband (John 4:4-30).

That is an example of supernatural knowledge.

When Yeshua was across the Jordan, far away from Lazarus and his family, by divine revelation, He said to His disciples, "Lazarus is dead." Only YHVH could have revealed this.

One of the most perfect examples of a word of wisdom is seen in a story about Yeshua in the Temple courts. He was with His disciples and some enemies shouted out, "Should we pay taxes to Caesar?"

Answering this question could potentially put Him in a "Catch 22" situation. If Yeshua were to say "yes," the Jewish leaders would not follow Him. If He were to say "no," the Roman soldiers would arrest Him and all of His followers.

Instead, Yeshua answered with a "word of wisdom." He said, "Give me a coin." When they did so, He wisely asked of them, "Whose picture is this on the coin?"

They said, "Caesar's."

Yeshua replied, "Render under Caesar that which is Caesar's and render unto God that which is God's."

A brilliant answer was given to a difficult question, and that answer is not easily forgotten. YHVH dropped His wisdom onto Yeshua at the moment in time in which it was needed.

Being Priests who Can
Light Up with Answers

Yeshua has now ascended to the right hand of the Father and has sent to us the Ruach haKodesh. So it is, that the Ruach can now drop a word of His truth and perfection on *our* hearts. As His priests, and like the High Priests who once wore the Urim and Thummim, which could light up with answers, we too, can now "light up with answers."

We are called to be the light of the world and to follow Yeshua, Who is the Way, the Truth, and the Life (Mat 5:14; John 14:6). He told us, when we are in difficult situations...

"Do not worry about how or what you should speak. For it will be given to you in that hour what you should speak; for it is not you who speak, but the Spirit of your Father who speaks in you" (Mat 10:19 -20). And, "When He, the Spirit of truth, has come, He will guide you into all truth; for He will not speak on His own authority, but whatever He hears He will speak; and He will tell you things to come. He will glorify Me, for He will take of what is Mine and declare it to you. All things that the Father has are Mine. Therefore I said that He will take of Mine and declare it to you" (John 16:13-15).

The Holy Spirit will guide us and tell us of things to come. He will reveal the truth to us, and that truth will always bring glory to the One we follow, the One Who is the Light and Perfect Truth.

WALKING IN KNOWLEDGE AND WISDOM

These are days of awe, and our movement, above all movements, needs to learn to properly walk in the supernatural giftings of the Ruach haKodesh. Our patriarchs and forefathers did it, and we need to do it too. We must no longer resist the workings of the Holy Spirit. The benefits of these blessings are too numerous to count. For example:

A word of wisdom can keep us from getting hung up on false doctrine. It can tell us how to walk wisely in a difficult situation. A word of knowledge from above can teach us the truth in any matter. A word of knowledge makes known the mind of the Ruach; it gives us knowledge beyond our natural understanding. With the words of knowledge and wisdom, we see not with the eye of experience, but with an eye that is divinely illuminated by the Almighty. A word of wisdom will reveal how the Ruach would have knowledge applied, so we can walk in light and truth.

Without these particular manifestations of the Ruach, our potential as Yah's people is greatly hindered. So we need to learn to walk with an eye open to God's supernatural gifts.

THE UNKNOWN VERSUS FOOLISHNESS

Granted that there is an element of the "unknown" in trusting the Ruach, for it written, "You do not know what is the way of the wind [Ruach]... you do not know the works of God who makes everything... you do not know which will prosper, Either this or that, Or whether both alike will be good" (Ecc 11:5-6).

It is difficult to learn to truly trust the Holy Spirit when we don't know exactly what might happen. But trust we must. Again, we must have our "senses exercised to discern both good and evil" (Heb 5:14). With practice, we can learn to discern the difference between our human voice and that of the Holy Spirit.

Nonetheless, many resist walking in this way due to mistakes they see in the "spontaneous" living habits of some. And, if ever there was a populace that lives spontaneously, we are they. Human beings live predominately moment to moment. But we Americans are perhaps the worst offenders. We often live by whims and sound bites, such as, "If it feels good do it" or "Go with gusto." We are bombarded with multi-media stimuli to "Live life to its fullest." Moreover, far too many Believers claim to "walk in the Spirit," contending they are being "led by the Spirit." But to many, it appears they are instead living a haphazard lifestyle, doing whatever they want to do, while attributing the reason for their erratic behavior to Almighty God. Sadly, they mistake their own "inner voice" for the voice of the Ruach. Such behavior is part of our human condition. We act, far too often, on impulse without truly inquiring of our God. We are all guilty on some level.

So it is that sometimes the Lord has to guide us through our mistakes. He keeps leading us until finally, we get it. We then realize what it is that He actually wants us to do.

We see an example of this type of behavior even in the great Charismatic, the Apostle Paul. He once said to his companion Barnabas, "Let us now go back and visit our brethren in every city where we have preached the word of the Lord, and see how they are doing" (Acts 15:36).

At first, it seems natural, logical, to revisit a community of Believers you were honored to bring into the kingdom. But we should always inquire of the Ruach, because we do not know which way will prosper (Ecc 11:6). For example, Paul and Barnabas had a falling out, so Paul asked Timothy to be his traveling companion, and off they went. But it seems they did not first seek God's counsel. They seem to instead have been operating spontaneously, impulsively. And when they had gone through Phrygia and Galatia, they were *forbidden by the Holy Spirit* to preach the word in Asia. After arriving in Mysia, they tried to go into Bithynia, *but the Spirit did not permit them*. Then they came to Troas and Paul had a vision in the night. A man of Macedonia pleaded with him, saying, "Come over to Macedonia and help us." So they sought to go to Macedonia, concluding that the Lord had called them there. They traveled to Phrygia, but again, *the Ruach forbade them to preach*. So they headed to Bithynia, *but the Holy Spirit stopped them again*. They then proceeded to Troas, a small port city. And at this point, *God told them to go to Macedonia* (Acts 16:6-10).

Sometimes, it is only after we run out of options, when our back is against the wall, that our God gives us the knowledge and wisdom we need to direct our lives. This is so because He does not want to turn us into puppets, but instead wants us to learn and to seek to do good. We are to minister one to another, and we often do that which appears to be logical. Yet there is always the chance that our actions might result in what we might call "mistakes."

But, in Abba's economy they may not be mistakes at all....

> Paul said," I now rejoice, not that you were made sorrowful, but that you were made sorrowful to the point of repentance; for you were made sorrowful according to the will of God, so you might not suffer loss in anything.... For the sorrow that is according to the will of God produces a repentance without regret, leading to salvation, but the sorrow of the world produces death" (2 Cor 7:9-10).

"Repentance without regret" sounds like an oxymoron, like opposites that do not go together, yet in the economy of the Holy One, the two add up to perfect repentance: We are sorry for our actions, but we learned valuable lessons from the experience. This knowledge, in turn, worked positive change in us, which makes it hard for us to "regret" having chosen that path. Even though it was a "wrong" path, due to our own choices, we had to walk it and learn certain things about ourselves. And, our experience led to "godly sorrow" that produced good in us. The result is that, in true Hebraic form, more so than what we are turning away from, our focus is on whom we are turning toward: the Holy One. [88]

In this way we see that the Father sometimes has to guide us through the "negative" choices we make. In Scripture we often see that He says, "Don't do this," or "Don't do that."

Also, sometimes we do not hear the Father's voice as often as we did when we were new Believers. When we are babes, the Father often reaches into our world and touches us. As we mature, He seems to get quiet and not to be reaching out to us as in times past. But the truth is, because of His great love for us, He is trying to get us to seek Him, because He wants us to grow up and learn to reach into *His world*. [89] Even so, we want to mature and learn to reach into our Father's world. And, words of wisdom and knowledge are key gifts that will surely help us as we seek to walk in the great end-time purposes of our God.

Apart from having the gifts of knowledge and wisdom, we are but theology students. We might be able to memorize the substance of the Bible, but without learning to operate in the supernatural spirituals offered by the Ruach haKodesh, we will be ill-dressed, ill-equipped priests; we will not be able to show to a hurting world the benefits of the Urim and Thummim.

---

88 *Israel's Feasts and their Fullness: Expanded Edition*, Batya Ruth Wootten, chapter 31, "Repentance and Returning— Tashlich and Teshuvah," (2008, Key of David Publishing, Saint Cloud, FL).

89 Thanks to Graham Cooke for this excellent point: www.grahamcooke.com

21

GIFTS OF HEALINGS
AND DIVINE HEALTH

N *ow concerning spiritual gifts....manifestation of the Spirit is* *given to each one for the profit of all ... to one is given the...* *gifts of healings... (1 Cor 12:1-11).*

The Father said, "If you diligently heed the voice of the LORD your God and do what is right in His sight, give ear to His commandments and keep all His statutes, I will put none of the diseases on you which I have brought on the Egyptians. For I am the LORD who heals you" (Exo 15:26).

Here we see that YHVH promises to heal us, albeit there is a huge "if" attached to His promise: *"If you diligently..."*

Too many people to count have been mistreated for what is perceived to be their failure to have enough faith to walk in this and other verses that promise divine healing. So, what is the truth about healing? Does our God always heal us when we ask?

This subject is so vast that it surely cannot be fully answered in this life, but we will note a few verses that suggest those who abuse people for a supposed "lack of faith" in regard to a sickness, may not have a full understanding of the promises given.

The Word says "*all* Scripture is given by inspiration of God, and is profitable for doctrine, for reproof, for correction, for instruction in righteousness" (2 Tim 3:16). Thus, we will try to take in its full counsel in this matter.

To begin, a few chapters after saying He is the LORD who heals us, YHVH established laws concerning caring for ailing people. He spoke of a man's being struck by another and said the offender must pay for the loss of his time, and provide for the stricken one "*until he is thoroughly healed.*" (After this, follows the famous eye for eye, tooth for tooth rule.) In this example, we see indication that not all will be immediately healed— even though the wounded ones appear to be innocent in the matter (Exo 21:18-27).

The righteous sometimes must suffer. The Almighty said, Job was "a blameless and upright man," yet he had to scrape his boils with potsherds as he sat in dust and ashes (Job 1:8; 2:8).

Chosen ones are sometime being taught a lesson. King David said YHVH "has chastened me severely, but He has not given me over to death. ... Before I was afflicted I went astray, but now I keep Your word." David also said, "It is good for me that I have been afflicted, that I may learn Your statutes.... Your judgments are right, and in faithfulness You afflicted me" (Psa 118:18; 119:67,71,75).

Powerful saints sometimes get sick unto death. Elisha had a double portion of Elijah's anointing, raised people from the dead, and did many miracles, yet he died from sickness (2 Ki 13:14).

Twice Yeshua said the reason for a sickness was so that the works of God might be displayed. He also said that in the world, we will have "affliction" (John 9:2-3; 11:4; 16:33).

The apostle Paul was afflicted by a thorn in the flesh, which the Lord refused to remove, so Paul, instead, learned to rejoice in his infirmity (2 Cor 12:8-10; Gal 4:13-14). Paul also was often used to heal people, yet all he could do for Timothy's stomach condition was advise him to use a little wine for his "frequent infirmities." Trophimus, too, was a companion of Paul, yet he "left him sick at Miletus" (Acts 20:9-10; 28:8-9; 1 Tim 5:23; 2 Tim 4:20). Paul exhorted suffering brethren to continue in the faith, because he knew that it is only after passing through "many tribulations" that we are able to enter into the kingdom of God (Acts 14:22).

HEALING: PROS AND CONS

Sin and sickness entered the world through Adam's disobedience. YHVH warned Adam that, in the day that he ate of the forbidden tree, he would begin to die (Gen 2:16-17; Rom 5:12).

In the end, all things must be attributed to the Almighty, because He is the Creator of all things. However, as Adam's heirs, we should not blame YHVH for our sickness nor for the death process. We brought these things on ourselves.

Our bodies are subject to sickness and decay— through the natural aging process, bad diet, lack of exercise, stress, afflictions by others, environment, genetics, disease, family curses, and more. Our bodies are perishable and weak, our outer man is decaying. Death, and the host of diseases that go with it, will be a part of the human condition until the perishable finally puts on the imperishable, until the corruptible puts on the incorruptible, until we receive resurrection bodies and are thereafter immune to the frailties of mankind (Exo 34:7; 2 Ki 15:12; 1 Cor 15:42-55; 2 Cor 4:16).

On one hand, it is true that the Father wants to heal us, wants us to be well and walk in health. He also wanted us to be with Him in the Garden— but mankind fell short of His glorious call (Exo 23:25; Psa 30:2; 107:20; Rom 3:23). For these and other reasons, telling sick Believers their problem is entirely due to *their* lack of faith, and that if *they* would but claim their healing, God would heal them, could be a matter of heaping unnecessary guilt on the ill and infirm. It also can serve as an excuse for impotent and ignorant prayer on the part of the one who led the prayer.

We know that without faith it is impossible to please God. Faith is essential to every aspect of our lives (Heb 11:6). However, we must not have faith in *our* faith— meaning, we must instead have faith that is truly rooted in the Father's ability, and not in our selves. We must not be deceived into having faith in "our" supposed giftings. And we must not, be beguiled into taking credit for healing— not in any way, shape, nor form.

We also must realize that praying for another's healing is a two-way street. To explain, we liken healing to pure water and mankind to a pipe through whom the healing flows. If our pipe is rusty, dirty, or corroded in any way, we risk contaminating the pure water that is the healing and thus harming the needy.

Moreover, a sudden rush of water can rupture rusty pipes. Pride can set in and ruin the one who prayed. We also can get filled up, or "stopped up" with "self." Such wrong attitudes can lead to spiritual sickness, in that pride always goes before a fall: "Pride goes before destruction, and a haughty spirit before a fall. Better to be of a humble spirit with the lowly, than to divide the spoil with the proud" (Pro 16:18-19). Having healings flow through our hands, having the purity of the Almighty course through our lowly pipes, is an awesome thing. Our hearts must be softened with humility and true compassion for the people, if we are to be prepared for the experience.

Compassion for the people and concern for Abba's purposes in their lives, must come first. Again, David felt sicknesses' bed of pain can teach and lead us to a deeper love of Yah and to spiritual growth. Before we dismiss people for a lack of faith, let us first try to truly discern the situation. Before we pray for people, let us first ask the Father *how* we should pray. Messiah Yeshua said, "I do nothing of Myself; but as My Father taught Me…. I speak what I have seen with My Father…" And, whatever "He sees the Father do… the Son also does in like manner" (John 5:19; 8:28, 38). Before Yeshua spoke or prayed, He knew what the Father wanted. For that reason, He always had success. We must do likewise.

22

GIFTS OF HEALINGS AND ATTITUDES...

The hidden and secret things of a man's frame belong to God (Psa 139:15). In each life, there are things that we do not understand or know anything about. Yet, we know that the revealed will of God is to heal His children. We also know that we are to pray for healing, for ourselves and for others. But, even if it doesn't happen the way we think it should happen, if the answer to our prayer is not what we expected, we must trust that the reasons and answers to the situation are hidden in the Almighty.

The Book of Job helps bring balance to the idea of healing. Through him, we hear the cry, "Why must the innocent suffer?" Job is one of the most interesting, elusive books in Scripture, and suffering of the righteous is its subject matter. In the second half of the book, God teaches the fundamentals of faith. He teases Job and asks, "Where were you when I formed the earth? Have you ever walked on the bottom of the sea? Have you ever said to the waves, come this far and no further?" With that, He then lists all the animals that He has made.

God was in essence saying, "Job, you do not even understand creation! How then can you understand my dealings with the human soul? You are in the first grade. When you get to high school, maybe we can talk. But right now, trust me. I am good, I am wisdom; just trust me!" (See Job 38-40.)

The revealed will of God is to heal, but when healing does not take place in the manner in which we think it should, we should not falter in our faith. We must instead cast ourselves, abandon ourselves, to the God who is infinitely wise and infinitely good. We must rest in the truth that we can trust in Him (Psa 46:10).

Healing appears to be one of the most widely dispensed manifestations of the Ruach haKodesh. Yeshua healed the sick wherever He went. So what are gifts of healings or divine healing?

WHAT IT IS NOT, AND WHAT IT IS...

Defining what healing is not will perhaps make it easier to understand what is divine healing. For example, divine healing is not healing by natural methods, with diet being an example of that. A diabetic who regulates his/her sugar properly feels better and enjoys relatively normal health.

Healing does not come through the medical profession— doctors only watch God heal. They can put bones together, but it is God who actually re-knits and repairs them. However, doctors can be used as part of the general desire of God for healing. Man knows that he is to be well, and doctors are urged on by that fact. Medical science though, is not divine healing. In the end, divine healing is a gift of the Holy Spirit. By the Spirit, a person is healed in a way that is beyond all human endeavors.

We read in 1 Corinthians 12:4, "There are diversities of gifts, but the same Spirit." The word translated *gifts* is from the Greek word *charisma* (khar'-is-mah), meaning a divine gratuity, deliverance, spiritual endowment, miraculous faculty, a free gift.

It comes from *charizomai*, meaning to freely grant as a favor, gratuitously, in kindness, pardon, rescue, deliver. This word comes from *charis*, meaning graciousness, divine influence on the heart, benefit, favour, gift, grace. [90]

Before Yeshua came, *charis* meant a present, such as a birthday gift, something you hadn't earned, you didn't merit, or something you may not have asked for. When Yeshua came and finished His work, a new dimension needed to be added to the word. The root definition fit to a point, because God does freely give without merit. He even wants us to ask of Him. He's in the giving business. But with Yeshua came the need to define the reverse of what we deserve. What we are given in the Spirit through Him is, not only unmerited and unearned, it is the opposite of what we deserve.

This means the giving of the gift is not based on the one who receives it. The word even implies unworthiness, which is why we are mercifully given the gift in the first place. The primary meaning of *charis* has to do with the Giver, which is YHVH. The gift is free and all attention is to be on the One who freely *gives gifts* to all.

The giftings of the Holy Spirit tell us God's love has become concrete. When we see a manifestation of His gifts, we are seeing the concrete love of God. No more is the love of God mere words. By His Spirit, He makes His love plain, physical, to be felt. He heals and thus His love is among us.

A gift of healing is a completely free bestowal of His favor. Regardless of our lifestyle, He can reach down and heal us. He "demonstrates His love own toward us, in that while we were still sinners, Christ died for us" (Rom 5:8). Even if we made ourselves sick through our own mistakes, He wants to heal us.

Bad lifestyles and behaviors result in long healing lines. Alcohol can lead to a bad liver and an ever increasing lack of brain cells. Diabetics often have poor vision and loss of mobility. Fats and sugars can lead to heart disease, and smoking can lead to cancer and breathing problems.

---

90 *Strong's* # G5486, from G5483, from 5485.

That people have been ministered to, and healed of, these problems and more, serves to prove healing is a *grace-based gift*. Otherwise, we could only minister by counseling people to change their diet and/or lifestyle. While such changes often are taught in the Torah, and often are logical solutions, we cannot forget that the mercy of God is much bigger than our sins. His mercy can come and cleanse our body of all the filth that we put into it.

His is a grace gift. Its manifestation tells us little about the recipient and much about God, especially that *He* is bestowing upon someone, *His* mercy and unmerited, unearned favor.

We cannot even define the word *grace* outside of the finished work of Messiah. Grace has no meaning outside the cross. It was on the tree that God dealt with us, but we did not even deserve that much. While Yeshua was on the tree, YHVH was dealing with our sin. When we come to the cross, we come face to face with Yeshua dealing with our sins and with the results of Adam's fall— which includes sickness and disease.

When Adam sinned, God said: "In the day that you eat of it, you will surely die." When Adam ate, he died, on the inside. Death began to take hold, starting in his spirit. Thus, all of his heirs live in the dimension of death. Each heir will ultimately have to experience physical death. This world age is under the dominion of the king of death, Satan, and under his rule, every human being dies. Satan is dead on the inside and his soul and emotions are dead too. However, hope is found in that we serve the King of Life Eternal: Messiah Yeshua.

In our day it is said that genius' use less than 10% of their brain power. Just imagine what Adam was like using 100% of his mental abilities! Man was created to be much greater, more accomplished, than he is today. But he is not as great at the moment as he is destined to be, because he is under the curse of death.

When death began to work in Adam's body, he had to come up with new words, like hurt, pain, sickness, and disease. These things were unknown until the fall— then his body began to die.

All sickness is indeed a result of sin, as in the archery term of *missing the bull's eye*, or *missing the high call of our Creator*. When we are laid to rest in death, our casket and its contents serve as a belated announcement that we have been dead all of our life. Our only hope lies in Yeshua and in His free gift of eternal life. In Isaiah 53 we see that He not only took our sicknesses and our pains but entered into death itself. When He rose from the dead, He personally defeated death and all that it entails. And one day, death also will be finally and forever defeated for us. The trumpet will sound and we will put on immortality, then the promise will be fulfilled, "Death is swallowed up in victory. O Death, where is your sting? O Hades, where is your victory?" (1 Cor 15:50-55; Hos 13:14).

On a long-ago First of First Fruits day, three days after Passover, in front of a freshly opened tomb, stood what was once a human body, but now, it was "glorified." Human bodies were initially made from the dust of the earth, and one had just passed through the bowels of the earth and come forth, in a new Heavenly form, never to die again. Death had been conquered in the dust. New, eternal life was offered by Yeshua to all who would believe.

HEALING AND ATONEMENT

Some teach that healing is in the Atonement, and that we should therefore claim healing for our earthly bodies. But in the First Covenant, *Atonement* was decided on the Day of Atonement, and it only *covered* sin from year to year. Conversely, Messiah, the Prince, puts an "end" to sin. In Him we are made "different"and forever "reconciled" to the Father."As far as the east is from the west... has He *removed* our transgressions from us" (Dan 9:24-25; Rom 5:11; Psa 103:12). Atonement only covered sins, but Messiah's Resurrection power puts an end to sin forever! Hallelujah! Our hope is in Messiah Yeshua's Resurrection Power! [91]

---

[91] Atonement: *Strong's* # H3722. Reconciliation: #G2643. See 2 Cor 5:18-19.
Healing: See the book, *Be in Health*, by Dr. Henry Wright: http://www.beinhealth.com

Yeshua did not die just to heal our sicknesses. Besides, a gift of healing only puts off death for a little longer. It doesn't deal with the real issue. We may receive gifts of healings over and over again, but at some point, we die. Apart from the Resurrection, complete healing does not exist for human bodies. Yeshua did not come to earth just to patch us up or to apply band-aids. He died so that one day, our bodies will be like His: eternal.

Many believe in the gifts of divine healing because they are afraid to die. But we are not ready to live until we are ready to die. Again, the highest divine gift is love, and the Word tells us that "perfect love casts out fear, because fear involves torment. But he who fears has not been made perfect in love" (1 John 4:18).

We are to be perfected in love, we seek earthly healing, but we are not afraid of death because we have the gift of eternal life.

THE HEALING ASPECTS OF LAUGHTER

To keep illness at bay, we note that Nehemiah 8:10 says, "The joy of the LORD is your strength." Restated, His rejoicing is our fortified place, His gladness our defense. Gladness and joy defend against illnesses that would take us captive. Rejoicing in the Rock gives us strength like a rock. Conversely, "by sorrow of the heart the spirit is broken," for, "a broken spirit dries the bones." Thus, we need to "Sing aloud unto God our strength: make a joyful noise unto the God of Jacob." Because, "a merry heart makes a cheerful countenance," it has "a continual feast," and it "does good, like medicine" (Psa 81:1, KJV; Prov 15:13,15; 17:22).

Laughter should be at the heart, in the "center" of YHVH's chosen ones. This truth is seen in the names of our patriarchs, Abraham, Isaac, and Jacob/Israel:

- Abraham: Father of many nations
- Isaac: Laughter
- Jacob/Israel: One who trips up/A Prince who Rules with the Almighty

In the meaning of these names we see that those who are heirs of the one called the father of many nations, shall laugh. They will cease to trip up or be tripped up, and ultimately be part of the chosen people of Israel— a people who are called to rule as a prince with YHVH.

GIFTS OF HEALINGS: PLURAL
GIFTS FOR THE SICK

In 1 Corinthians 12:9 and 28, we see the words, "gifts of healings." This plural translation is correct according to *The Fourth Revised Edition of the Greek Testament* (United Bible Society, 1994), and *The Greek Testament According to the Majority Text, Second Edition* (Thomas Nelson, 1994). Both sources show the same Greek phrase for these verses: *charismata iamatone*— and both words are in the *plural.* [92]

Seeing this point helps us realize that these are not a singular gift that we can own, but are instead plural gifts given to the people for their good. Thinking we can own a singular gift leads us to ask for the "gift of healing," as though we can dispense it (singular) at will. It can also lead us to get puffed up because of the importance of "our gift." But, the Word says there are "diversities" of gifts, ministries, and activities, but the same Spirit "works all in all." It tells us that manifestation of the Spirit is given to each one "for the profit of all."

Emphasis is not to be on the one through whom one of the many gifts flowed, but on the good of the Body of Messiah as a whole. After explaining that gifts are distributed as the Spirit wills, Paul repeatedly emphasizes that the Body of Messiah is "one." His point being, concerning gifts, we must keep in mind, the good of the whole Body. Paul then sums up his explanation concerning the distributions of the plural gifts of the Holy Spirit by pointing us to the greatest gift of all, which is love (1 Cor 12:4-13:13).

---

92 Thanks to Cathy Geever for help with the Greek sources.

> HEALINGS
> ARE
> PERSONAL
> TOUCHES
> OF LOVE
> FROM GOD,
> BESTOWED
> ON
> HURTING
> PEOPLE

For every sickness, God has a healing. The Holy Spirit has different healings for different diseases. To each sick person is given a particular gift of healing. When we are healed, it is because one of those gifts has been given to us. The *pray-er* does not own the gift, but is instead a conduit for it. Such gifts of healings are personal touches of love from God, bestowed on hurting people.

Every sickness is an opportunity for the Holy Spirit to make manifest the finished work of Yeshua. We do not earn these gifts because we have enough faith, but simply receive them.

It is not a matter of us, "confessing" our healing, as in having faith in our faith. That is not true faith. True faith is a matter of placing our lives in the hands of the Father. That is what "resting in Him" means. Real Shalom. No struggles. We rest in Him and get well. We don't *try to believe*, but *rest*. We take our sick bodies and rest in the arms of the Father, knowing that the Son has accomplished all on the tree, and that the Holy Spirit brings to us the free gift of healing. We don't try to make it happen. We don't try to "quote our faith into being." We simply rest in God, we give Him our body, and we don't take it back (Psa 46:10).

HEALING THE WHOLE MAN

Scripture has been revealing healing truths for ages. It tells us man is a composite: body, soul, and spirit. And it indicates that problems in the body can affect the soul and spirit, and vice versa (see footnote 91, book by Wright). In Scripture we often see that the total person was delivered and healed, not just their bodies. When the diseased had an encounter with Yeshua haMashiach, He not only healed bodies, but the soul and spirit man as well.

When the whole man is healed, the peace and joy of God fill their whole person, they become a manifestation of God's grace.

Our "job," so to speak, is to find out what kind of healing is needed, because, in sickness, the whole man is affected.

Thus, when praying for healing, it is good to have words of knowledge and wisdom in action, along with discernment of spirits. These giftings will often work in tandem when we pray for people. One gift can quickly lead to the operation of another, with each one building us up in the faith.

For instance, we see that with the man stricken with palsy, Yeshua said "Your sins are forgiven." In the natural we might say, "Let's heal the man, then we'll discuss the Gospel with him." But Yeshua looked beyond the sick body and saw with the eyes of the Holy Spirit. He saw that there was something wrong on the inside of the man that caused him to lie there in a condition of sin as well as in physical sickness.

Yeshua dealt with the whole man and so should we. He dealt with the spirit, the inside man, then He told the palsied individual to take up his bed and walk. Once delivered from his sin, the man did as he was told and was healed in a total sense.

TWO KINDS OF HEALING

We see two kinds of healing in Scripture, healing when God's power goes forth, and healing by God's wisdom.

In this sense, the whole Bible is a healing book because its wisdom gives us direction. It helps us to live a life that is free of anger, bitterness, envy, jealously, and pride.

Such negative emotions are scientifically proven to cause illness. More than thirty years ago the British Medical Association declared, "No tissue in the human body is totally removed from spirit." The way we are in spirit shows up in our bodies.

For example, "An excellent wife is the crown of her husband, but she who causes shame is like rottenness in his bones." And, "A sound [tranquil] heart is life to the body, but envy is rottenness to the bones"(Prov 12:4 14:30). Similarly, anger can raise one's blood pressure and cause strokes. Bitterness is a poisonous plant called wormwood, and it is more than a metaphor; it can be an actual poison in your body— and it can even be measured in a test tube.

Harmful poisons flow through our bodies when we lie in bed and entertain feelings of anger, envy and jealousy (Eph 4:26-27).

The Word tells us to "let all bitterness, and wrath, and anger, and clamour, and evil speaking, be put away from you, with all malice." We must look "diligently lest any man fail of the grace of God; lest any root of bitterness springing up trouble you, and thereby many be defiled" (Heb 12:15; Eph 4:31, KJV).

If we are in bitterness, let us trust God to come with healing and deliverance. Let us also realize that, while the poison of bitterness can be measured, to counteract such things, the Father gives the Spirit "without measure" (John 3:34, NASB).

When we have problems, the Spirit comes to us with wisdom, which teaches us a dimension of love, and love actually sends healing balm into our bodies. Faces "light up" when people are released from negative emotions, especially in the area of forgiveness. As we forgive, whoever it may be, friends, family, spouses, etc., we feel freeing, healing power enter into our bodies.

LOVE AND COMPASSION

We have seen that prophecy comes via the path of revelation. God reveals to the prophet His word for that moment. Healing, too, comes by a path or a roadway, and that road, that conduit, the trigger pulled that begins a healing flow, is *compassion*.

In studying the life of Yeshua, we find that He was moved with compassion when He healed the sick. Furthermore, He tells us that He prefers mercy and compassion over sacrifice (Mat 9:13).

Yeshua felt compassion for the people because they were distressed, dispirited, like sheep without a shepherd. He also felt compassion because He knew they were hungry, blind, needed cleansing, teaching, and were weeping with sadness. [93]

We must have the same type of compassion. As chosen ones, we are to put on a heart of compassion, kindness, humility, gentleness and patience (Col 3:12).

Harshness, condemnation and cruelty must not be allowed. It quenches the Spirit, and that is sin (1 Th 5:19). Putting people down can be given no place. God is love. To be used in divine healing, we must move in His love and compassion. Like the Good Samaritan, we must truly care about the hurting ones we find in the ditches of life.

LAYING ON OF HANDS

Compassion and gifts of healings are ministered to the sick through a spoken word— or a touch. We read in Mark 16:17, "These signs shall follow those who believe. They shall *lay hands* on the sick and they shall recover."

In the natural, when we see someone that is sick or in distress, immediately, our hands reach out. It's innate in human beings, we somehow know that our feelings can be transmitted through our hands. Mothers especially know this. When a baby cries at night, the mother puts her hand on it. Hers are hands that bring quiet and comfort. If we see someone sobbing, even if we do not know them, our instinctive reaction is to reach out and touch them in some way. Even so, there are organizations, operating apart from Christianity, that practice imparting strength through their hands. They have found that you can relieve pain by touching the sick.

If they can impart feelings by the laying on of hands, how much more, when we are baptized in the Holy Spirit, can we have His great power flowing through us? It is for us even as promised: "Out of his heart will flow rivers of living water" (John 7:38). Through our touch, healing rivers of living water will flow to the needy. When Abba instructs us to lay hands on someone, we need to believe this truth and impart His healing life.

---

93 Mat 9:36; 14:14; 15:32; 20:34; Mark 1:41; 6:34; Luke 7:13.

SPIRIT-INSPIRED WORDS

When we pray for people, we must not think we will be heard because of our many and supposedly eloquent words. Messiah Yeshua said, "When you pray, do not use vain repetitions as the heathen do. For they think that they will be heard for their many words." The New American Standard reads, "Do not use meaningless repetition as the Gentiles do…. Do not be like them; for your Father knows what you need before you ask Him" (Mat 6:7-8).

Yeshua spoke simply and directly, and the job was done. Like Him, we, too, want to use only the necessary, yet powerful, Spirit-inspired words. He said, "The words I speak to you are spirit and life" (John 6:63). We too want to use words that impart true life.

We can lay hands on people without their knowing it. We can do it with a passing pat on the back. We do not have to have a healing line to pray for the sick. One nurse tells the story that, when with her patients, she silently prays for them and seeks to impart life to them. Even so, some would comment about how they felt uplifted when she was around.

We can do the same. When opportunity arises, we can pray for people without making a "spiritual fuss." We do not need to draw attention to ourselves. We just need to pray in faith.

CALLING FOR THE ELDERS

James, the Lord's brother writes, "Is anyone among you sick? Let him call for the elders of the church, and let them pray over him, anointing him with oil in the name of the Lord" (James 5:14).

Unfortunately, this verse is often taken out of context.

The Greek word translated *sick* has strong meaning, like feeble, diseased, impotent, weak, without strength. More than something like a cold, it means to be extremely ill, even bedridden. [94]

When we are sick and weak, we often feel bad spiritually. Body, soul and spirit are close relatives, and when any one of them is out

---

[94] *Strong's* # G770; from G772.

of sorts, they all suffer. For this reason, Abba, in His mercy, instructs us to have others who are "stronger" to pray and believe for us.

His is a fantastic plan: When we get sick and despair, when it is hard for us to find the strength to pray, we are to call for the elders of the Church. This means, the elders are not to hear about our illness and show up with a bottle of olive oil. The sick person is supposed to *call*— because calling is an act of faith on their part.

This plan reveals healthy, positive inter-dependence: The sick one calls for the elders, which shows dependency, and corporately, all depend on God. When we are sick, we can call a doctor, but the Word specifically tells us to call for our elders and have them pray. In this way, we first submit ourselves to the Father.

ANOINTING OIL AND TZIT-TZIT

Tzit-tzit

Anointing with oil is symbolic of the Ruach haKodesh. We see the connection of anointing with oil and healing in Scripture (1 Sam 16:13; Mark 6:13). However, oil does not heal, but is a symbolic point of contact that can help our faith. The same is true with the *tzit-tzit*, or *fringe* on Messiah Yeshua's garment (worn on the Jewish prayer shawls of today. See example at right). The woman with an issue of blood touched the fringe of Yeshua's garment and was healed. Her healing did not come from Yeshua's tzit-tzit, but from her faith (Mat 9:20-22). [95] Also, a paralyzed man was carried on his bed, and since they could not get to Yeshua because of the crowds, they let the man down through the roof. This effort was indicative of their faith, and the man was delivered and healed (Lk 5:18-26). Even so, we are told that "the prayer of faith will save the sick, and the Lord will raise him up."

---

95 *Strong's* # G2899. *kraspedon*, a fringe or tassel, called *tzit-tzit (tsiytsith)* in Hebrew. This Greek word is used in Numbers 15:38 in the Greek Septuagint to describe the *tzit-tzit*.

WE MUST NOT CALL IT ALL "SIN"

Concerning the sick, we are told, "And if he has committed sins, he will be forgiven" (James 5:15). The "if" in this verse indicates that all sickness is not the result of "personal sin."

Sickness did come into this world as a result of sin, but that does not mean every illness is a result of personal sin. Due to our fallen state, viruses and bacteria float in the air. It is part of the curse of this world that we live in. At least for the time being...

Nonetheless, when someone is sick, our first thoughts tend to be, *"What did they do wrong? What sin do they have in their life?"* If we think this way, we need to remember that YHVH said of Job: "There is no one like him on the earth, a blameless and upright man, fearing God and turning away from evil" (vs. 1:8, NASB).

We also remember that James continued his prayer instructions, saying, "Confess your trespasses to one another, and pray for one another, that you may be healed" (James 5:16). This verse can mean repentance and confession of sin help keep us in right order with Abba, so we will not get sick due to sin. However, it also can mean, if we are preparing to pray for someone, and the Holy Spirit reminds us of sin in our own lives, we too need to openly repent.

We must not hold ourselves aloof; elders especially must be humble, open and honest.

> THE "IF"...
> INDICATES THAT ALL SICKNESS IS NOT THE RESULT OF "PERSONAL SIN"

Finally, we note that James continues with: "The effective, fervent prayer of a righteous man avails much" (James 5:16).

We are more *effective* when we understand the problem at hand. We are *fervent* when we truly care about solving it. And we are *righteous* when we are covered by Messiah's blood.

May it be that we become men and women whose prayers are very effective! Amen!

23

WORKING OF MIRACLES

N ow concerning spiritual gifts....manifestation of the Spirit is
   given to each one for the profit of all ... to one is given the...
working of miracles.... (1 Cor 12:1-11).

Messiah Yeshua worked miracles among the children of Israel.
He was "attested by God to you by miracles, wonders, and signs
which God did through Him." He, and the apostles, were confirmed "with signs and wonders, with various miracles, and gifts
of the Holy Spirit" (Luke 19:37; Acts 2:22; 2 Cor 12:12; Heb 2:3-4).

The Greek word for *miracles* is *dunamis* (doo'-nam-is); meaning
force, miraculous power, mighty work. In Hebrew, the word for
miracles or wonders is *pala'* (paw-law'), which means to separate,
distinguish, great, wonderful, things too high, marvelous. [96] In
English, a *miracle* is an extraordinary event, thing, or accomplishment that manifests a perceptible interruption of law that can only
be explained by divine intervention.

---

96 *Strong's #* G1411 and H 6381, respectively.

WORKING OF MIRACLES

"Working of miracles" (1 Cor 12:10) is translated from two words: *energema*, meaning working, deed, act, and *dunamis*, power, or strong ability. Together they mean "acts of powers."

Like baptisms and healings, "miracles" also is plural, which, in turn, indicates *repeated* works. Hebrews 2:4 speaks of *"various/poikilos /manifold miracles."* [97]

> THE PROMISE IS, "YOU SHALL RECEIVE POWER WHEN THE HOLY SPIRIT HAS COME UPON YOU..." (ACTS 1:8)

So it is that some miracles are unique and may never be repeated, such as walking on water and crossing the Red Sea. However, every Believer is promised *dunamis-miracle-working-power.* The promise is, "You shall receive *power* when the Holy Spirit has come upon you..." (Acts 1:8).

We are promised power to witness, abound, endure, handle suffering, overcome, power to preach, heal, and most important, the power to love. [98] Thus, we can expect to see the power of God at work in our lives.

THE PURPOSES OF MIRACLES

Miracles are spoken of in relation to bringing people to repentance. Again, convincing signs, wonders and miracles confirmed the ministries of our Messiah and His apostles. [99]

Miracles are by definition rare. They are not magic tricks that can be purchased, as Simon the Magician seemed to think (Acts 8:9–13). Miracles are beneficial, resulting in health, safety, and encouragement, and they are given to bring honor to God. The story of the

---

97 *Strong's* #'s G1755; 1411 and 4164.

98 Mk 16:17–18; Acts 1:8; 4:33; Rom 15:13; 1 Cor 2:4; Eph 1:19; 3:14-19; Phil 3:10; Col 1:11; 1 Thes 1:5; 2 Tim 1:8; Heb 2:4.

99 Mat 11:4-6; 11:20-21; Lk 10:13; Acts 2:22; 6:8; 8:6; 9:11; Rom 15:19; 2 Cor 12:12; Heb 2:3.

rich man shows us that miracles in themselves do not necessarily convince people of truth but can awaken and encourage faith. [100] Yet, in the end, we must *first* have a grain of faith. For, "without faith it is impossible to please Him, for he who comes to God must believe that He is, and that He is a rewarder of those who diligently seek Him" (Heb 11:6).

For those who do not believe, no proof is possible; for those who do believe, no proof is necessary.

Miracles and wonders are often mentioned together. Their difference being that, miracles are signs, and signs give a sense of direction. Miracles are signs that point people toward God. Miracles also fill people with amazement.

Wonders create a sense of worship. They are convincing and compelling acts that give a sense of the unending power of our God. [101]

We are not to think these wonders are too hard for us to attain, but instead are commanded to earnestly desire supernatural spiritual gifts (1 Cor 12:31; 14:1). But on the other hand, we must not seek them for the wrong reasons...

> MIRACLES ARE SIGNS... THAT POINT PEOPLE TOWARD GOD.... WONDERS CREATE A SENSE OF WORSHIP... AND... GIVE A SENSE OF THE UNENDING POWER OF OUR GOD

WANTING SIGNS FOR THE WRONG REASONS

Messiah Yeshua once told some followers, "Most assuredly, I say to you, you seek Me, not because you saw the signs, but because you ate of the loaves and were filled. Do not labor for the food which perishes, but for the food which endures to everlasting

---

100 Lk 16:31; John 12:37; Acts 3:16; 14:14-15; 1 Cor 12:7; 14:12.
101 Mat 12:28; Mk 1:27; 2:2; 7:37; Lk 4:36; John 2:11; Acts 2:22; 8:13; Heb 2:4.

life, which the Son of Man will give you, because God the Father has set His seal on Him." Yeshua also sternly warned some questioning Scribes and Pharisees when they said, "Teacher, we want to see a sign from You." But He answered them, "An evil and adulterous generation seeks after a sign" (John 6:26-27; Mat 12:39).

Let us beware. It is *evil* to seek signs for the wrong reasons. Such seeking leads to *spiritual adultery*: We want the signs because we think they will cause others to seek us, and should want them so they will seek the Holy One. We become *adulterous* in that we encourage others to be intimate with us; we seek a place in their lives that should belong to the Father alone. We thus become self-serving and prideful. We become users of God instead of being used by God. For this reason, we must continually search our hearts, asking the Father to reveal to us any wrong motives: "The heart is deceitful above all things, and desperately wicked: who can know it?" (Jer 17:9). Our hearts must be right in these matters. We must earnestly desire to see signs and wonders, but only because they point people to the Holy One.

As those who seek the restoration of the whole house of Israel, we especially need to be armed with the advantage of miracles, signs and wonders. We see their benefits when preaching the Gospel of the Kingdom. Our Messiah was armed with these things, as were many of His disciples. Thus people were brought to repentance (Mat 4:23; 9:35; 24:14; Mark 1:15; Luke 16:16).

For example, when Philip went to Samaria and preached, multitudes heard him and saw the miracles he did. The result was that "unclean spirits, crying with a loud voice, came out of many who were possessed; and many who were paralyzed and lame were healed. And there was great joy in that city." Indeed, "notable miracles" make the truth "evident," and we desperately need that joy-giving evidence in our lives (Acts 4:16; 8:5–8). [102]

Let us therefore desire these things with a pure heart.

---

[102] Thanks to http://www.wesleymission.org.au/ministry/chant/050501.asp for making available their helpful study on the subject of miracles.

24

DISCERNING OF SPIRITS

*C*oncerning spiritual gifts.... To one is given... discerning of spirits.... (1 Cor 12:1-11).

Discerning of spirits is more than having a hunch about someone. Discerning of spirits, or discernment, as some call it, is not the gift of suspicion. It is not natural knowledge, nor is it an insight that comes from experience. It is not mere suspicion or intuition. It is instead a supernatural inner-knowing, it is knowledge of a matter that comes from the Holy Spirit.

This endowment often seems to be counterfeited and abused by Believers who are mistakenly thought to be "more mature." It also is sometimes employed to manipulate the naive. Some, who claim to have discernment, when all they have is suspicion, have left a trail of ruin. For the sake of "appearing spiritual," and wanting to focus attention on self, they claim to discern things about an individual, and it may or may not be true. True discerning of spirits is given by the Ruach haKodesh to *help* others, not to embarrass or destroy the lives of fellow Believers. Whenever possible, negative insights should be shared in private (Mat 18:15). Discerning of spirits must not be confused with criticism, faultfinding, suspicion and judgmental attitudes.

PSYCHICS AND SUCH...

Psychics, palm readers and fortune tellers often claim to have the gift of discerning of spirits; they claim to have a supernatural ability to see into the spirit realm, and they claim their gift is given to them by "God." However, theirs is not the gift of discerning of spirits as given by the Holy One. Palm reading, soothsaying, fortune telling, psychic seances and such are forms of witchcraft — which is strictly forbidden (Deu 18:10-12). Those who are involved in ghost hunting and psychic phenomena are not operating by the Holy Spirit of God.

Paul was once being followed by a woman who kept crying out, "These men are the servants of the most high God, who proclaim to us the way of salvation." She was actually possessed by a demonic spirit of divination and by it, gained money for her masters. She did this for many days, and Paul, being greatly annoyed, said to the spirit, "I command you in the name of Jesus to come out of her." And he came out that very hour. But, when her masters saw that their hope of profit was gone, they seized Paul and Silas and drug them off to the authorities (Acts 16:16-9).

The spirit of divination is a demonic spirit by which sooth-sayers, palm readers, fortune tellers and those who practice such things work to deceive others into accepting false reports or false "fortunes" that are *not* given by the Spirit of God.

Such things are strictly forbidden and must not be confused with the manifestation of the Ruach known as discerning of spirits. They are not the same.

For every true endowment of the Holy Spirit, Satan has a counterfeit for the purpose of deception. Divination is just one such perverted imitation.

DISCERNING THE DRIVING FORCE

The manifestation of discerning of spirits, like all of the other spiritual endowments is given and operated as the Lord wills, not as man wills. Discerning of spirits is the supernatural ability to discern the driving force in a given situation. It is a gift that allows one to know whether a situation or person is being affected by an evil spirit or by the Holy Spirit. It can be used to identify heavenly beings, as well as the character and heart of a man. It is the supernatural ability to see into what is often called the fourth dimension, to see into the spirit realm. This realm coexists with the natural realm in which we live today. To better understand this spirit realm dimension where celestial creatures exist, we will use an illustration about a fish and his pond.

Consider a typical pond where there are fish swimming, frogs croaking, lily pads and cattails growing along the bank. The fish have never been out of the pond. As far as they are concerned, nothing exists outside of it. Their pond is their entire world; it is the realm in which they live. The dimension in which they exist consists of water, plants, fish, insects, and anything else that enters into the pond. On occasion they see drops of water that cause the tops of the lily pads to move, but they have no concept of rain or anything else outside of life in their pond. Never having been outside, they lack the ability to see or understand that their realm/ dimension coexists with another, unknown realm. They do not see, understand, or know of it, but it nonetheless clearly exists alongside their world.

Now let's imagine that one day, a fisherman catches one of the fish and he ends up outside his pond. Suddenly, he sees that, strange and inhospitable as it may seem, there is an existence beyond his known realm. If we transfer human emotion to this fish, we can imagine that his is a frightening experience.

Mankind is like the fish. Men who have not seen into the spiritual realm have little concept of what exists around them, because that dimension is hidden from them.

Discerning of spirits is God's discretional opening of spiritual eyes whereby He imparts to us an ability to supernaturally see into the spirit realm that exists all around us. In this other dimension, in this spirit world, we find YHVH's earlier creation of righteous angels, and we find fallen demons. This dimension is commonly referred to as the *heavenly realm*. However, that term is misleading in that, the spirit realm does not exist *only* in the heavens. It coexists with the realm in which we live in, in the *natural realm*. It also exists everywhere, on earth, in heaven, and in hell itself.

When YHVH wills to give one of His servants the ability to discern spirits, He is allowing that individual to see into this realm for a period of time and for His purposes. The individual will sometimes observe angels or demons or both. The gift is given to impart wisdom and knowledge regarding a situation, or to inform of spiritual battles taking place, or to see demonic attacks. This gift also can be used to reveal if and when sickness is the result of demonic oppression. It is even used to bring encouragement.

ENCOURAGEMENT

When the roll is called up yonder, when the great shofar is sounded, the dead in Messiah will rise first, and all who are alive and in Messiah Yeshua meet Him in the air. One day, when our mortality puts on immortality, we will have a body like Yeshua's resurrected body (1Cor 15:53; 1 Thes 4:16). And, it appears that we will not only be able to see into the spirit realm, but will traverse back and forth even as the angels do today.

When Yeshua rose from the tomb as the firstborn of the resurrection, He was raised with a glorified body. All who find salvation in Yeshua will, one day, have the same kind of body. "For our citizenship is in heaven, from which we also eagerly wait for the Savior, the Lord Jesus Christ, who will transform our lowly body that it may be conformed to His glorious body, according to the working by which He is able even to subdue all things to Himself" (Phil 3:20-21).

A glorified body seems to be at home in the spirit and natural realms. Yeshua seems to have moved between them, because He suddenly appeared when doors were shut, for fear of some Jews. He stood before His disciples and said, "Peace be with you" (John 20:19). Then He vanished. Luke tells of Yeshua meeting two disciples on the road to Emmaus. "Their eyes were opened and they knew Him," then He vanished from sight (see Luke 24:13-53).

When Yeshua returns and we are given new immortal bodies, just like His, we too will be able to traverse between the natural realm and spirit realms. Our eyes will be opened to see and commune with the angels. This is certainly most encouraging!

For now, we note that the gift of discernment does not always entail seeing into the spiritual realm, but often manifests as a "knowing" in one's spirit. Discernment is given to identify the nature, or character, of spirits, including those seen and those not seen. It includes discerning the presence of the Holy Spirit, angelic spirits, demonic or satanic spirits, and the human spirit.

Various Visions

In Scripture, we see that people often saw into the spirit realm. For instance, the angel of the Lord appeared to Moses in a blazing fire from the midst of a bush. Balaam saw the Angel of the Lord standing in the way with His drawn sword in His hand. The Angel of the Lord appeared to Gideon and said, "The Lord is with you, you mighty man of valor!" One having the likeness of the sons of men touched Daniel's lips and strengthened him. And, the women at Yeshua's tomb said they had seen angels (Exo 3:2; Num 22:31; Judg 6:11-12; Dan 10:16-18; Luke 24:22-23). Peter experienced an angelic visitation concerning Cornelius. And Peter, James, and John all saw Elijah and Moses speaking with Messiah Yeshua. They even heard the Father saying, "This is My beloved Son. Hear Him!" John the Revelator similarly saw and spoke with an angel (Acts 10:3; Mark 9:2-9; Rev 22:8-9). These are but a few of the many examples that can be found in Scripture.

A WARNING

We need to be careful about what we ask for. Discerning of spirits is not for the timid or weak of heart. In today's world people love angels. They are the latest fad. Everybody wants to see angels. People are taken by them, fascinated by the idea of being able to see them. But we must keep in mind that the spiritual endowment of discerning of spirits doesn't just allow us to see into a realm of good things, such as current concepts of angels. Instead, or included, are visions of demons as well. So let us not seek this gift for the purpose of seeing only the "good side." That is unwise. We will surely see evil spirits as well. [103]

Balance is often key to understanding Scripture. Yet, some Believers become obsessed with the idea of demons. They blame everything on Satan. They even seem to think he is more powerful than the Almighty. They do not seem to take in the works of the flesh and find demons under every bush and in every corner.

We must not get out of balance with such things. We must be diligent to maintain balance and not allow seeing into the spirit realm to cause us to be overly zealous, wanting to see demons or angels all the time and convincing ourselves that every flicker of light is an angel or every shadow a demon.

There is a danger in "pressing in" to the spirit realm— when it is not a true and Godly call. Satan will surely show us things for his own deceptive purposes. True discernment by the Spirit will allow us to see what God wants us to see. To press into the spirit realm without true guidance from the Holy Spirit, is to press in without permission. We can be deceived, a door for demonic attack can be opened, a deceptive or familiar spirit of divination can attempt to imitate the Ruach. To try to see into the spirit realm outside of God's will, falls under the category of witchcraft. We need to be sensitive to the moving of God's Holy Spirit and use discerning of spirits only as YHVH wants the gift used.

---

103 Thanks to Cheri D. Holt of *Hope of Glory Ministries:* www.hopeofgloryministry.com
For more information, see Addendum B— Demons and Deliverance, page 209.

25

RELEASING THE SPIRIT WITHIN

We want to be people through whom the Holy One of Israel can release the greatness of His Holy Spirit. When we are obedient to the eternal truths of Torah, the Spirit can operate more fully in our lives. However, we must realize that it is not our good works that release His awesome power. Instead, it is our trust, belief, dependence and faith in the Almighty that lead to the release His miraculous works in our lives.

Paul asked a question in Galatians 3:2, "Did you receive the Spirit by the works of the Law, or by hearing with faith?"

He asked this question knowing its answer was obvious: No matter how good they might be, works of the Torah do not cause us to receive the Spirit. This does not mean we are then free to be disobedient or negligent in regard to its truths, because we are called to obedience. It instead means we look to Yeshua to heal us, deliver us, and build us up. The Canaanite woman who came to Him for healing for her daughter was rewarded, because of her great trust in Yeshua's ability to heal.

We need to have the same attitude.

We see healing and supernatural manifestations when we are in love with and believe absolutely in Yeshua. When we seek His face, we begin to see His hand at work with miracles. When we walk in His love, it proves the "weighty matters of Torah" are important to us. Our love gives evidence to the fact that we value things like justice, mercy and faithfulness.

We must be madly in love with Yeshua. Torah is a straight path to Him, but we need to beware getting off course by taking pride in our observance of it or in external acts of piety. If we go down that mistaken path, our eyes will be fixed on our selves and not on Yeshua. Such errant attitudes will short-circuit the power of the Spirit today, even as they did in Yeshua's day. [104]

THE KEY TO RELEASING THE GIFTS: LOVE

We must realize that life is but a job-placement program; it helps to prepare us for eternity. Life also is a series of problems. Either we are in one now, we're just coming out of one, or we're getting ready to go into another one. Life is like that because our God is more interested in our character than He is in our comfort. He is more interested in making our life holy than He is in making our life happy. We can be reasonably happy here on earth, but that is not the goal of life. Our goal is to grow in character, in Christ-likeness. Our goal is to learn to love even as He loved.

If we focus on our problems, we become self-centered: We focus on *our* problems, *our* issues, *our* pain. The best way to get rid of pain and problems is to get our focus off ourselves and onto God and others, to instead focus on loving Him, and our fellow man.

We have to deal with both the good and bad of life. In so doing, we need to know that Abba is more interested in what we are than He is in what we do. That's why we're called human beings and not human doings. What we need to *be*, is, people who love others.

---

104 John Conrad (Messianic Israel Alliance Shepherd), Messianic Israel Talk Group (yahoo.com), 01/12/09.

WE ARE EQUIPPED—
WITH EVERYTHING WE NEED

In the Second Book of Timothy, an aged apostle Paul writes a letter to his beloved son in the faith, Timothy. In it, Paul says he is being poured out as a drink offering and that the time of his departure is at hand. He says he has fought the good fight, finished the race, and kept the faith. Paul is preparing to leave this world, so he gives some sound advice to a precious son whom he trusts to continue the work (see chapter 4).

In chapter three, Paul warns:

"Know this, that in the last days perilous times will come: For men will be lovers of themselves, lovers of money, boasters, proud, blasphemers, disobedient to parents, unthankful, unholy, unloving, unforgiving, slanderers, without self-control, brutal, despisers of good, traitors, headstrong, haughty, lovers of pleasure rather than lovers of God, having a form of godliness but denying its power. And from such people turn away! For of this sort are those who creep into households and make captives of gullible women loaded down with sins, led away by various lusts, always learning and never able to come to the knowledge of the truth. Now as Jannes and Jambres resisted Moses, so do these also resist the truth: men of corrupt minds, disapproved concerning the faith.... But you have carefully followed my doctrine, manner of life, purpose, faith, longsuffering, love, perseverance, persecutions, afflictions, which ... persecutions I endured. And out of them all the Lord delivered me. Yes, and all who desire to live godly in Christ Jesus will suffer persecution. But evil men and impostors will grow worse and worse, deceiving and being deceived. But you must continue in the things which you have learned and been assured of, knowing from whom you have learned them, and that from childhood you have known the Holy

Scriptures, which are able to make you wise for salvation through faith which is in Christ Jesus. All Scripture is given by inspiration of God, and is profitable for doctrine, for reproof, for correction, for instruction in righteousness, that the man of God may be complete, thoroughly equipped for every good work" (2 Tim 3:1-17).

Surely we live in the last days of which Paul warned, and it is even as he said it would be. Moreover, our Messiah essentially warned the same thing: "Because lawlessness will abound, the love of many will grow cold" (Mat 24:12).

The love of many is now waxing cold; an abundance of evil now surrounds us. Yet, we remember that our Messiah continued His discourse with these words, "But he who endures to the end shall be saved."

We must endure to the end, and it is the Holy Spirit that will help us do that. We also must remember that Messiah said, "This gospel of the kingdom"— specifically, the gospel that tells of the raising up and full restoration of the fallen house of David— "will be preached in all the world as a witness to all the nations, and then the end will come" (Amos 9:11; Mat 24:12-14; Acts 15:16).

We, those who want to see the kingdom restored to the whole house of Israel, have a job to do. We have been given a mandate to preach the gospel of the kingdom, *with transforming power*. And, we cannot do the job we are called to do apart from being imbued with, clothed from on High, empowered by, the Holy Spirit.

Our first martyr, Stephen, cried out saying, "You stiff-necked and uncircumcised in heart and ears! You always resist the Holy Spirit; as your fathers did, so do you" (Acts 7:51).

As children of Israel we must move to a place where it is no longer said that we resist the Ruach haKodesh. To get there, we must realize that, while truths about the Holy Spirit may not be as some have taught in the past, we absolutely know we need Him and His transforming power. Israel simply cannot get where she needs to go apart from the power of the Holy Spirit.

We also must realize that it is not a matter of whether we have this or that gift, as though we could possess such holy things. Instead, it is a matter of, in the Spirit, we are made complete, and we are thoroughly equipped for every good work. We can trust that the God of peace, who brought up from the dead the great Shepherd of the sheep through the blood of the eternal covenant, even Messiah Yeshua, will "equip" us in every good thing to do His will. He will work in us that which is pleasing in His sight and give us what we need to do our part (Heb 13:20-21).

The Father will throughly *equip/katartizo* us. He will repair, adjust, and mend us. He will do whatever is necessary to make us fit for the job He sets before us. Even as promised, in the last days, He will perfectly join His two houses together. He will restore us (Eze 37:15-28). As His children, we can trust that He will perfect us for every good work to which He calls us. In and by the power of His Spirit, we will be *thoroughly furnished* (2 Tim 3:17). 105

Thus, we conclude that: We have available to us *all* of the Holy Spirit, and that is to be our focus. We need His transforming *power*. We want *genuine* giftings and not anything that is counterfeit. Moreover, what we yearn for, man has not yet seen!

What we seek has not been manifested in the earth. If it were already found in this world the problem would be solved, and we would not be searching. As stated earlier, we cannot fully comprehend our incomprehensible God. He said through Isaiah, "As the heavens are higher than the earth, so are My ways higher than your ways and My thoughts than your thoughts" (Isa 55:9).

His ways and thoughts are higher than ours. Thus, it is impossible for mortal man to provide an all-encompassing description of the ways of His Holy Spirit.

---

105 *Strong's* #'s G2675. katartizo, kat-ar-tid'-zo; from G2596 and a der. of G739; to complete thoroughly, i.e. repair (lit. or fig.) or adjust:--fit, frame, mend, (make) perfect (-ly join together), prepare, restore. G2596. kata, speaks of being "joined." Also, G1822. exartizo, ex-ar-tid'-zo; from G1537 and a der. of G739; to finish out (time); fig. to equip fully (a teacher):--accomplish, thoroughly furnish.

To help in our search and growth in understanding of spiritual endowments, rather than claim to be able to adequately define what they are, we often have to resort to defining what they are not. But this much we do know: *When we cry out, the Holy One hears us from Heaven and responds to our needs.*

> Our forefathers said, "We cried to the LORD, the God of our fathers, and the LORD heard our voice and…He brought us out of Egypt with a mighty hand and an outstretched arm and with great terror and with signs and wonders…" (Deu 26:7-8; also see Num 20:16; Neh 9:9, NASB).
>
> King David said, "In my distress I called upon the LORD, Yes, I cried to my God; and from His temple He heard my voice, and my cry for help came into His ears" (2 Sam 22:7. Also, see Psa 18:6). And, "I waited patiently for the LORD; and He inclined to me and heard my cry" (Psa 40:1, NASB). [106]

Our Father looks upon our distress and responds— *when He hears our cry!* He says, "Call to Me, and I will answer you, and show you great and mighty things, which you do not know" (Jer 33:3). He says, "I am the LORD your God, who brought you out of the land of Egypt; open your mouth wide, and I will fill it" (Psa 81:10). He has great and mighty plans for us. They are plans of peace that give us "a future and a hope" (Jer 29:11). In the Spirit, He has given us talents, and we want to be servants who are wise enough not to bury them but to instead make good use of them (Mat 25:14-30).

Let us therefore cry out and ask our Father to fill us with the fullness of His Holy Spirit— and to show us great and mighty things that bring Him glory. Let us open our mouths wide, knowing that He will fill and empower us with His Holy Spirit. Let us trust Him to lead, guide, and use us mightily in the exciting times that surely lie just ahead.

Amen and Amen!

So Be It!

---

106 Also see Psa 31:22; 106:44; Lam 3:56; Mark 10:47-49.

ADDENDUM A—
A NEUROSCIENTIFIC LOOK AT
SPEAKING IN TONGUES

The following article appeared in the New York Times Newspaper. For the sake of further study, we reproduce it here, as well as the complete scientific Report from which the article was taken.

A Neuroscientific Look at Speaking in Tongues
by Benedict Carey
November 7, 2006, The New York Times, Health, Correction Appended
The Measurement of Regional Cerebral Blood Flow During Glossolalia:
A Preliminary SPECT Study (Psychiatry Research: Neuroimaging)

The passionate, sometimes rhythmic, language-like patter that pours forth from religious people who "speak in tongues" reflects a state of mental possession, many of them say. Now they have some neuroscience to back them up.

Researchers at the University of Pennsylvania took brain images of five women while they spoke in tongues and found that their frontal lobes— the thinking, willful part of the brain through which people control what they do— were relatively quiet, as were the language centers. The regions involved in maintaining self-consciousness were active. The women were not in blind trances, and it was unclear which region was driving the behavior.

The images, appearing in the current issue of the journal Psychiatry Research: Neuroimaging, pinpoint the most active areas of the brain. The images are the first of their kind taken during this spoken religious practice, which has roots in the Old and New Testaments and in Pentecostal churches established in the early 1900s. The women in the study were healthy, active churchgoers.

"The amazing thing was how the images supported people's interpretation of what was happening," said Dr. Andrew B. Newberg, leader of the study team, which included Donna Morgan, Nancy Wintering and Mark Waldman. "The way they describe it, and what they believe, is that God is talking through them," he said.

Dr. Newberg is also a co-author of "Why We Believe What We Believe."

In the study, the researchers used imaging techniques to track changes in blood flow in each woman's brain in two conditions, once as she sang a gospel song and again while speaking in tongues. By comparing the patterns created by these two emotional, devotional activities, the researchers could pinpoint blood-flow peaks and valleys unique to speaking in tongues.

Ms. Morgan, a co-author of the study, was also a research subject. She is a born-again Christian who says she considers the ability to speak in tongues a gift. "You're aware of your surroundings," she said. "You're not really out of control. But you have no control over what's happening. You're just flowing. You're in a realm of peace and comfort, and it's a fantastic feeling."

Contrary to what may be a common perception, studies suggest that people who speak in tongues rarely suffer from mental problems. A recent study of nearly 1,000 evangelical Christians in England found that those who engaged in the practice were more emotionally stable than those who did not. Researchers have identified at least two forms of the practice, one ecstatic and frenzied, the other subdued and nearly silent.

The new findings contrasted sharply with images taken of other spiritually inspired mental states like meditation, which is often a highly focused mental exercise, activating the frontal lobes.

The scans also showed a dip in the activity of a region called the left caudate. "The findings from the frontal lobes are very clear, and make sense, but the caudate is usually active when you have positive affect, pleasure, positive emotions," said Dr. James A. Coan, a psychologist at the University of Virginia. "So it's not so clear what that finding says" about speaking in tongues.

The caudate area is also involved in motor and emotional control, Dr. Newberg said, so it may be that practitioners, while mindful of their circumstances, nonetheless cede some control over their bodies and emotions.

Correction: Nov. 11, 2006

An article in Science Times on Tuesday about brain images of people speaking in tongues misstated the origins of the practice in America. It is thought to have begun in Pentecostal churches established in the early 1900s, not in charismatic churches. The charismatic movement began decades later.

Related Web Link: The Measurement of Regional Cerebral Blood Flow During Glossolalia: Preliminary SPECT Study (Psychiatry Research: Neuroimaging). [107]

---

[107] See: ww.nytimes.com/2006/11/07/health/07brain.html?_r=1
www.nytimes.com/imagepages/2006/11/06/health/20061107_BRAIN_GRAPHIC.html

The New York Times

Evidence for a Religious State

Scientists found notable changes in brain activity when people speak in tongues. The brain scans below show blood flow in the brain (blue lowest, red highest).

SINGING GOSPEL SONG

SPEAKING IN TONGUES

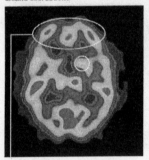 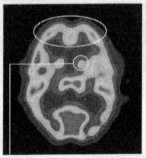

Frontal lobes Involved in the willful control of behaviors; more activity when singing than when speaking tongues.

Left caudate Involved in motor and emotional control; less activity in those speaking in tongues.

Source: Andrew B. Newberg, University of Pennsylvania

The New York Times

BRIEF REPORT

The following is a published "Article In Press" at Science Direct (www.sciencedirect.com).

By: Andrew B. Newberg et al., The Measurement of Regional Cerebral Blood Flow During Glossolalia: a Preliminary SPECT Study, Psychiatry Research: Neuroimaging (2006), doi:10.1016/j.pscychresns.2006.07.001.

Brief Report:
The measurement of regional cerebral blood flow during *glossolalia:* [108]
A preliminary SPECT study

Andrew B. Newberg, [109] Nancy A. Wintering, [110] Donna Morgan, [111] Mark R. Waldman [112]

Received 9 May 2006; received in revised form 20 July 2006; accepted 25 July 2006

1. Introduction

---

[108] Glossolalia (or "speaking in tongues") is an unusual mental state that has great personal and religious meaning. Glossolalia is experienced as a normal and expected behavior in religious prayer groups in which the individual appears to be speaking in an incomprehensible language. This is the first functional neuroimaging study to demonstrate changes in cerebral activity during glossolalia. The frontal lobes, parietal lobes, and left caudate were most affected.

© 2006 Elsevier Ireland Ltd. All rights reserved. Keywords: Glossolalia; Cerebral blood flow; Single photon emission tomography

[109] Division of Nuclear Medicine, Department of Radiology, University of Pennsylvania Medical Center, 110 Donner Building, 3400 Spruce Street, Philadelphia, PA 19104, United States

Center for Spirituality and the Mind, University of Pennsylvania, Philadelphia, PA, United States

Corresponding author. Tel.: +1 215 662 3014; fax: +1 215 349 5843.

E-mail address: andrew.newberg@uphs.upenn.edu (A.B. Newberg).

[110] Division of Nuclear Medicine, Department of Radiology, University of Pennsylvania Medical Center, 110 Donner Building, 3400 Spruce Street, Philadelphia, PA 19104, United States

Center for Spirituality and the Mind, University of Pennsylvania, Philadelphia, PA, United States

[111] Division of Nuclear Medicine, Department of Radiology, University of Pennsylvania Medical Center, 110 Donner Building, 3400 Spruce Street, Philadelphia, PA 19104, United States

[112] Center for Spirituality and the Mind, University of Pennsylvania, Philadelphia, PA, United States

Glossolalia, sometimes referred to as "speaking in tongues," is an unusual mental state associated with specific religious traditions. The individual appears to be speaking in an incomprehensible language over which he or she claims to have no control. Yet, the individual perceives glossolalia to have great personal meaning. The individual also describes a lack of voluntary control over the vocalizations. Studies have shown that the vocalizations, which often are part of singing, are not related to any clear linguistic structure (Samarin, 1972). It is unclear whether glossolalia is related to psychopathology (Hine, 1969; Lovekin and Malony, 1977), and one study suggested that abnormal temporal lobe activity could be a possible cause of glossolalia (Persinger, 1984). Since there are no imaging studies of this phenomenon, we wanted to determine if glossolalia was associated with specific changes in cerebral activity.

We present the ^{99m}Tc-Bicisate (Bristol Myers Squibb, N. Billerica, MA) SPECT data from five practitioners of glossolalia. We compared glossolalia to a religious singing state since the latter is similar except that it involves actual language (English). The SPECT technique used in this study measures regional cerebral blood flow (CBF) that correlates closely with cerebral activity.

This technique was previously validated (Newberg et al., 2005) and also used in our similar study on meditation (Newberg et al., 2001).

We tested several hypotheses regarding glossolalia: (1) it is known that the frontal lobes are involved in willful control of behaviors (Frith et al., 1991; Pardo et al., 1991). We hypothesized that glossolalia, associated with the perceived loss of intentional control, would be associated with decreased activity in the frontal lobes compared with singing; (2) we previously argued that in practices such as meditation, there is decreased activity in the superior parietal lobe (SPL) because of the altered sense of self (Lynch, 1980; Newberg et al., 2001). This is not described in glossolalia, and thus we expected no such decrease; (3) glossolalia is a highly active state, and hence we expected increased CBF in the thalamus related to overall increased cerebral activity; (4) we expected increased activity in the limbic areas such as the amygdala since glossolalia is a very emotional state.

2. Methods

2.1. *Subjects and imaging acquisition*

We recruited five women ranging from 38 to 52 years with a mean of 45 years (both men and women perform glossolalia, but in our community, there is a preponderance of women). Each subject described herself as a Christian in a Charismatic or Pentecostal tradition who had practiced glossolalia for more than 5 years. All were active, stable members of their communities. On the study day, informed consent (approved by the Institutional Review Board) was obtained. Structured clinical interviews excluded current psychiatric conditions, without considering the practice of speaking in tongues.

Thus, none of the subjects reported visual or auditory hallucinations, mood disorders, or exhibited any clear evidence of current Axis I or II disorders (American Psychiatric Association, 1994). It should be noted that one subject reported a history of substance abuse but had been abstinent for 4 years. In addition, subjects did not have any active neurological or medical conditions, or take medications that would affect cerebral function.

Subjects had to have a negative pregnancy test. Initially, an intravenous cannula (IV) was placed in one arm with a long IV line to permit relatively free range of movement, needed for singing and glossolalia.

The subject began singing in the room while standing, with her eyes closed, matching her condition during glossolalia. Earphones were used to play music to sing and to perform glossolalia (the same music was used for both). The subject sang for 5 min at which time she was injected through the IV with 7 mCi of ^{99m}Tc-Bicisate. The subject continued singing for 15 min, at which time the singing state was terminated and she was brought to the SPECT scanner for a 40-min scan.

Images were acquired on a Picker-Prism 3000 XP (Picker Inc, Cleveland, OH) triple-headed scanner using high resolution fan beam collimators. Projection images were obtained at 3° angle intervals on a 128×128 matrix (pixel size 3.56 mm $\times$ 3.56 mm) over 360°. SPECT images were reconstructed using filtered backprojection, followed by a low pass filter and 1st order Chang attenuation correction.

Following the "singing" scan, the subject returned to the room to perform glossolalia. It began with the music playing and the person initially singing, and then relatively quickly entering into the glossolalia state (usually within 5 min). Once the subject was observed performing glossolalia for 5 min, she was unobtrusively injected with 25 mCi of ^{99m}Tc-ECD. The subject continued to perform glossolalia for 15 min and then the session was ended. The subject was then scanned ("glossolalia" scan) for 30 min using the same imaging parameters as above.

It should be noted that we observed all subjects to ensure that the two conditions (singing and glossolalia) were as similar as possible in terms of patient vocalization and motion with the exception of the glossolalia itself. Both conditions involved listening to music and singing, which was voluntary and performed while listening to gospel music. The glossolalia was perceived to be non-voluntary by the subjects. Subjects were standing throughout both conditions and were moving both their arms and legs in a similar rhythmic manner during both conditions. We did not observe any particular changes in the motor cortex, which suggests that the patient's motion was not significantly different between the two states. The phonemic structure was different between the two conditions since the singing was associated with clear grammatical sentences, although they were often brief utterances such as "Praise God" or "Thank you, Jesus" in both conditions. The phonemic structure during the glossolalia state was variable with periods of increased and decreased intensity, volume, and speed, although certain "phrases" were repeated a number of times.

2.2. *Image analysis and statistics*

The singing and glossolalia scans were resliced and coregistered. A previously validated template consisting of regions of interest (ROIs) corresponding to major cortical and subcortical structures was placed over the singing scan (Resnick et al., 1993). Each ROI was adjusted manually to achieve the best fit. ROIs were then copied directly onto the glossolalia scan. Count values for the glossolalia scans were obtained by determining the counts in each ROI and subtracting the number of counts in the same ROI on the singing scan (decay corrected to the midpoint of the two scans). Counts per pixel in each ROI were normalized to whole brain activity yielding a CBF ratio. A percentage change was calculated for each region. A laterality index (LI) representing the percentage difference between the right and left side was also calculated.

CBF ratios were compared between the glossolalia and singing state using a paired t-test (Minitab Statistical Software, 2000). The LI for each homologous pair of ROIs in the singing and glossolalia states was compared using paired t-tests as well. Our results were hypothesis driven so comparisons were only tested for the major structures of the frontal, temporal, and parietal lobes, as well as the amygdala, hippocampus, striatum, and thalamus, and thus a correction for multiple comparisons was not performed.

3. Results

The data between the glossolalia and singing state revealed several significant rCBF differences (see Table 1 and Fig. 1). There were significant decreases in the prefrontal cortices, left caudate and left temporal pole while there were increases in the left superior parietal lobe (SPL) and right amygdala. There was a significant negative correlation (R=-0.90, P=0.03) between the singing and glossolalia thalamic LI, indicating that the more the thalamic activity was asymmetric to begin with, the more the asymmetry reversed during glossolalia.

4. Discussion

References to speaking in tongues–or glossolalia, as it is technically called–can be found in the Old and New Testaments, but until the 20th Century, only brief references have been made. Its more recent rise in use is believed to have originated at the Azusa Street Mission when a woman named Agnes Ozman first began to speak in tongues and initiated the charismatic movement in the United States (Balmer, 2001). More recently, researchers at the University of London identified two distinct forms of glossolalia (Grady and Loewenthal, 1997). The first, which we studied in this report, is the more dramatic form, involving singing, vocal utterances, and ecstatic bodily experiences. However, the researchers found that many practitioners engage in a gentler, almost silent glossolalic prayer that is associated with calm, pleasant emotions.

Originally, it was thought that glossolalia was related to some form of psychopathology by the biomedical community. However, the limited number of reported studies have suggested that people who speak in tongues show no differences in personality traits from other population groups— no increases in depression, anxiety, mania, or psychosis (Hine, 1969; Richardson, 1973). In fact, only a small percentage of mentally ill people exhibit glossolalia, and when they do, the hallucinations often have a religious content (Hempel et al., 2002). One recent study involved nearly a thousand clergy members of a British evangelical group. The researchers found that the 80% who practiced glossolalia had greater emotional stability and less neuroticism (Francis and Robbins, 2003). Other studies have not supported the finding that glossolalia has health benefits, but neither did they find any negative psychological effects (Louden and Francis, 2001).

The present study is the first we are aware of that has evaluated changes in cerebral activity during the practice of glossolalia. Regarding our hypotheses, we observed decreased activity in the prefrontal cortices during the glossolalia state. This finding was clearly distinct from our previous study of meditation using the same imaging technique (Newberg et al., 2001). Neuroimaging studies have also shown increased frontal lobe activity during attention-focusing tasks (Frith et al., 1991; Pardo et al., 1991). It is interesting that the frontal lobes showed decreased perfusion during glossolalia, but this is consistent with the subjects' description of a lack of intentional control over the performance of glossolalia. A left lateralization in the frontal lobes might be expected since singing and glossolalia are related to language functions. While such a lateralization was not robust, the left hemispheric structures appeared to have significant decreases that were not observed in the right hemisphere. However, the lack of a clear lateralization in the frontal lobes suggests that the expressive language parts of the brain may not be as directly affected by glossolalia as might be expected.

Our second hypothesis predicted no change in the SPL. We have previously argued, and found, decreased activity in the SPL during meditation in which there is a described loss of the sense of self. However, glossolalia was not associated with a loss of the sense of self and there were no significant decreases in the SPL.

We did not observe the hypothesized increase in thalamic activity. However, there was a shift in thalamic LI between the singing and glossolalia scans. It is not clear what such a finding may represent from a physiological perspective, but the thalamus is a major cortical and cortical–subcortical relay, serving as a gating function of neuronal information. This might be important for altering the sense of control in which practitioners no longer feel as if they are willfully making the vocalizations.

Our fourth hypothesis was that there would be increased activity in the limbic structures, and there was a trend towards increased activity in the right amygdala. An earlier report described seizure-like electrical activity in a subject during prolonged glossolalia (Persinger, 1984). The marginally increased activity observed in our study does not elucidate the exact relationship between the limbic system and glossolalia, nor does it rule out the possibility of seizure activity. The significant decrease in the left caudate is of uncertain significance but may relate to the altered emotional activity during glossolalia.

Potential confounding problems with this study include the fact that the subjective sense reported during glossolalia is difficult to measure.

However, it is easy to observe when an individual is performing glossolalia, so there is little doubt that the injection of Bicisate occurred during that state. Future studies should also evaluate the phonemic structure of the vocalizations in glossolalia to understand the basic units of this vocalization and to compare these to imaging results. This study measured CBF at a single point during glossolalia, at a relatively early time point. Future studies might determine whether there are different changes after a longer time performing glossolalia. The study has a limited number of subjects since it is difficult to find experienced practitioners willing to perform glossolalia in a laboratory setting. While this complicates the statistical analysis, the number of subjects was sufficient to reveal statistically significant results.

The results from this preliminary study have begun to elucidate the neuophysiological correlates of glossolalia. That there were changes in several brain structures suggests that there is complex brain activity during this unusual practice. Future studies should explore the cerebral correlates of glossolalia in a larger sample incorporating physiological and neurophysiological measures in addition to a more elaborate analysis of the phonemic structure of glossolalia.

References:

American Psychiatric Association, 1994. Diagnostic and Statistical Manual of Mental Disorders, fourth edition. APA, Washington, DC.

Balmer, R., 2001. Religion in 20th Century America. Oxford University Press, Oxford.

Francis, L., Robbins, M., 2003. Personality and glossolalia: a study among male evangelical clergy. Pastoral Psychology 51, 5.

Frith, C.D., Friston, K., Liddle, P.F., Frackowiak, R.S.J., 1991. Willed action and the prefrontal cortex in man. A study with PET. Proceedings of the Royal Society of London 244, 241–246.

Grady, B., Loewenthal, K.M., 1997. Features associated with speaking in tongues (glossolalia). British Journal of Medical Psychology 70, 185–191.

Hempel, A.G., Meloy, J.R., Stern, R., Ozone, S.J., Gray, B.T., 2002. Fiery tongues and mystical motivations: glossolalia in a forensic population is associated with mania and sexual/religious delusions. Journal of Forensic Sciences 47, 305–312.

Hine, V.H., 1969. Pentecostal glossolalia: toward a functional reinterpretation. Journal for the Scientific Study of Religion 8, 212–226. Louden, S.H., Francis, L.J., 2001. Are Catholic priests in England and Wales attracted to the charismatic movement emotionally less stable? British Journal of Theological Education II, 65–76.

Lovekin, A., Malony, H.N., 1977. Religious glossolalia: a longitudinal study of personality changes. Journal for the Scientific Study of Religion 16, 383–393. 4 A.B. Newberg et al. / Psychiatry Research: Neuroimaging xx (2006) xxx–xxx study, Psychiatry Research: Neuroimaging (2006), doi:10.1016/j.pscychresns.2006.07.001.

Lynch, J.C., 1980. The functional organization of posterior parietal association cortex. Behavioral and Brain Sciences 3, 485–499.

Newberg, A.B., Alavi, A., Baime, M., Pourdehnad, M., Santanna, J., d'Aquili, E.G., 2001. The measurement of regional cerebral blood flow during the complex cognitive task of meditation: a preliminary SPECT study. Psychiatry Research. Neuroimaging 106, 113–122.

Newberg, A.B., Saffer, J., Farrar, J., Pourdehnad, M., Alavi, A., 2005. Stability of cerebral blood flow measures using a split-dose technique with ^{99m}Tc-exametazime SPECT. Nuclear Medicine Communications 26, 475–478.

Pardo, J.V., Fox, P.T., Raichle, M.E., 1991. Localization of a human system for sustained attention by positron emission tomography. Nature 349, 61–64.

Persinger, M.A., 1984. Striking EEG profiles from single episodes of glossolalia and transcendental meditation. Perceptual and Motor Skills 58, 127–133.

Resnick, S.M., Karp, J.S., Tretsky, B.I., Gur, R.E., 1993. Comparison of anatomically defined versus physiologically based regional localization: effects on PET-FDG quantitation. Journal of Nuclear Medicine 34, 201–208.

Richardson, J.T., 1973. Psychological interpretations of glossolalia: a reexamination of research. Journal for the Scientific Study of Religion 12, 199–207.

Samarin, W., 1972. Variation and variables in religious glossolalia. In: Haymes, D. (Ed.), Language in Society. Cambridge University Press, Cambridge.

A.B. Newberg et al. / Psychiatry Research: Neuroimaging xx (2006) xxx–xxx 5
ARTICLE IN PRESS
Please cite this article as: Andrew B. Newberg et al., The measurement of regional cerebral blood flow during glossolalia: A preliminary SPECT study, Psychiatry Research: Neuroimaging (2006), doi:10.1016

Addendum B—
Demons and Deliverance

Messiah Yeshua often commanded unclean spirits to come out of Israelites. And, He gave His disciples "power and authority over all the demons." And, He told Paul that He would send him to the Gentiles, and use him to "open their eyes so that they may turn from...the dominion of Satan to God" (Mark 1:25; 9:25; Luke 4:36; 9:1; 10:19; Acts 26:15-18).

After *Paul,* a New Covenant Believer, was baptized in water and the spirit, he was "buffeted" by "a messenger of Satan." Moreover, Peter *warned us* to be sober and vigilant. He said, "Your adversary the devil walks about like a roaring lion, seeking whom he may devour" (2 Cor 12:7; 1 Pet 5:8).

Clearly, Satan can buffet and devour us.

Yet, some argue that Spirit-filled Believers cannot be *possessed* by a demon. They say this, because, our "body is the temple of the Holy Spirit, who is in us, and whom we have from God" (1 Cor 6:19).

Giving of the Holy Spirit did mark a pivotal point in history. Now, Believers are living stones in the Temple that is Messiah's Body. Yet, our enemy looks for opportunities to devour us.

To reconcile these seemingly opposing facts some say a Believer can be *oppressed* by a demon but cannot be *possessed* by it— that they can be buffeted on the outside, but cannot be possessed from the inside. However, *oppressed* and *possessed* are English words that, due to our associations with their meaning may not convey the Greek meaning of the word, which is to *vex and exercise power*. [113]

When a demon vexes, or exercises power, over us, we have a problem.

The thief, Satan, comes to steal, kill, and destroy (John 10:10). So let us imagine that we are in our house and cannot leave it, a robber has a gun and a clear view of us, and he wants to kill us.

Our first line of defense should be to disarm the robber. And, our immediate and primary problem is not whether the robber is *inside* or *outside* our house, but that he has a gun and wants to *shoot* us with it. Granted, the closer he is to us, the better his chances, but we still want to *take away his gun*. Regardless of where our enemy is located, we must disarm him. As long as he has a gun pointed at us, he is vexing us and exercising a certain power over us.

As for in or out, we note that Yeshua's command for demons to *"Come out,"* has more to do with *the action of leaving/departing* than it does with the location they are being commanded to vacate. [114]

Nonetheless, to help us expose our enemy, we examine possible locations. We begin by noting that we are comprised of *spirit*, *soul*, and *body* (1 Thes 5:23).

As members of Yeshua's congregation of firstborn our *spirit* is made "perfect," it is "sealed," meaning, it is *marked for preservation* (2 Cor 1:22; Eph 1:13; 4:30; Heb 12:22-23). [115] (From this we assume that, while our imagined robber may be able to shoot us, he will not be able to mortally wound us, because we are *sealed*.)

---

113 *Strong's* # G1139. To be exercised or vexed by a devil or devils.

114 *Strong's* # G1831. *Exerchomai*, leave, come out, depart, go (i.e., Mat 17:18; Mark 1:25).

115 *Strong's* # G4972. To stamp with a private mark for security or preservation.

The *soul* includes *mind*, *will*, and *heart/emotions*. YHVH formed man's body from the dust, then, He breathed life into him, and Adam became a living soul. Adam sinned, and as his heirs, the Word can save our fallen souls. But, we must not conform ourselves to worldly ways, but instead be renewed and transformed by the Word, in our mind/soul. We must watch over our heart/soul, because, from it, spring the issues of life. The Word also can divide soul and spirit and reveal our heart's true thoughts and intent (Gen 2:7; Pro 4:23; Eph 4:23; Rom 12:1-2; Heb 4:12; James 1:21).

Our *bodies* are to be presented as a living "sacrifice." And herein lies the problem: "Nothing good" dwells in our flesh. We can joyfully concur with Abba's Law in our spirit man, yet see a different response in our body. Sin dwells in our flesh. There, evil is present. For this reason, on a daily basis, we must crucify our flesh. We can do this, in Messiah, and by the power of His Holy Spirit (Rom 7:19-25; 1 Cor 15:31).

OUR HOLY OF HOLIES AND COURTS

Demons most often find an opening through our flesh— which, when out of order, can affect both soul and spirit.

A blueprint of Israel's ancient Temple will help us visualize our problem. It had an *Outer Court*, an *Inner Court*, and a *Holy*

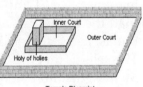

Temple Blueprint

of Holies. One moved from the Outer to the Inner Court, but only the High Priest could enter into the Holy of Holies (also called the *Most Holy Place*). We have seen that man is a triune being. And in our analogy, we will liken our body to the Outer Court, our soul to the Inner Court, and our spirit man to the Holy of Holies. [116]

When we are born of the Spirit, He resides in our Holy Place. He seeks to lead our spirit man in righteousness while Satan seeks to destroy us through attacks against our Outer Court flesh man.

---

[116] See *Recognizing the Real Enemy* by Miguel A. Demelli, Ocala, FL, 2009, pages 52-56.

 While we live in the flesh, our war is not really with the flesh. Instead, we wrestle against principalities, powers, rulers of darkness, and spiritual hosts of wickedness in heavenly places. They want to rule our flesh (2 Cor 10:3-4; Eph 6:12).

In this war of flesh against spirit, our soul is the "tie-breaker." As Israelites, we are "chosen to choose." Every day, we need to refuse evil and choose good (see Chapter 3; Isa 7:15). [117]

When we are born of the Holy Spirit, He resides in our Holy of Holies. Only the High Priest, Messiah Yeshua and His Spirit, can enter there. However, even as there were those who wanted to make the Father's Temple a den of robbers, and had to be cast out of the Outer Court, so the Robber, Satan, sometimes needs to be cast out of our Outer Court (Eze11:15-17; Mark 11:15-17).

We see a similar principle in Ezekiel's Temple. YHVH told Ezekiel to "describe" the Temple so we would be "ashamed" of our iniquities. That Temple has three levels. Its unique design reveals that, the higher up one goes, the less room there is for earthly things. Its Most Holy Place is found at the top (Ezek 43:10-12). [118] This tells us that the more we *depend* on, and the *higher up we go in Messiah*, the more holy will be the area in which we dwell.

In the Outer Court of Solomon's Temple we see the Brazen Altar and the Golden Laver. Here, we remember Messiah's blood sacrifice in our behalf. Here, by His grace, we begin our salvation journey.

Here, before moving into the Inner Court, the priest would wash himself. Similarly, we want to be constantly washing ourselves with the Word. For, even as little foxes can spoil the vine, so little sins can lead to demonic strongholds (Song 2:15).

---

117 Chosen/Choose: See, Exo 19:4-6; Deu 4:37; Josh 24:15; John 16:13; 1 Pet 2:9-10; *Strong's* # H 977. Also see, *The Voice... Hearing the Almighty* by Batya Wootten, chapter 5.

118 The design of this Temple makes it all but impossible to build. But, its details provide a blueprint of Abba's plan for our salvation. See *Restoring the Kingdom to Israel*, "Ezekiel's Temple— It's Real Meaning," by Angus Wootten, St. Cloud, 2009, Key of David Publishing.

Having experienced salvation, we move to the Inner Court, to the inner recesses of our mind and to various places of "ministry." Here, we see the Menorah. It speaks of Messiah's Light, of us as branches that must abide in Him, and of our need to always keep the oil of the Spirit in our lamps— so we can see the truth (Mat 25:1-14; John 15:5).

We see, too, the Table of Showbread and its twelve loaves. These speak of Israel's Twelve Tribes, and of YHVH's covenant with, and, constant provision for them (Lev 24:5-9).

The Altar of Incense sends forth a sweet savor, as do our prayers as they rise heavenward. Prayer helps to preserve us as Abba's covenant people (Psa 141:2; Luke 1:10). In this place of ministries, and in our minds, among many other things, Satan tries to turn our living relationship with Abba into the dead religion of man. Thus we trust in Yah, and we set our faces like flint toward Him and His ways. Then, we will not be made ashamed (Isa 50:7).

Next, we move into the Holy of Holies. Many believe this area is off-limits to evil. Yet, we must not be "high-handed" about sin or continue in it. Paul asks, "What agreement has the temple of God with idols?" The answer is, "None." We are to be dead to sin, to come out and be separate, and cleanse ourselves from all filthiness of "flesh and spirit." If we do *not* do that, YHVH will send us a "strong delusion," so we will believe the lie and be condemned— *because we did not believe the truth but had pleasure in unrighteousness* (Num 15:30; Rom 6:1-11; 2 Cor 6:16-17; 7:1; Col 3:5; 2 Th 2:11-12).

Scripture warns of an abomination of desolation, of evil in the Holy Place, and it tells us YHVH's house was destroyed, with not one stone left upon another. *Evil wants the same for us, so cannot be complacent about sin!* (Dan 12:11; Mark 13:2,14; Heb 10:31; Rev 21:27).

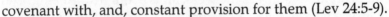

FLESH: ITS WEAKNESSES AND DESTINY

We also can liken our earthly situation to a ship. We have a flesh exterior, a soul that is the captain that determines direction, and a spirit, or radar system, through which we both send and receive signals from on High. Satan works on our mind and tries to get us to obey our body and its lusts, to sail through life based on what we see and on what feels good. The Holy Spirit sends direction to our spirit, and tries to get us to sail according to His guidance. He knows things that are hidden from our view, and He is always trying to lead us— in complete safety.

Our flesh/mind/soul are the weak links in our triune being. Our flesh and its lusts wage war against our mind/soul and make us a prisoner of its sins. Our spirit is willing, but our flesh and its emotions are weak. So, our flesh, in its present state, "cannot inherit the kingdom." Thus, we watch and pray against its temptations. We work to strengthen our inner man and must not lose heart in the process. Although our outward man is perishing, our inward man is being renewed day by day— in the Holy Spirit. [119]

On the other hand, Yeshua and the Father want us to have life abundantly, and they want to sanctify us completely: spirit, soul, and body. But, to inherit their Kingdom, our mortal body first must put on an immortal body; perishable must put on imperishable, then death will be swallowed up in victory. For now, we are being transformed into the image of our Messiah, as we pass from glory to glory. [120]

So it is that life is a test. We might even liken it to a job placement program— so we want to do well on our exams.

In life, we experience betrayals, tests, trials, physical and spiritual assaults, and sometimes, we give in to sin. So it is that, even as we ask Abba for our *daily* bread, at the same time, we also need to ask, *"Lead us not into temptation, but deliver us from evil...."*

---

[119] Mat 26:41; Luke 11:4; Rom 7:17-23; 1 Cor 15:50; 2 Cor 4:16; Gal 5:19-25; Eph 3:16; Heb 5:14; 1 Pet 2:11.

[120] John 10:10; Rom 8:29-30; 1 Cor 15:51-55; 2 Cor 3:18; Phil 3:21; 1 Thes 5:23.

Demons are real. Satan, serpents, snakes, demons, devils, and dragons, are mentioned more than 200 times in Scripture. We are foolish not to recognize the reality and activities of these enemies of our souls. They wage war against us and want to prevail over us (2 Cor 10:2-4; Eph 6:12).

However... While we need to accept that reality, we do not want to "see demons in everything." We do not want to be people who are always "blaming everything on the devil." Such attitudes can lead to not taking responsibility for our own fleshy weaknesses. If we make that mistake, we miss the point of our being tested in the first place. The Father says, sin is crouching at the door and "*we* must master it" (Gen 3:7). [121] He also says, "Resist the devil and he will flee from you," and, "Draw near to God and He will draw near to you." When His Light comes in the devil's darkness goes out. Light eliminates darkness. We belong to the Light. He paid a price for us. His Spirit resides in us. Even so, John said, "You are of God, little children, and have overcome them, because He who is in you is greater than he who is in the world" (James 4:7-8; 1 John 4:4). [122]

YHVH is Greater, and yet, Satan demanded, and was granted, permission to "sift" Peter (Luke 22:31-32). Moreover, if we give the devil a "place" in our lives, our sin will find us out. Abba will allow our sin to be exposed— because He wants to give us opportunity to repent, before it is too late (Num 32:23; Eph 4:27).

THE AUTHORITY OF EVIL AND ITS LIMITS

As for Satan's authority, he is given permission to make war with and overpower the saints— but only in this life. Even if we do experience tribulation or death, we do not die without hope. Like Messiah, we choose to overcome evil. And we choose to do so, even if it costs us our life in order to maintain our testimony to the end (John 16:33; 1 John 4:4; 5:4-5; Rev 11:7; 13:7).

---

121 See, *A Door of Hope for the Last Days* by Batya Wootten, Key of David, 2009.
122 John 3:6; 8:12; 1 Cor 6:20; 1 Pet 1:17-19; 5:8-9; 1 John 1:5.

We overcome by the blood of the Lamb, by the word of our testimony, and by not loving our earthly lives, even unto death. It is the "second death," and the One Who can cast us into it, that we are to fear. We must only fear/revere the Holy One. And, we trust that great rewards await all who overcome according to His plan (Luke 12:4-7; Rev 2:7-26; 3:5-21; 12:11; 20:6,14; 21:7-8).

When dealing with evil influences, we would do well to ask, did we somehow give the devil an opportunity? If so, when and where did we open a door to him? We want to ask these things of the Spirit, and when He shows us the problem, in repentance we close that door. Moreover, we know that we can close it ourselves because we have control over our "ship." In the end, we decide our direction. Nonetheless, if we do open a door to the Devil, and he beats up on us, we can find ourselves in a weakened state and in need of other Believers to help us overcome our problem.

DEALING WITH DEVILS IN OTHERS

Messiah Yeshua sent His disciples out in pairs (Mark 6:7). When dealing with demons, we too, might want to be in pairs and have a second witness. We also want to ask the Holy Spirit to give us discernment of sprits, and words of wisdom and knowledge, so we will know how to best deal with each individual situation.

As for deliverance that involves others, Believers have authority over unclean spirits, but not over the will of others. Generally, YHVH will not violate our will. So, before seeking to help someone, it might be good to know if they really want help. Unless they want deliverance, our efforts could be in vain. The individual too, needs to know that, in the end, *they* have authority in the matter. They need to be encouraged to rise up and take a stand against the evil that is vexing them.

In deliverance encounters, we want to take "authority," but we do not want to be arrogant. Our authority is in the LORD, and in His Holy Name, and we might want to ask Him to do the rebuking (Zec 3:1-2; Jude 1:9).

Casting out demons demonstrates the presence of the kingdom of God. But, let us seek to do so with the same dignity our Messiah showed when He cast them out. This means, we do not necessarily need to yell at them. They can hear us. (However, they may come out with a loud voice.) While Messiah Yeshua did once ask a demon for his name, we need to be careful with this technique too, because we are talking to entities that follow the father of lies. [123]

We must not attribute undue authority to Satan. Only the Holy One is all-knowing and omnipresent. We must not have overly long conversations with, or give undue attention to evil. We do not want to "put on a show," nor do we need to shout. We need to speak with true authority, and only the demon needs to hear us.

We also must not allow misguided people to use deliverance situations to draw attention to self— whether they have demons or claim to be chasing them away. Drawing attention to self detracts from Yah's glory, and from His power to deliver man from the one who wants to destroy him. Remember, it is *His* power and authority that demons obey. We do not want to usurp that power in any way, lest the demons find a place in us due to unconfessed sin (see page 180). We want to be sure we are in right order with Abba before we take on demons. And we remember that they can use the one under their control to exhibit supernatural strength. [124]

FILLING OUR HOUSE WITH THE RUACH

Yeshua said, "When an unclean spirit goes out of a man, he goes through dry places, seeking rest." *Dry* places are places that do not have the "water of the Word." Yeshua also said, when the demon does not find a new dry place, he returns to his old house/person. And, if he finds that house is "swept and put in order," he goes and gets seven other spirits more wicked than himself to join him. And, the last state of that man is worse than the first.

---

123 Mat 8:16; Mark 1:26,34; 5:7; Luke 11:15-27; John 8:44.
124 Mat 8:28; 15:22; 17:15; Luke 9:42; Acts 19:13-16.

At first, this does not seem right. Then we see that the man's last state is worse because he only *swept* his house, and he should have *washed* it with the water of the Word. He also *garnished* his house (KJV)— which speaks of *cosmetic decoration*.

Superficial, cosmetic faith and religious ritual will not save us. Cursory acceptance of the Messiah will not do. We need to truly *know* Him. Neither will head knowledge or fleshy righteousness save us. We need to be washed, sanctified, and justified in Messiah Yeshua's Name. We need to be reborn of His Spirit. We must be washed, regenerated and renewed by the Spirit, and in the Word. To prevail over our enemy, we must be cleansed by the blood of the Lamb. Apart from this, we will not know true deliverance (Luke 11:24-26; 1 Cor 6:11; Eph 5:26; Titus 3:5).

Yeshua said some spirits come out only by "prayer and fasting" (Mark 9:29). We likewise want to fast and pray. However, we also see that Messiah Yeshua was successful because— *He only did that which He saw the Father doing.*

Similarly, to be successful, we first need to know what the Father wants done in a given situation. Thus, we first want to pray for words of knowledge and wisdom when dealing with demons (John 5:19-20; Rom 8:14). We also want to resist supposed *formulas*. Believers can be oppressed for countless reasons and they need to be ministered to as unique individuals.

As led by the Spirit, we must try to bring to light the issues that are causing the problem. We do this through the golden avenues of true repentance, forgiveness, reconciliation, and restoration. In this way, we help remove vulnerable spots in the individual and the evil departs.

Finally, we trust that, as the Father's beloved children, whatever the problem might be, we can come boldly before His throne, and there, find mercy and grace to help in our time of need (Heb 4:16).

Amen!

Greater— Much Greater— is He Who is in us!

Amen!

ABBREVIATIONS AND BIBLIOGRAPHY

Abbreviations:
ArtScroll: ArtScroll Tanach Series
BDBL: New Brown-Driver-Briggs-Gesenius Hebrew-Aramaic Lexicon
ISV: International Standard Bible
NIV: New International Version Bible
S&BDB: Strong's Exhaustive Concordance and Brown-Driver-Briggs Lexicon
Strong's: Strong's Exhaustive Concordance
TWOT: Theological Wordbook of the Old Testament

The following is a listing of writings used in making this book.

Adler, Mortimer J. *Ten Philosophical Mistakes* . NY: Macmillian, 1997.
Aharoni, Yohanan; Michael Avi-Yonah. *The Macmillan Bible Atlas* . NY: Macmillan, 1977.
Bacchiocchi, Samuele. *From Sabbath To Sunday*. Maplewood NJ: Hammond, 1979, 2000.
Barna, George. *Revolution*. Tyndale House Publishers, Inc: Wheaton, IL, 2005.
Barraclough, Geoffrey. *Times Atlas of World History*. Pontifical Gregorian University Press: Rome, 1997.
Brown, Frances. *The New Brown-Driver-Briggs-Gesen ius Hebrew- Aramaic Lexicon*. Peabody, MA: Hendrickson, 1998.
Carta's Historical Atlas of Israel. Jerusalem: Carta, 1983.
Cohen, A. Rev. Dr. *Ezekiel*. NY, London: Soncino, 1999.
    . *Isaiah*. NY, London: Soncino, 1999.
    . *The Twelve Prophets*. NY, London: Soncino, 1999.
DeHaan, M. R.. *The Chemistry of the Blood* . Grand Rapids: Zondervan, 1971, 1989.
Dowley, Tim. *The Kregal Pictorial Guide To The Bible*. Grand Rapids: Kregal Publications, 2000.
Eckstein, Yechiel, Rabbi. *What Christian Should Know About Jews and Judaism*. Waco, TX: Word, 1984.
Edersheim, Alfred. *The Life and Times of Jesus the Messiah* . Grand Rapids: Eerdman's, 1979, 1997.
Edersheim, Alfred. *The Temple*. Grand Rapids: Kregal, 1997.
Edidin, Ben M. *Jewish Customs And Ceremonies* . NY: Hebrew Publishing, 1987.
Edidin, Ben M. *Encyclopaedia Judaica, 16 Vols* . Jerusalem: Keter, 1972.
Even-Shushan, Avraham. *New Concordance of the T anach*. Jerusalem: Sivan, 1983, 1999.
Fay, Frededrick L. *A Map Book For Bible Students* . Old Tappan, NJ: Revell, 1966.
Fellner, Judith. *In the Jewish Tradition, A Year of Food and Festivities*. Middle Village, NY: Jonathan David Publishers. 1995.
Frank, Ephraim. *Return to the Land: An E phraimite's Journey Home* . St. Cloud, FL: Key of David, 2004.
Frankel, Ellen, and Betsy Platkin Teutsch.*The Encyclopedia of Jewish Symbols*. Northvale, NJ: Jason Aronson Inc., 1992.
Gesenius' Hebrew-Chaldee Lexicon To The Old Testament. Grand Rapids. Baker, 1979, 2000.
Gilbert, Martin. *Atlas of Jewish History* . NY: William Morrow, 1993.
Gilbert, Martin. *Israel: A History* . NY: William Morrow, 1998.
Green, Jay P. *The Interlinear Bible* , Hebrew, Greek, English. Grand Rapids: Baker, 1979.
Gruber, Daniel. *Rabbi Akiba's Messiah* . Hanover, NH: Elijah Publishing House, 1999.
Harris, R. Laird, Gleason L. Archer Jr., and Bruce K. Waltke, eds. *Theological Wordbook of the Old Testament, 2 Vols* . Chicago: Moody, 1998.
Hatch, Edwin, and Henry A. Redpath. *Hatch and Redpath Concordance to the Septuagint, 2 Vols*. Grand Rapids: Baker, 1983.

Holladay, William L. Editor. *A Concise Hebrew and Aramaic Lexicon of The Old Testament*. Grand Rapids: Eerdman's, 1991.
House of David Herald. Lakewood, NY - White Stone, VA - Saint Cloud, FL: 1982-2000.
Interpreter's Dictionary of the Bible, 5 Vols . Nashville: Abingdon, 1983.
Jablonowski, Paul. *Sons to Glory*. www.sonstoglory.com: 2008.
Jahn, Herb. *The Aramic New Covenant* . Orange, CA: Exegeses, 1996.
Jenkins, Simon. *Bible Mapbook*. Herts, England: Lion, 1985.
Knapp, Christopher. *The Kings of Judah & Israel* . Neptune NJ: Loizeaux, 1983.
Kolatch, Alfred J. *The Jewish book of Why* . Middle Village NY: Jonathan David, 1981, 1995.
Kolatch, Alfred J. *The Second Jewish Book of Why* . Middle Village NY: Jonathan David, 1996.
Isaacson, Ben, Dr. David Gross, ed. *Dictionary of the Jewish Religion* Englewood, NJ: Bantam, 1979.
Lamsa, George M. *The Holy Bible From Ancient E astern Manuscripts*. Nashville: Holman, 1968, 1984.
Leil, C.F.; F. Delitzsch. *Commentary on the Old Testament In Ten Volumes*. Grand Rapids: Eerdman's, 1981.
Lisman, Lee. *What Kind of "Holiday Memories" Does God Have?* . P.O. Box 1501 Brush Prairie, WA 98606
Messianic Israel Herald . Saint Cloud, FL. 1999-2002.
Mordecai, Victor. *Is Fanatic Islam A Global T hreat?* Jerusalem, 2002. Fifth Edition.
The New Encyclopaedia Britannica, 29 Vols . Chicago: Encyclopedia Britannica, 1985, 2003.
The New English Bible With the Apocrypha . Oxford, England: Oxford University Press, 1994.
New International Version Study Bible . Grand Rapids: Zondervan, 1985, 1995.
Newsome, James D. Jr., ed. *A Synoptic Harmony of Samuel, Kings and Chronicles* . Grand Rapids: Baker.
Norcross, Paul D. *Dining at the Master's T able*. 1997. Charlemont, MA. Kingdom Presence Publishing.
Pearl, Chaim, ed. *The Encyclopedia of Jewish Life and T hought*. Jerusalem: Carta, 1987.
Pfeiffer, Charles F., Howard F. Vos, John Rea, eds. *Wycliffe Bible Encyclopaedia*. Chicago: Moody, 1983.
Richards, Lawerence O. *Expository Dictionary of Bible Words* . Grand Rapids: Zondervan, 1985.
Scherman, Nosson, and Meir Zlotowitz, eds. *Genesis. ArtScroll Tanach Series*. Brooklyn: Mesorah, 1987.
Scherman, Nosson, and Meir Zlotowitz, Rabbis. *The Wisdom In The Hebrew Alphabet*. Brooklyn: Mesorah Publications, 1993.
Scherman, Nosson, and Meir Zlotowitz, Rabbis. *Stone Edition The Chumash*. Mesorah, 1993-2001.
Smith, Wallace E. *By the Power of His Ruach.* Las Vegas: 2008.
Smith, Wallace E. *Are Christian Holidays… Holy Days?* Las Vegas: 2005.
Smith, Wallace E. *The Revelation of Yeshua, A First Century Look at a First Century Book* . Las Vegas: 2004.
Smith, William, L.L.D. *Smith's Bible Dictionary*. Peabody, MA: Hendrickson, 1997.
Strong, James. *The New Strong's E xhaustive Concordance* . Nashville: Thomas Nelson, 1984, 2002.
Stern, David H. *Jewish New Testament Commentary*. Clarksville, MD: Jewish New Testament Pub. 1995.
TenBoom, Corrie, Sherrill, Elizabeth. *The Hiding Place*. Chosen Books, 1996.
Tenny, Merrill, ed. *Zondervan Pictorial Encyclopedia of the Bible, 5 Vols*. Grand Rapids: Zondervan, 1976.
Thayer, Joseph Henry. *Thayer's Greek-English Lexicon of the New Testament*. Grand Rapids: Baker, 1983.
Thomas, Winton, ed. *Documents from Old T estament Times*. New York: Harper & Row, 1961.
Turner, Nigel *Christian Words*. Nashville: Thomas Nelson, 1981.
Unger, Merrill F. *Unger's Bible Dictionary*. Chicago: Moody, 1974, 1996.
Vaughn, Curtis, ed. *26 Translations of the Holy Bible* . Atlanta: Mathis, 1985.
Vincent, Marvin R. *Vincent's Word Studies of the New T estament*. McLean, VA: MacDonald.
Vine, W.E. *Expanded Vine's Expository Dictionary of New Testament Words*. Minneapolis: Bethany, 1984.
Walton, John H. *Chronological Charts of the Old T estament* . Grand Rapids: Zondervan, 1978.
Webster's Third New International Dictionary, 3 Vols . Chicago: Encyclopedia Britannica, 1981.
Whiston, William, trs. *The Works of Flavius Josephus, 4 Vols* . Grand Rapids: Baker, 1974, 1992.
Wilson, William. *Wilson's Old Testament Word Studies, Unabridged Edition*. McLean, VA: MacDonald.
Wootten, Angus. *The Restoration of the Kingdom to Israel* . Saint Cloud, FL: Key of David, 2000.
Wootten, Angus. *Take Two Tablets*. Saint Cloud: Key of David, 2002.
Wootten, Batya Ruth. *Israel's Feasts and their Fullness: Expanded Edition*. Saint Cloud: Key of David, 2008.
Wootten, Batya Ruth. *Redeemed Israel— Reunited and Restored* Saint Cloud: Key of David, 2006.
Wootten, Batya Ruth. *The Voice… Hearing the Almighty* . Saint Cloud, FL: Key of David, 2009.
Wuest, Kenneth. *Weust's Word Studies From the Greek New Testament*. Grand Rapids: Eerdman's, 1981.
Yaniv, David. *Birth of the Messiah* . Lynnwood, WA: New West Press, Ltd. 1997.

INDEX

Congregation(s): xiv, 35, 101, 144, 210
Connection: ix, 77-78, 93, 106-108, 179
Control: ix, 14, 21, 97, 98, 101-116, 134, 140, 144, 193, 198-202, 206, 214-216
Cosmetic: 218
Counted Out: 31
Court(s): 158, 211-212
Counterfeit(s): xiii, ix, 20, 23, 186, 195
Covenant: viii, xvii, 10, 16, 30, 32-34, 42-47, 61, 84, 88, 91, 118, 123, 124, 132, 148, 150, 171, 195, 209, 213
Curse(d)(ing): 9, 44, 89, 104, 170, 180
Daniel: 85, 189, 219
Darkness: 24, 122, 212, 215
David(s): iv-xix, 6, 9, 16, 34, 46, 61-89, 101, 134, 142-153, 162-166, 196, 219, 220
Day of the LORD: 69
Death: 4-5, 27, 33, 44, 71, 96, 115, 119, 123, 124, 137, 161-172, 214-216
Deceive(d): 6, 18, 21, 24, 28, 31, 40, 44, 130, 166, 186, 190, 193
Deluded (Delusion): 27-33, 207, 213
Demon(s): 20-38, 76, 186-190, 209-218
Deliverance: 84-85, 168, 176, 190, 209, 216-218
Deposit: 41-42, 46, 48, 58
Destroy: 6, 25, 45, 98, 112, 186, 210-217
Devil(s): 13, 18, 24, 29, 55, 111, 119, 209, 215-216
Discerning of Spirits: x, 50, 104, 145, 185-188, 190
Discern(ment): 108, 116, 175, 185-190, 216
Disobedient: ix, 12, 23, 30, 193
Divided (Division): xv, 36, 59, 61, 93, 108, 110, 116, 131, 157, 201, 211
Door: 78, 190, 215-216
Double Portion: 164
Dress(ed): 41, 162
Dwell: xv-xx, 46, 60, 131, 143, 211-212
Egypt: 42, 47, 60, 85, 137, 196
Elementary: 3

Elijah: 27, 153, 154, 164, 189, 219
Elohim: vii, 74, 127
Empower(ment): vi, ix, xi, xii, 2-6, 13, 19, 22, 32, 50, 55, 71, 101, 110, 116, 196
Ephraim: vii, xi-xx, 37-39, 43, 68, 131-134, 219
Equal: 77, 82, 99, 101, 113, 118
Eternal: viii, xii, xvii, xix, 3, 4, 10, 15, 31-35, 43-46, 68, 81, 90, 91, 114, 121, 125, 130, 144, 170-172, 191, 195
Evidence(d): 6, 11, 20-24, 43, 51, 76, 92, 106, 184, 192, 203
Evil: 6-15, 24-29, 38, 89-98, 119, 138, 160, 176-187, 190-194, 211-218
Exercise Power: 210
Ezekiel: xiv, xv, xviii, 64-66, 121, 133, 212, 219
Fast(ed)(ing): 137, 153, 218
First Fruits: 42, 48, 83, 171
Firstborn: 61, 188, 210
Flesh(y): xv-xviii, 5-11, 34, 42, 53-54, 62, 69-71, 115-129, 164, 190, 211-218
Foreign: xv, xvi, 64, 111
Former(ly): 43, 72, 101
Foundation(al): 3, 50, 123-132, 156
Fruit(s)(Fruitful): vii, 6, 15, 16, 30, 39, 44, 67, 68, 84, 88, 91, 96
Fruit(s) of the Spirit: 83, 96
Fulfill(ed): 39, 42-45, 53, 120, 123, 132, 156, 171
Fullness: ix, 13, 41-43, 46, 58, 67, 109, 130, 131, 162, 196, 220
Gentile(s): vii, 30, 43, 67, 72, 103, 104, 115, 124, 130, 131, 178, 209
Gifts: x-xiii, 19-24, 32-38, 48, 50, 56, 76, 78, 92-117, 130, 138, 141, 145, 148, 153-169, 172-177, 181, 183, 192
Gift(s) of Healing: 50, 104-110, 145, 163-168, 172-177
Gifts (Nine): 108, 109, 116
Glossolalia: 76, 197, 199, 201-208
Goal: ix, xi, xii, 3, 4, 13, 96, 192

WALLACE E. SMITH

W allace E. Smith (Wally) was born in Los Angeles, California and moved to Las Vegas, Nevada at the age of 8. He gave his life in the service of YHVH at the age of 25.

In preparation for pastoral ministry, Wally began teaching Junior and Senior youth at Grapevine Fellowship under the mentorship of the late Bud Higginbotham. In 1994 Wally received his first appointment as Senior Pastor by the International Church of the Foursquare Gospel.

September 1996, on the Feast of Tabernacles, Pastor Wally and his wife Kathy and a few faithful Bible students pioneered, what has come to be known as, the House of Israel Fellowship in Las Vegas, Nevada.

The House of Israel Fellowship is a free congregation of Messianic Believers recognizing that the sovereignty of the church belongs to King Yeshua, and to Him alone, as guaranteed by the First Amendment of the United States Constitution.

Pastor Wally and Kathy have both been recognized and Ordained with the Messianic Israel Alliance.

Today, Pastor Wally is actively engaged in his continued study of Yeshua's Word, and pastoral duties with the House of Israel Fellowship.

Wally also has compiled and edited two previous books: *Are Christian Holidays... Holy Days?* and, *The Revelation of Yeshua, A First Century Look at a First Century Book.*

His wife, Kathy, recently retired from a rewarding career as a school administrator with the Clark County School District. She now works hand in hand with her husband at the House of Israel. Kathy now has the time to lovingly spoil her grandchildren and to volunteer as a counselor at one of the busiest crisis pregnancy centers in the country.

Wally and Kathy will soon happily celebrate their 25th wedding anniversary.

Wally Smith
hoif@cox.net
www.houseofisraelfellowship.org

BATYA RUTH WOOTTEN

B atya Wootten and her husband, Angus, were early pioneers in the Messianic movement. Decades ago they began publishing the first Messianic Materials Catalogue, created to serve a fledgling new interest in Israel and the Jewish people. Batya read countless books about these subjects so she could write descriptions of them for the catalogue. She discovered the great diversity of opinions about Israel's role and identity. Hungering to truly know the truth of the matter, she began to cry out in desperation to her Heavenly Father and asked Him to show her *His* truth. As promised, He answered: "Call to Me and I will answer you, and I will tell you great and mighty things, which you do not know" (Jer 33:3). The Holy One began to open up the Scriptures to her. His answers led to the writing of many books about Israel and her full restoration.

Batya's challenging books represent decades of study on the crucial issues of identifying Israel, celebrating her feasts, honoring Torah, and the role of women, and now – books about the role of the Holy Spirit, the Ruach haKodesh.

Many have given testimony about having been transformed by her writings. Lives are changed as they see the truth about Judah and

Ephraim, their broken brotherhood and coming restoration. Batya's emphasis on the need to show mercy and grace to both houses is helping to heal the wounds that began with Israel's division into two Kingdoms.

Her book, *Israel's Feasts and Their Fullness: Expanded Edition*, represents years of meticulous research, study, and prayerful writing. It is a book that is helping Believers to be liberated into glorious celebrations of the feasts. Several people have said of it, "This is the best book about the feasts that I have ever read." Her book, *Mama's Torah: The Role of Women*, has likewise received high acclaim from both men and women. She now offers the book you have in your hands, plus its "companion" work, *The Voice… Hearing the Almighty*.

Batya is married to her best friend, Col. Angus Wootten (Ret.), author of the visionary books, *Restoring Israel's Kingdom* and *Take Two Tablets Daily*. Together they have ten children who have blessed them with many beloved offspring.

Working as a team, Angus and Batya moved forward from the early days of the *House of David Catalogue* and began publishing a Newsletter, the *House of David Herald*. They also founded the informative Messianic Israel web site: *www.messianicisrael.com*. This led to the birth of the Messianic Israel Alliance, a rapidly growing, and loosely affiliated Alliance of fellowships based on agreement with "The Hope of Messianic Israel," their broad statement of faith.

Together Angus and Batya continue to publish books that serve the growing army of Believers who are discovering the truth about their Hebraic heritage. They work together to help raise up new leaders and to draw out their giftings. For this assignment they have been uniquely prepared by the God of Abraham, Isaac, and Jacob. We know you will be blessed as you read their works.

Batya posts the following notice in all of her books:

> *The Word tells us to " let the one who is taught*
> *share all good things with him who teaches" (Gal 6:6).*
> *If through this book a good thing has been accomplished in your life,*
> *please write and share your good news with me.*
>
> Batya Wootten, PO Box 700217, Saint Cloud, FL 34770
> *e-mail: batya@mim.net*

Israel— Empowered by The Spirit by Wallace E. Smith and Batya Ruth Wootten: If you understand your Hebraic roots, yet long for a true move of the Holy Spirit, this book is for you! It explains why we need the Holy Spirit. It addresses issues like counterfeit moves, prayer languages, prophecy, singing in the Spirit, words of wisdom and knowledge, gifts of healing, working of miracles, discerning of spirits, and deliverance.
You want this handbook on your library shelf!
Paper, 192 pages, $14.95   ISBN 1-886987-28-9

Ruth and Esther: Shadows of our Future by Frank Morgan, M.D. The divine destiny of Ephraim and Judah is foretold in the stories of Ruth and Esther. They tell of Israel's redemption and restoration, they tell of a widow and a maiden, and give glimpses of Yah's great love for us— and give insights into His latter-day plan for us.
Paper, 144 pages, $9.95   ISBN 886987-19-X

Return to the Land: An Ephraimite's Journey Home by Ephraim Frank As a new Believer, Ephraim could not explain what he felt burning in his soul. He only knew that he was being wooed by His God and had gone on a tour that had forever changed his life...
From the farm lands of America to the Holy Land of Israel, this compelling autobiography tells of a "stranger" who felt divinely drawn to both the Promised Land and the God of Abraham, Isaac, and Jacob. It tells of the birthing of a new and fresh move of the Spirit, it reveals what YHVH is doing in today, it tells of the blessed redemption of the whole house of Israel. A blessed and encouraging book. You will not want this story to end!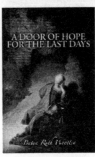
Paper, 240 pages, $12.95   ISBN 1-886987-18-1

A Door of Hope for the Last Days by Batya Wootten This book addresses the various "Rapture" theories and offers a unique perspective that is based on "doors," the days of Noah, and Israel's full restoration. An inspiring work. Paper, 160 pages, $9.95 ISBN 1-886987-32-7

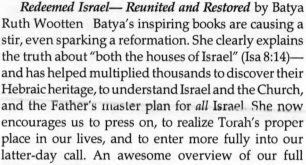

Redeemed Israel— Reunited and Restored by Batya Ruth Wootten Batya's inspiring books are causing a stir, even sparking a reformation. She clearly explains the truth about "both the houses of Israel" (Isa 8:14)— and has helped multiplied thousands to discover their Hebraic heritage, to understand Israel and the Church, and the Father's master plan for *all* Israel. She now encourages us to press on, to realize Torah's proper place in our lives, and to enter more fully into our latter-day call. An awesome overview of our full restoration. Includes illustrations, maps, and charts. Paper, 256 pages. $14.95   ISBN 1-886987-17-3
Also Available in an Audio CD Set!

Ephraim and Judah: Israel Revealed by Batya Wootten Inexpensive. Succinct. Easy to read. This condensed overview of the material presented in Batya's classic works includes illustrations, maps, charts. It clarifies misconceptions about Israel and helps Believers see that they too are part of Israel. This encouraging work shows how and where both the houses of Israel fit into the Father's divine plan. An invaluable tool for Believers. It quickly outlines the essence of the phenomenal truth about all Israel— Ephraim and Judah.
Paper, 80 pages, $3.95   ISBN 1-886987-11-4

Spanish! Espanole: ¿Quién es Israel? The classic book, *Who is Israel?* is available in Spanish. (Some maps and charts continue to be in English only.) To help get the word out, this 320 page book is offered at the special price of only $9.95   ISBN 1-886987-08-4

One Stick in His Hand Print by Crystal Lenhart. Fine quality white linen paper suitable for framing. Inspiring vivid sunset background in burgundy, red, blue, and purple tones. Size: 21x29" (3" white border, 15x23" image).
Signed/ numbered (1500 prints), $25.00.
Not Signed, $15.00.

Israel's Feasts and their Fullness: Expanded Edition by Batya Ruth Wootten This book is an informative, liberating classic. Written especially for those who understand about both houses of Israel, it is well researched, insightful, and highly enjoyable. Encourages freedom in Messiah, yet shows reverence for Scripture and due respect for Judaism's honorable traditions. Addresses Shabbat and the seven Feasts. Includes simple "Instruction Guides" for Sabbath, Havdalah, Passover, plus charts, tables, graphics. Batya's style has endeared her to many readers, and now she invites us to celebrate in the presence of the Almighty! Paper, 384 pages, $16.95   ISBN 1-886987-29-7

Passover in all its Fullness Includes Passover related chapters from the above Feast book plus helpful Passover Guides. Explains the Four Passovers and the meaning of the Day of the Wave Sheaf. Makes an ideal gift at Passover celebrations. 96 pages, $4.95
ISBN 1-886987-15-7-3

Come! Let us Rehearse the Four Passovers— DVD!
A dance filled two-hour drama narrated by Angus and Batya Wootten. Presents Passover based on Scripture. Depicts the four types of Passover (described in Batya's books): Family, Congregational, Personal, and Kingdom. Seeing Passover in dance and drama, while hearing related verses, is exciting, enlightening, encouraging. Watch this DVD and be inspired to celebrate Messiah's Passover like never before!
DVD: $10.00

Package of Pamphlets— One Each: Erev Shabbat, Havdalah, The Four Passovers, Messianic Jewish Passover, and Ten Days of Prayer all by Batya Wootten.
Each paper is printed on a folded 8 ½ x 11 size paper, and will fit nicely in your Bible. Five Pamphlets, one each: $5.00.

The Voice... Hearing the Almighty by Batya Wootten Israel's Patriarchs all heard the voice of the Holy One— and, we should too. However, man tends to fear hearing Him. This eye-opening book explains why— and why it's time to change our attitude about "Hearing from on High." YHVH said, *"In the latter days you will return to the LORD your God and listen to His voice"* (Deu 4:30). Difficult times are at our door. We truly need to learn to hear His voice! *Now!* An inspiring book. Paper, 160 pages, $9.95 ISBN 1-886987-27-0 *Available on Audio CD!*

Mama's Torah: The Role of Women (Expanded Edition) by Batya Wootten Insightful and compelling. Defines "help meet." Delightfully depicts the different roles of husband and wife. Shows how women in Scripture were used, addresses difficult verses, and unveils Abba's call to women in this hour, especially in regard to Israel's full restoration to the *spirit of Torah*. A wonderful book that is receiving rave reviews from both men and women. Paper, 160 pages, $9.95 ISBN 1-886987-20-3 *Available on Audio CD!*

One Nation Under God by Crystal Lenhart Good News for children! Illustrated, fun (fifth grade level). Share your faith with your children. Teach them in a family-oriented Bible study. Read a story and let the little ones do a work page. Elementary age to young teens. Pages to color, graphics, maps, illustrations, lesson overviews, summaries. Paper, Spiral Bound, 8x11, 76 pages, $12.00 ISBN 1-886987-16-5

My Beloved's Israel by Gloria Cavallaro A personal journal. Embark on an intimate journey into the heart of our Bridegroom, have a relationship with Him like David described, know intimacy with Him like that of the Song of Songs. Gloria chronicles her visions and dreams, then interprets them in light of scriptural reflection. She concludes that Israel must be reunited if she is to be prepared for her latter-day challenges. Gloria's exhortations help us prepare our hearts for the days ahead. Paper, 384 pages $16.95 ISBN 1-886987-05-X

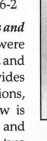

ABOUT THE COVER PAINTING
BLESSED MOVE OF THE RUACH

As the Holy Spirit descends upon our lives, we welcome Him with open arms. We ask Him to be our Comforter and to grant us empowerment, as He guides us in a blameless walk before YHVH.

We, who are a part of the once broken staffs of Zechariah, Favor and Union, are now being gracefully covered in Messiah's crimson blood. May it be that, like an almond branch, we "bud quickly forth." Like its blossom, may we, too, be used to help pollinate YHVH's truth. As branches are used in a fire, may we be used to help rekindle a fire of revival for the whole house of Israel.

David Hardin
Artist